This new volume of philosophical papers by Bernard Williams is divided into three sections: the first, 'Action, freedom, responsibility', the second, 'Philosophy, evolution and the human sciences', in which appears the essay which gives the collection its title, and the third, 'Ethics', some of the essays in which are closely related to his 1985 book *Ethics and the limits of philosophy*.

Like the two earlier volumes of Williams's papers published by Cambridge University Press, *Problems of the self* and *Moral luck*, this volume will be welcomed by all readers with a serious interest in philosophy. It is published alongside a volume of essays on Williams's work, *World, mind and ethics: essays on the ethical philosophy of Bernard Williams*, edited by J. E. J. Altham and Ross Harrison, which provides a reappraisal of his work by other distinguished thinkers in the field.

Making sense of humanity

Making sense of humanity

and other philosophical papers

1982 – 1993

BERNARD WILLIAMS

CAMBRIDGE
UNIVERSITY PRESS

Published by the Press Syndicate of the University of Cambridge
The Pitt Building, Trumpington Street, Cambridge CB2 1RP
40 West 20th Street, New York, NY 10011–4211, USA
10 Stamford Road, Oakleigh, Melbourne 3166, Australia

First published 1995

Printed in Great Britain at the University Press, Cambridge

A catalogue record for this book is available from the British Library

Library of Congress cataloguing in publication data
Williams, Bernard Arthur Owen.
Making sense of humanity and other philosophical papers,
1982–1993 / Bernard Williams.
p.   cm.
ISBN 0 521 47279 2 (hardback) ISBN 0 521 47868 5 (paperback)
1. Ethics. 2. Man. 3. Philosophy.   I. Title.
BJ1031.W47 1995
192–dc20   94–30859   CIP

ISBN 0 521 47279 2 hardback
ISBN 0 521 47868 5 paperback

For
Jonathan

Contents

Preface

This is a collection of philosophical papers that I have published since 1982. It includes one paper, 'Resenting one's own existence', that has not been published before (though some of the material in it has been). I have made small revisions, at least, to most of the papers, and one or two, in particular the first chapter, have been substantially rewritten.

I have not included reviews, replies, or pieces that seemed too closely tied to their occasions. I have also left out some essays in the history of philosophy, because their topics were too distant from the rest of the collection, and one or two papers that overlapped too much with my book *Ethics and the Limits of Philosophy*, which was published in 1985. I have included, however, some papers that are quite closely related to that book but which, I hope, contain enough that is independent of it: in particular, 'The point of view of the universe' (about Henry Sidgwick), and 'Ethics and the fabric of the world' (about J. L. Mackie). I have added some cross-references between the chapters, to *Ethics and the Limits of Philosophy*, and to a more recent book, *Shame and Necessity* (published in 1993).

The chapters originally appeared as follows, and I am grateful to those who have given permission to reprint:

(1) the Lindley Lecture, University of Kansas, 1985; (2) the Hart Lecture, Oxford, 1987: 10 *Oxford Journal of Legal Studies* (1989); (3) *Logos* 10 (1989), Santa Clara University, CA; (4) *Proceedings of the Aristotelian Society* 92 (1992/3); (5) in *Virtues and Reasons*, ed. R. Hursthouse, G. Lawrence and W. Quinn (Essays for Philippa Foot) (Oxford: Oxford University Press, 1995); (6) *European Journal of Philosophy* 1:1 (1993); (7) lecture given to the Stanford University Centennial Conference, 1987, and published in James Sheehan and Morton Sosna (eds.), *The Boundaries of Humanity: humans, animals, machines*, (Berkeley, CA: University of California Press, 1991); (8)

shortened version of a Herbert Spencer Lecture, given at Oxford in 1986, under the title 'Evolutionary theory: epistemology and ethics', and published in *Evolution and its Influence*, ed. Alan Grafen (Oxford: Clarendon Press, 1989); (9) lecture in a Darwin Centennial series at Cambridge, and published in *Evolution from Molecules to Men*, ed. D. S. Bendall (Cambridge: Cambridge University Press, 1983); (10) in *Trust: making and breaking co-operative relations*, ed. Diego Gambetta (Oxford: Blackwell, 1988); (11) *Proceedings of the Aristotelian Society* 85 (1984/5); (12) inaugural lecture at Oxford: a shortened version published in *London Review of Books*, 29 August 1991; (13) the Henry Sidgwick Memorial Lecture, Newnham College, Cambridge, published in *The Cambridge Review*, 7 May 1982; (14) in *Morality and Objectivity*, ed. Ted Honderich (Essays for J. L. Mackie) (London: Routledge and Kegan Paul, 1985); (15) in *Human Agency: language, duty and value*, ed. J. Moravscik and C. C. W. Taylor (Essays for J. O. Urmson) (Stanford University Press, 1988); (16) in *The Good Lawyer*, ed. David Luban (Totowa, NY: Rowman and Allenheld, 1983); (17) a Royal Institute of Philosophy Lecture, 1992, in *Ethics*, ed. A. Phillips Griffiths (Cambridge: Cambridge University Press, 1993); (18) in *Moral Dilemmas in Modern Medicine*, ed. Michael Lockwood (Oxford University Press, 1988), and incorporating additional material from 'Types of moral argument in embryo research', in *Human Embryo Research: yes or no?* (CIBA Foundation, 1986); (19) unpublished, but based in part on 'Who might I have been?', in *Human Genetic Information: science, law and ethics* (CIBA Foundation, 1990); (20) in *Ethics and the Environment*, ed. C. C. W. Taylor (Corpus Christi College, Oxford, 1992); (21) in *Moral Luck*, ed. Daniel Statman (Albany, NY: State University of New York Press, 1993).

Oxford, May 1994

I

Action, freedom, responsibility

1

How free does the will need to be?

1 The irrelevance of constraint

Locke said[1] that the question was not whether the will be free, but whether we have a will. *A fortiori*, it cannot be a question of how free the will may be. Locke's remark reminds us that the freedom of the will that has been the subject of the classical problem, if it comes at all, does not come in degrees. People's freedom, however, in more everyday senses, obviously enough does come in degrees.

This point raises a question not only about the classical problem of freewill, but also about the classical compatibilist answer to it, based on the idea that freedom is opposed to constraint and not to necessity. That position certainly deploys an idea of freedom, but of a freedom that may be more or less extensive, and that fact in itself should make us ask whether the position does not miss the point of the problem it is supposed to resolve. It is far from clear what exactly constraint is,[2] but in the kinds of cases usually invoked, somebody brings it about, by intentional application of threats or force, that an agent either cannot attain his original goal at all, or can attain it only at an increased cost. The agent may be confronted by a highwayman who (whatever the standard formula says) does not, in fact, offer him a choice between his money and his life, but rather a choice between losing merely his money, and losing his money together with his life; in that case, he cannot attain the goal of keeping his money at all. On the other hand, a man who possesses a valuable secret may be able to attain at least part of his objectives, and frustrate his captors, if their threat to kill him leaves him with the option of dying with his secret.

But what significance is there in the fact that the cases standardly invoked are cases of *constraint* – that is to say, cases in which the

3

limitation of effective choice is deliberately imposed, for their own ends, by other agents? These are merely one sort of what Aristotle rightly and relevantly identified as 'actions done through fear of greater evils', such as that of the sailors who throw the cargo overboard to save themselves and the ship.[3] In the cases that do not involve other people's hostile intentions, the agent's original objective may equally be made more costly, or it may become inaccessible, or his objectives may need to be modified in one way or another.

Now in all cases of things done through fear of greater evils, whether that fear is imposed by other agents or not, there is no loss of *freewill* in any sense that has to do with the agent's capacity to choose, or with his being held responsible. The agent is responsible for his action. He may not be to blame for the loss of the goods or whatever, in the sense that a course of action that would have been unreasonable or blameworthy in ordinary circumstances is reasonable and not blameworthy in the constrained circumstances. This is very obvious when the agent's original objective is accessible, though at greater cost, but similar points apply to the cases in which a course of action usually or previously thought available becomes unavailable. People are indeed seen as responsible for their actions in such circumstances, as when Aristotle's sailors are complimented for their prudence, or alternatively told off for panicking. In such circumstances you can of course be excused for not doing something that you would otherwise be blamed for not doing; more than that, you can be complimented for not trying to do it.

If we look at the larger class of things done through fear of greater evils, we are not going to learn much relevant to freewill or to ideas of compatibilism. It might be said that these are things that people do 'against their will'. But things done against one's will, in such circumstances, are not even (except in a very everyday sense) things that one does when not wanting to do them. They are things that one did not originally want to do, or which one would not want to do unless the circumstances were exceptionally disadvantageous, and their possibility does not shed any more light on the question of compatibilism than that which is shed by other actions that are performed under limiting circumstances.

If we are not to count as exercising freewill in cases of this kind, then we never exercise it, since all choices operate in a space of alternatives constrained by the contingent cost of various possibilities, and these exceptional cases are simply dramatic cases of that, where the space has been unexpectedly restricted. It makes no difference to this central aspect, so far as the agent's decisions and their status are concerned, whether the space of possibilities has been altered by a human being with the intention of doing just that. But the cases in which that is so are the ones that count as cases of constraint. So constraint is a red herring so far as freewill is concerned.

There are of course some important differences between actions done under constraint, and other actions done from fear of greater evils. If the restrictions are humanly imposed, they are likely to elicit resentment as well as frustration. Moreover, constraint is peculiarly related to the deliberative conclusion that one *must* or *has to* do a certain thing (a kind of conclusion to which I shall return). Conclusions reached under constraint are not always of that form, but they often are. When such conclusions are reached in other situations, they characteristically express some project or objective with which the agent is deeply identified, for instance (though by no means exclusively) requirements of morality. What is peculiar about these conclusions, when they are reached under constraint, is that they witness to the agent's vital interests or deepest needs only negatively, as things to be protected: the actions required are the expression of someone else's intentions and can lie indefinitely far away from anything with which the agent is identified.

Such considerations can indeed help to explain why constraint – restrictions imposed by other people, rather than by nature – is perceived as specially opposed to *freedom*. It constitutes being in someone else's power, which is a paradigm of unfreedom. But the very fact that decisions taken under constraint are decisions – and that, further, they can take the form of practical necessity, a form that belongs to some of the most serious and responsible decisions we take – shows why constraint cannot provide the clue to understanding freewill.

Why does freewill, unlike freedom, not come in degrees? Presumably it is because its assertion consists only of an existence claim. How exactly that claim should be expressed is notoriously disputed, but it is something to the effect that agents sometimes act voluntarily, and that when they do so they have a real choice between more than one course of action; or more than one course is open to them; or it is up to them which of several actions they perform. I shall leave the claim in this indeterminate form, and give it a label that preserves its indeterminacy, *the Plurality Principle*. Why the Principle takes the form of an existence claim will become clearer later. The present point is that it merely requires that there be, in the appropriate sense, alternatives for the agent, and that it is indifferent to their number, their cost, and so forth. That is why the freewill that it introduces is different from the freedom that comes in degrees and is opposed to constraint.

5

2 What the reconciling project must be

The old compatibilism made a lot out of the opposition between freedom and constraint. If the argument of section 1 is right, it was looking in the wrong direction. But that is not the only reason why we have to recast the question of compatibilism, or, as we may say, the reconciling project. As it is usually described, the reconciling project involves an important, structural, misconception. Its task is explained in terms of taking two recognizable items – determinism (or something like that), on the one hand, and on the other hand, something that is often called 'moral responsibility' – and trying to reconcile them with one another. But this account of the task underdescribes it, because there are not two but three items or sets of items to be accounted for. They are, first, determinism (or something like that); second, a class of psychological items such as choice, decision, or rational action; and, third, some ethical items such as blame or responsibility. Since there are three items or classes of items involved, there is more than one way of understanding what would be involved in reconciliation. It may be thought that what need to be reconciled are determinism and choice, where choice is understood as a psychological item, and that if this can be achieved, the ethical notions will be able to live with determinism. Alternatively, it may be thought that even if the psychological items can be reconciled with determinism, this may not be enough to save the ethical notions, which require something more; something that excludes determinism. If this further demand is put in terms of *choice*, it might be expressed by saying that responsibility and similar ethical notions require real choice, and real choice is not a purely psychological notion, but a metaphysical one. I shall come back to this idea.

As well as undercounting the items involved, reconcilers have tended to make the further mistake of thinking that we understand the ethical items at least as well as we understand the psychological items. A similar mistake is often made by their opponents as well. Of course, the reconcilers and their opponents do not necessarily think that they have the *same* determinate understanding of the ethical notions; notions such as, in particular, 'moral responsibility'. Because of these differences, the opponents sometimes say that the reconcilers have failed to show that our actual ethical notions are compatible with determinism, but, rather, have changed the subject and brought in a reductive and inadequate version of those notions. Both parties, however, do tend to agree on two things: that we have a determinate understanding of the relevant ethical notions; and that what we have to worry about, if anything, is just the relation of those notions to determinism (or something like that).

The truth is that we have other reasons to worry about many of our moral notions, and if we have come to have difficulty in understanding ideas such as 'moral responsibility', this is not simply because of our suppositions, hopes and fears about naturalistic explanations of action. It is to some extent because of this, and inasmuch as compatibilism was, like its opponents, wedded to 'moral responsibility' as the ethical term that had to be reconciled to naturalistic explanation, it has failed. But, more significantly, we have reasons *anyway* for being doubtful about 'moral responsibility'.

I said that the first item to be considered in relation to the reconciling project was 'determinism' (or something like that). The important feature of this item is that it should be some general doctrine about the world's workings, which is thought, unless the reconciling project is successful, to conflict with the Plurality Principle. It is this item, in fact, that determines the shape that the Plurality Principle takes. The feared effect of the doctrine in question is to reduce in every case the actions open to the agent in the relevant sense to one, and it is this that the Principle denies.

It is much less important that the doctrine in question should be universal determinism. There may have been a time when belief in a universal determinism looked like the best reason there was for expecting strong naturalistic explanations of psychological states and happenings, but, if that was once the case, it is no longer so. It now looks a great deal more plausible and intelligible that there should be such explanations than that the universe should be a deterministic system, and it is the possibility of those explanations that itself creates the problem. 'Strong naturalistic explanation' is an extremely vague phrase, and it may be said that a good deal more needs to be known about what it means, before we can know what the problem is supposed to be. It may be said, in particular, that only tight nomological explanations can generate the problem. I doubt that this is correct. As Daniel Dennett[4] has pointed out, the chance of being able to cash in the nomological claim at the only level to which it could apply – that of a repeatable microstate – is vanishingly small. But the mere failure to do so (because of randomness, for instance) would be uninteresting in itself, while strong psychophysical explanations that did not meet that standard could equally create unease for the Plurality Principle, if anything of that sort could.

This follows from the nature of the Plurality Principle itself, which is expressed in terms of 'courses of action'. How many courses of action are 'open to' the agent (or whatever the preferred formulation may be) must be considered in terms of what can be counted, in relation to a given agent on a given occasion, as relevantly different courses of action. There is a complex question of how we should understand this, but it seems to be a sufficient condition of an agent's enjoying on a given occasion the freewill defined by the Principle that the courses of action *which present themselves to that agent as deliberative alternatives* are in the required sense open to him. (Some of the complexities lie in the fact that this is not also a necessary condition: there may be various courses of action relevantly open to him, but he may have overlooked or misidentified them in his deliberation. But these problems need not be pursued in the present argument.)

Suppose that the Plurality promised by the Principle, so understood, fails: only one of the courses of action that present themselves to the agent in his choice is actually open to him. It is compatible with this that various different movements might still be possible, any of which would constitute this course of action, and that no microdeterministic set-up determined which set of movements would come about. This would not restore the required Plurality. On the other hand, the reason why Plurality failed might be found in strong psychophysical explanations operating at a level, perhaps, at which actions were specified. If so, it will be the strong explanations that matter, rather than microdeterminism.

It certainly remains unclear what the strongest kind of psychophysical explanations might be like. But I do not think that so far as these questions are concerned, it matters a great deal what exactly they might be like. It must in any case be sensible to test the psychological and ethical notions against the strongest hypotheses we could possibly entertain about psychophysical explanation. Further, there is a substantive reason for this policy. So far as these issues are concerned, the answers to questions about psychophysical explanation will matter only if the outlook for the psychological items is sensitive to those answers. But one respect, as it seems to me, in which the reconciling project has been a success is that the outlook for the psychological items has been shown not to be sensitive to those answers. Work by Brian O'Shaughnessy[5] and others seems to me to have shown that those concepts can function compatibly with the strongest hypotheses about explanations. We have good reason to believe that, insofar as they are psychological notions, all the following are compatible with any conceivable possibility of naturalistic explanation: choice; reasoned choice, and decision; action; intentional action; reasoned intentional action; and what is entailed by that, trying.

3 Determinism, fatalism, and an incompatibilist argument

If this work has achieved the reconciling project so far as the psychological items are concerned, the remaining task should consist of bringing the ethical items into an intelligible relation to the psychological items.

However, opponents of the reconciling project – call them 'incompatibilists' – may say that to go about things in this way is to beg the question. They may say that it is a mistake to suppose that we can do with a purely 'psychological' conception of choice, or (perhaps) of intentional action, if that means a concept lacking the kinds of metaphysical implications that are relevant to this problem. They may say that the concepts we have do have such implications, and if a 'psychological' concept of choice or intentional action lacks them, then it is not an adequate concept. Alternatively, the incompatibilist may say that there is perhaps a purely psychological concept of choice under which choices or deliberated action can be reconciled with strong psychophysical explanation, but this concept is inadequate to our ethical purposes, which do require a concept with stronger metaphysical implications.

Sometimes it is hard to tell which of these views an incompatibilist is offering. This is particularly likely to be so when the concept under discussion is 'free action'. This is the concept standardly associated with the Plurality Principle, but what work exactly is this concept expected to do? It is most often mentioned in connection with ethical demands, especially the demands of blame, and this might imply that 'free action' is above all an ethical concept. On this showing, if the Plurality Principle fails for metaphysical reasons, we may have to revise our ethical practices, but we could still be left with functioning psychological concepts of choice and intentional action. Some incompatibilists, however, seem to proceed on the assumption that, even apart from ethical considerations, 'free action' represents a basic category of action: much the same, perhaps, as 'chosen action' or 'deliberated action' or 'intentional action'. It may even be claimed that it is coextensive with action itself, at least when that is understood in the strictest sense. On this account, the metaphysical implications of the Plurality Principle are such as to leave the whole conceptual structure of action in ruins if they turned out to be false.

This more radical incompatibilist line gives rise to a rather uneasy dialectical situation. Suppose that the incompatibilist argues that deliberated action (say) is incompatible with determinism (or something like that: for simplicity, I shall take the item to be determinism). It may seem that it is absolutely obvious that there is such a thing as deliberated action – because, for instance, we all go in for it. Then, if the incompatibilist argument is correct – more particularly, if it can be made obvious that it is correct – it will be obvious that determinism is false. But how could that be? You would suppose that if determinism were coherent at all, it would be a large task to establish its truth or falsehood. Faced with the obvious existence of deliberated action and the unobviousness of the truth or falsehood of determinism, the most economical assumption is that there is something wrong with this style of incompatibilist argument: for instance, the incompatibilist, for ultimately ethical reasons, has interpreted the familiar concept of deliberated action in too ambitious a way. (It can be helpful to bear in mind the truism that if determinism is true at all, it is true *already*.) It is a product of this unstable situation that many incompatibilist arguments, including some of those most familiar from the tradition, prove (if anything) more than their authors can want. They turn out, for instance, not to distinguish satisfactorily between determinism and fatalism, even if the incompatibilist wants, reasonably, to be able to make this distinction.

This is illustrated by the version of a familiar incompatibilist argument that has been presented by David Wiggins.[6] Wiggins starts from the idea of what an agent can or cannot bring about at a given time, where this involves the idea of the steps that an agent may or may not be able to take at one time in order to bring about an outcome at a later time. It is uncontentiously illustrated by a situation in which at 9.55, being where I am, I may (still) be able to catch the train that leaves at 10.15, but at 10.03 I am no longer able to do so. In terms of this idea of a tensed capacity, Wiggins defines a notion of *historical inevitability at t*:

By 'it is historically inevitable at time t' that p' is intended something like this: whatever anybody does at t' or thereafter, it cannot make any difference to whether p ...[7]

Let '$Nec_{t'}$' represent 'it is historically inevitable at t' that ...' Then, under determinism, for each action, R, of an agent A, there will be some truth of the form

(1) $Nec_{t'}$ (if C at t then A does R at t'),

which is a consequence of some law of nature, and expresses an inevitability because no-one can change the laws of nature. Moreover, for the appropriate set of conditions, C,

(2) $Nec_{t'}$ (C at t),

simply because C obtained at t, and no-one can change the past. So if we take '$Nec_{t'}$' indeed to represent a modality, we can use 'the uncontroversial modal principle'

(3) If Nec(p), then [if Nec(if p then q), then Nec(q)]

to reach the conclusion

(4) $Nec_{t'}$ (A does R at t'),

and 'how', Wiggins asks, 'does this consist with'

10

(5) A could at t' have done something other than R?[8]

How indeed, since by the definition of inevitability (4) entails

(6) Whatever A does at t', A does R at t'

and (6), on a natural reading, expresses a contradiction. This may just be a failing of the definition of 'historical inevitability'. But what interpretation of (4) will give the result that the argument needs? I cannot see any, constructed from these materials, that will not express a fatalistic conclusion.

Wiggins denies that his argument involves fatalism, but his ground for this is simply that it involves contingent premises, and is not 'a mere logical puzzle'.[9] But this is to reduce fatalism to the type that has been called 'logical fatalism'. 'Fatalistic' does not pick out a class of arguments, but a class of beliefs or attitudes: those that involve the idea that action, choice, and so forth have no effects; that everything will be the same whatever you do.[10] In many cases, such a belief is manifestly false, which is the main reason why incompatibilists want to keep determinism and fatalism apart: if determinism, by their argument, is as manifestly false as fatalism, then, as I just suggested, this casts doubt on their argument. With Wiggins's argument, however, the attempt to keep fatalism and determinism apart has failed.

This comes out if we reflect that, on the basis of the directions and the examples we have been given, we can read 'Nec$_t$(p)' as saying 'no thought or intention of any agent, occurring at t or later, has an effect on the obtaining of the state of affairs that makes p true'. In this sense of the operator, not only are (1) and (2) true, but so are

(1!) Nec$_t$ (if C at t then A does R at t')

and

(2!) Nec$_t$ (C at t),

so by the modal principle we can derive

(4!) Nec$_t$ (A does R at t'),

where t can be an arbitrarily long time before t'.

(4!), together with the explanation of the operator, entails that no thought or intention of A in an arbitrarily long period before t' has an effect on what A does at t', and this is a nakedly fatalistic conclusion.

Unless one wants to argue that determinism simply does entail an absurd fatalistic conclusion, it is reasonable to conclude that there is something wrong with this argument. It seems fairly clear what is wrong.

11

Given that (3) expresses a sound modal principle, then a question that Wiggins himself raises, whether 'Nec$_t$' expresses a modality, should receive a negative answer. At least, it is not well defined for the values crucial to the argument. While we have a good enough idea, for many purposes, of what it is for an agent's thoughts to be unable to have an effect on a state of affairs, we have been given no instructions on how to interpret the idea of an agent's thoughts having no effect on a state of affairs which includes something that is the effect of his thoughts. We have no idea of how relevantly to read (4), and hence cannot be licensed to apply (3) so as to arrive at it.

This is, of course, only a version of the equally traditional reply to these traditional arguments, that they fail to distinguish between causality that runs through the agent and causality that does not. Wiggins indeed discusses this distinction,[11] but in effect he says that a compatibilist who wants to make anything of it has first to deal with the 'circumstantial demonstration' offered by the modal incompatibilist argument. However, the distinction directly affects that argument. One could hope to understand the non-standard application that the argument makes of its (supposed) modal operator, namely to the agent's capacities in relation to situations involving his own actions, only if one had already thought through questions of what it is for causality to run through an agent's thoughts; the differences between an agent's acting and his being conscious of the causality of that very action, and so forth. This is precisely the kind of question that has been discussed in the work that I earlier claimed had given enough reason to think that there is no incompatibility between determinism (or something like it) and such things as deliberated action.

4 Choice as objectively determining

Some incompatibilists have interpreted the Plurality Principle as implying that when we (really) choose, we, for the first time, bring it about that a certain event will occur, or at any rate that a certain event will have certain properties; we determine, by or through our choice, that the course of events will have one character rather than another. Incompatibilist arguments of the kind I considered in section 3 are sometimes intended (though not by Wiggins) to encourage some such picture. The argument may be driven by supposed ethical demands on the voluntary, or simply by a metaphysical idea of what real choice must be. What is involved in this can be conveniently represented in a temporal model with forward-looking branches. An event that is possible at t is to be found in at least one branch later than t. Any event that has already been determined at t to happen is to be found in every branch later than t – that is to say, is necessary at t. To choose (really) at t that E will happen is to determine that E will happen, and requires that up to the moment of choice it was possible that E should happen and also possible that it should not happen. It trivially follows that E, if it is really chosen at t, cannot, at t, have been already determined.

Incompatibilists often try to persuade us that we *must* use such a conception of choice. I shall not take that issue further; I turn, rather, to the question of whether anyone could really want such a conception, and whether it could give its defenders what they need. Let E be the event that consists in A's doing a certain action, say G-ing. Then what exactly is it, on this account, that determines for the first time that E will happen? The point of the argument seems to be that A's choice should do this. But if *determining* means the closing of objective possibilities, then it will follow that if A chooses at t to G at some later time, then it is impossible from t on that A should not G; and that is absurd. No-one can need or want a notion of choice that leads to this result.

There are, then, two options, either to bring the thing determined up to the choice, thus identifying it as something other than the action; or else to move the determination down to the action. The latter course means that if this is a doctrine about choice at all, it applies only to those choices that coincide with the action chosen. Prior choices will not count as (real) choices. But this does less than justice to prior choosing, leaving it beached, so to speak, and out of relation to the real choosing that supposedly occurs only when one acts. Prior choice becomes a mere harbinger of later action. Can this be what is wanted by those who have this picture? To judge from their writings, it is precisely such things as the experience of prior choosing, apparent self-determination through deliberation, that help to encourage the picture in the first place.

So perhaps we should rather take the first option. We shall then say that a prior choice does, for the first time, determine something, and that what it determines is that there exists a state of affairs which will, other things being equal, issue in the agent's G-ing at the appropriate later time. The state of affairs presumably consists in a state of the agent. But if the picture is going to yield an account of free action, only some such states will count. The ones that count – the ones that we call states of intention – will have to be distinguished from such things as somnambulistic or drugged conditions into which, equally, A might put himself (if not quite so directly), and which, equally, might be expected to issue in his G-ing. (We all need to make such a distinction, and those who are drawn to this picture will be particularly keen to do so.) But in order to make that distinction, it looks as though we need to bring in two further conditions. One is that when A's state is the required one, intention, he could still change his mind. Another is that *issuing in* should not simply be equivalent to *causing*.

These further conditions, however, make it unclear again what, in the picture, choosing is supposed to effect. The first condition means that even after A has chosen there is still an objective possibility that E will not happen, and, moreover, whether that possibility is realised is still up to A. So how can his choice have done anything to shut any possibilities off? As for the second condition, it may be that *issuing in* is understood as at any rate a special case of *causing*. If it is understood in this way, then it will have been admitted that one can consistently say both that A is in a state which will cause his G-ing, and that he has the power even then not to G. Once that much has been admitted, the picture itself surely begins to seem less compelling. (The fact that, according to the picture, A put himself into that state, though it supplies a consideration, does not supply it at the right point to weaken the force of the admission.) If, on the other hand, *issuing in* does not even imply *causing*, we are still in the dark about the difference that A's getting into this state is supposed to make. It looks as though A still has to do everything that he has to do in order to G, and we are back with the first option, by which prior choice is at best only a harbinger of action.

The picture of choice objectively determining outcomes is not unwelcome merely to someone who has a prejudice in favour of determinism or parsimony. Rather, in its own terms it makes no sense of the relations between prior choice, intention, and action. It could not deliver what is wanted by those who are attached to it.

5 Blame

I come now to the relations between the second and third items that I picked out earlier, the psychological and the ethical. The item from the third area most favoured in these discussions, is, of course, 'moral responsibility', and that is usually explained in terms of *blame*. This is conceived as the rough analogy in the moral realm to legal penalties and denunciations. It is supposed to demand, more stringently than in the legal case, that the agent could have acted otherwise. (This is an application of the Plurality Principle.)

Faced with the problem of accommodating these notions to determinism, or at any rate to strong psychophysical explanations, the standard reconciling strategy does two things. It tries to find, or at least postulates, a sense of *could have acted otherwise* that will be compatible with those explanations. But, in addition, it tries to find a function or point for blame, and this is characteristically found in some forward-looking reason for it, such as the modification of the agent's motives.[12] It is interesting that the need should be felt for some such justification. The underlying idea seems to be that if blame *were* related to a non-naturalistic *could have*, it would not need any other explanation or justification; but since it is not, it does. Why should that be so? If it is said that it needs justification because it is to some extent unpleasant, that would be just as true if there were a non-naturalistic *could have* as if there were not. I think that the search for an appropriate account of blame is motivated by a rather shifty thought that if the non-naturalistic story were true, blame would be really or straightforwardly justified, but since that story is false, it is not, and we shall have to find something else to justify it.

The standard reconciling account, in terms of blame's effects, is too generous to blame, and at the same time sells it short. It sells it short by trying to base the justification of blame just on its efficacy. No such account can be adequate, because it collides with one of the most obvious facts about blame, that in many cases it is effective only if the recipient thinks that it is justified. Blame that is perceived as unjust often fails to have the desired results, and merely generates resentment. This shows that the idea of blame's justification is not the same as the idea of its efficacy. When a recipient thinks that blame is unjustified, the content of his thought cannot be that the blame will be ineffective. This does not show that the purpose of blame may not in fact lie in the modification of behaviour; it means only that if this is true, it cannot be obvious to those who are effectively blamed. Like many such Utilitarian proposals, it is not so much self-destructive as inconsistent with ideals of social transparency, and most naturally fits a situation in which those who understand the justification, and those whose behaviour is being modified, are not the same people.[13] These complexities do mean, however, that if you are trying to say what blame is, you cannot simply cite its aims of modifying behaviour. If blame is an instrument of social control, it is a peculiar one, and its peculiarities must be allowed for in the account of what it is.

The need to find something useful for blame to do illustrates the way in which the standard reconciling strategy has been, also, too generous to blame. Just like most of the libertarians who reject the reconciling project, it takes blame to be enormously important, the real thing. Indeed, there is a special form of ethical life, important in our culture, to which blame is central: we may call this special form of the ethical 'morality'.[14] Much discussion of freewill, on all sides, has shared the assumptions of morality, particularly about the central significance of blame. To correct those assumptions, there are several points to be borne in mind about blame itself.

Judgements that express blame are only one kind of ethical judgement among others. Inasmuch as blame is an ethical force, it is only one kind of ethical force, and it could not have its effects if it did not rely on other kinds. We have to learn what it is to be blamed, and (in line with a pattern familiar in ethical learning) we learn this by being blamed: by being, relative to the standards of later on, *unjustly* blamed. As soon as we look at blame not as a uniquely appropriate expression of truly moral judgement, and not, on the other hand, simply as an instrument of social control, but see it as part of a concrete ethical life, we shall be helped to understand the other psychological forces (such as love, perhaps) that are needed to make blame possible as a manifestation of the ethical dispositions.

Blame rests, in part, on a fiction; the idea that ethical reasons, in particular the special kind of ethical reasons that are obligations, must, really, be available to the blamed agent. (This is not the same as the fiction of a non-naturalistic *could have* but it is connected to it.) *He ought to have done it*, as moral blame uses that phrase, implies *there was a reason for him to do it*, and this certainly intends more than the thought that we had a reason to want him to do it. It hopes to say, rather, that he had a reason to do it. But this may well be untrue: it was not in fact a reason for him, or at least not enough of a reason. Under this fiction, a continuous attempt is made to recruit people into a deliberative community that shares ethical reasons, and the truth misperceived by the reconcilers' causal story is this, that by means of this fiction people may indeed be recruited into that community or kept within it. But the device can do this only because it is understood not as a device, but as connected with justification and with reasons that the agent might have had; and it can be understood in this way only because, much of the time, it is indeed connected with those things. Blame, like some other ethical institutions, operates in a space between coercion and full deliberative co-operation.

Blame is expressed in the most *tightly focussed* of ethical judgements. It tries to relate itself, typically, to this very act, in these very circumstances (though the acts themselves may, of course, belong to various orders, such as adopting a policy). It is a good question, why our culture should have evolved an institution that has just this character. It is also a very large question, and I shall not try to discuss it here. But the fact that blame tries to work in this way is doubtless connected with the fiction of the agent's having reason to act in the required way, and with the fact that the stance of the scrupulous blamer is that of a transferred or identifying deliberator, a fellow member of the community of reason. These features lead blame, too, towards an ideal of the absolutely voluntary act; but, as I have already said, that consequence is not the first source of its difficulties.

6 Freedom and practical necessity

The deepest exploration in philosophy of the requirements of morality is Kant's (which of course does not mean that those who disagree with Kant, such as Utilitarians, may not be deeply entangled with morality). Kant believed not only that there was an unconditional possibility for action, or at least for trying to act, but also that there was an unconditional necessity to be found in a certain kind of deliberative conclusion. This is a conclusion naturally expressed in the form 'I must'; it may be called a conclusion of practical necessity.[15]

Kant understood practical necessity in terms of a reason for action that was not conditional on any desire at all, and he thought that there could be such a thing because he thought that the reasons of morality were based on reason alone. That is why he identified practical necessity as uniquely moral necessity, and why, for him, unconditioned possibility and unconditioned necessity ultimately coincide, so that he could be led to say that the only truly free acts were those done for the sake of duty.

I do not think that many of us believe this. There are certainly such things as conclusions of practical necessity, but it is not that they are determined by no desires or projects of the agent at all. Rather, they are determined by projects that are essential to the agent. In well socialized agents, many of these projects will be compatible with, indeed expressive of, ethical considerations, and we can understand why that should be so. But not all or everyone's are, and it may not be at all clear which are, and which are not, and how. One form of moral luck lies in never having to find out.

Daniel Dennett has invoked practical necessity, as one among other kinds of example, to show that we care less than theorists suppose about whether the agent could have acted otherwise.[16] Such conclusions are surely paradigm examples of accepting responsibility, and yet, as with any other kind of necessity, 'I must' implies 'I cannot not', and 'I had to' implies 'I could do nothing else'. So it looks as though responsibility does not entail 'I could have acted otherwise', and the search for some reconciling explication of that formula loses some of its urgency.

It would be a mistake to reject this argument on the supposition that practical necessity is a purely 'normative' modality that has nothing to do with how things will be. It is plausible (though, as we shall see, it is not quite correct) to say that if a person rightly concludes that he must do a certain thing (has no alternative, cannot not, etc.), then it is impossible, not that he should fail to do it, but that he should intentionally fail to do it. Equally, if his conclusion is that he cannot do a certain thing, then it is, roughly, impossible that he will intentionally do it (for convenience, I shall from now on keep to this negative case). His conclusion does, then, have implications about the way the world will be, but the modality that occurs in them is still essentially deliberative, in the sense that the statement expresses the agent's intentions, and does not merely report an antecedent fact about the agent. If it did report an antecedent fact, then the agent's acceptance of it, if it did not express an unintelligible form of fatalism, would have to represent his recognition of a limitation on his powers; but in that case he could not do the thing in question even unintentionally.[17]

What this modality represents is a recognition that one cannot intentionally do this thing when one has taken everything available to one into account, *including this very deliberation*. This helps to explain why the impossibility applies only to the intentional action. It also explains something else, that the conclusion 'I cannot do this' does not imply that there is no possible world in which I figure as doing this thing intentionally. For, granted that there are other possible worlds in which I figure, I figure in some of them without my actual projects, and without my actual projects this practical necessity will not arise. This shows something further again; that my conclusion does not after all imply without qualification that the actual world will not contain my intentionally doing this very thing, where 'this very thing' refers to the most specific description available to me of what I have decided I cannot do. If the demon scientist or a bolt from the blue radically changes my character and projects between now and the time of action, it may be that I shall intentionally do this very thing, but it will (*pace* certain theories of personal identity) still be me.

We can see, I think, how these various points hang together, if we take seriously the point that statements of practical necessity express intentions. Those statements bear much the same relations to a class of possible worlds as ordinary statements of intention do to predictions about the actual world. When I say 'I will ...' or 'I am going to ...', I make an assumption which is presupposed in arriving at any deliberative conclusion, that I can reasonably count on certain future happenings being brought about by this very conclusion, and by the projects and desires that have issued in this conclusion. When I say 'I cannot', I imply that no possible world contains my acting in this way, if it contains me with these projects, and permits the general conditions for my projects to be expressed in action.

So is the *could not* of practical necessity the negation of the *could* in 'he could have acted otherwise', as Dennett's use of it in his argument implies? I doubt it. I think that the latter, the *could* that belongs with the institution of blame, must be meant to represent a possibility available to the agent in deliberating, that is to say, one that he could in principle recognize antecedently.[18] But this is a difficult question, one that is made more difficult, perhaps insoluble, by the fact that the institution of blame, because it involves the fictional features I have mentioned, leaves it indeterminate what it does demand in the way of *could* (which may help to explain why so much difficulty has been found in analysing it).

But the phenomenon of practical necessity does certainly show this at any rate, that my acknowledgement of responsibility can coexist with, indeed be grounded in, a consciousness that I am not in the position of choosing between courses that I shall continue to see as equally open to me. Once one recognizes this, one will see that the acknowledgement of responsibility has less to do with the concerns of blame, with regard to *could have* or anything else, than is made out. The phenomena of agent regret and of our capacity and need to acknowledge responsibility for what we have unintentionally done, are other examples of the same thing.

7 What have we got?

Can the reconciling project succeed? Between determinism (or as much naturalistic explanation as you like), and relevant psychological concepts, yes. Between both of these, and the ethical conceptual scheme, no, not as it stands: or rather, the question is often indeterminate because it is indeterminate to what extent that scheme is committed to all the aspirations and misunderstandings of morality.

We need to recast our ethical conceptions. But that is not in order to escape or adjust ourselves to determinism or naturalistic explanation. We need to do so in order to be truthful even to what we know already about our psychology, and to much of our ethical life. It is a basic misrepresentation of the problem to pretend that it is only in the light of what we might discover about ourselves or our actions that we might need to reconsider our ethical ideas. But if we bring our ethical ideas nearer to reality, then assuredly we shall find that they are consistent with naturalistic explanations of our choices and actions.

The will is as free as it needs to be. That does not mean, as libertarians would take it, that it is able to meet all the demands of the morality system as they present themselves to the uncritical consciousness or, perhaps, conscience. Nor does it mean that it is free enough to keep the morality system in adequate business, as reconcilers usually take it to mean. It means that if we are considering merely our freedom as agents, and not the more important question of our political or social freedom, we have quite enough of it to lead a significant ethical life in truthful understanding of what that life involves. A truthful ethical life is, and always has been, one that can include our best understanding of our psychological life, and we know that such an understanding is compatible with naturalistic explanation.

Notes

1 John Locke, *Essay on Human Understanding*, II, 21, 14.
2 See Robert Nozick's subtle discussion, 'Coercion', in *Philosophy, Science and Method: essays in honour of Ernest Nagel*, ed. S. Morgenbesser, P. Suppes and M. White (NY: St Martin's Press, 1969).
3 Aristotle, *Nicomachean Ethics*, 1110 a4 seq.
4 Daniel Dennett, *Elbow Room* (Cambridge, MA, and London: MIT Press, 1984), p. 136.
5 Brian O'Shaughnessy, *The Will: a dual aspect theory* (Cambridge: Cambridge University Press, 1980).
6 David Wiggins, 'Towards a reasonable libertarianism', in his *Needs, Values and Truth* (Oxford: Blackwell, second edition 1991): page references cited refer to this edition, which is a revised version of an article first published in 1973. I am indebted to Wiggins for helpful discussion of an earlier draft of this section.
7 *Ibid.* p. 285. Despite its informal introduction, this is called, on the same page, a 'definition': the symbolism that follows differs from Wiggins's, but this is only a matter of typography.
8 *Ibid.* p. 284. I have slightly shortened Wiggins's presentation of the point.
9 *Ibid.* pp. 283 and 302, Longer Note 20.
10 I have discussed fatalism more generally in chapter 6 of my book *Shame and Necessity* (Berkeley, Los Angeles and London: University of California Press, 1993). In connection with the conclusion (6), compare the idea of 'immediate fatalism' on pp. 138–9 of that chapter.
11 In part 5 of his article. Wiggins points out (p. 285) that it is not an objection to his definition of inevitability that it uses the notion of possibility. That is correct. The objection is not that it uses notions of possibility or, indeed, capacity, but that the use made of the operator tries to apply the notion of (in)capacity where we have no clear idea of how to apply it.
12 It is notable that Hume, in some ways an archetypal reconciler, refused to ascribe any such restricted role to blame. This is closely connected with his striking resistance to some central tenets of what I call 'morality': in particular, his refusal to take seriously what he called the merely 'grammatical' distinction between virtues and talents. See *Treatise* III, iii.4, and the admirable discussion in appendix IV to *An Enquiry Concerning the Principles of Morals*.
13 I have discussed this idea and its relation to some versions of utilitarianism in my book *Ethics and the Limits of Philosophy* (Cambridge, MA: Harvard University Press, 1985), pp. 101, 108–10: further citations of this book use the abbreviation *ELP*. See also 'The point of view of the universe', and for the account of blame that follows, 'Internal reasons and the obscurity of blame'.

14 See *ELP*, chapter 10: for further suggestions about blame's relation to the morality system, and to ideas of freewill, see 'Nietzsche's minimalist moral psychology'.

15 See *ELP*, p. 133 seq; 'Practical necessity' in *Moral Luck* (Cambridge: Cambridge University Press, 1981); and, for further development of the points made here, 'Moral incapacity'.

16 Dennett, *Elbow Room*, p. 133 seq. Dennett is not only, or principally, concerned with deliberative conclusions of practical necessity; he mentions them in discussing, very relevantly, impossibilities grounded in character. My questions concern the relations between the two.

17 I take it that if it is possible that I should G unintentionally, then it is not beyond my powers to G: there can, of course, be more than one kind of reason why I should be unable to G intentionally, though it is possible for me to G unintentionally. This is explored in 'Moral incapacity', where I also take further the distinction, made below, between impossibilities that present themselves to the agent's deliberation as limitations, and those that emerge from the deliberation.

18 The question is related, further, to the matters discussed in section 3, and to the distinction between determinism and fatalism.

2

Voluntary acts and responsible agents

Voluntary acts

Particular actions may have various things wrong with them. I shall be concerned only with people's actions and not with things that happen to people; and I shall not be concerned with the question of where that line itself should be drawn. Everyone will agree that it is something that happens to a person if he is thrown through a window by others, even if he asked them to do it, or (differently) asked for it. But if the doctor strikes my knee with his little hammer and my leg moves, some would say that this was a reflex action of mine, as opposed, for instance, to peristaltic movements of the gut, which are reflex changes that happen to me.[1] For the present purpose, I shall move the frontier of action one stage further out than the reflex: action must manifest some degree of control. That still leaves room for actions done in a variety of untypical states.

The agent may be asleep, yet the language, not just of action, but of purposive action, be appropriate beyond dispute:

- ... Lo you, here she comes! This her very guise; and, upon my life, fast asleep. Observe her; stand close ...
- You see, her eyes are open.
- Ay but their sense is shut.
- What is it that she does now? Look, how she rubs her hands.
- It is an accustom'd action with her, to seem thus washing her hands. I have known her continue in this a quarter of an hour.

This example, described with such absolute precision,[2] is, like hypnosis, a radical case. At one level, the agent does not know what she is doing at all, though at another she knows, as is revealed by the effective intentional contour of what she does: for instance, she had brought the light from her bedroom.

There is another kind of case, where agents do at an everyday level know what they are doing, but the cause of their doing it does not bear the usual relation to their reasons. This would be the case, paradigmatically, with post-hypnotic suggestion.[3] Both this case, and that of somnambulism, are examples of action that has an inherent defect – a defect simply from the point of view of the theory of action. Other cases, again, are peculiar with respect to the theory of deliberative action. They are cases in which the agent straightforwardly knows what he or she is doing, but the relation of the action to relevant deliberation is awry.

The notorious cases of incident passion provide examples of deliberation being *suppressed*; passion also may bring it about that deliberation is *skewed*, and so, typically, do obsessions. What is often vaguely discussed under the general heading of *akrasia* is an example, in its most spectacular form, of something different again, deliberation being *decoupled*: the agent deliberates, arrives firmly at a practical conclusion, and straight off intentionally does something different.[4] There are various ways of describing and distinguishing these possibilities, guided by interests in the philosophy of mind, and to some extent it does not matter for the present purpose how this is done; but a more general point does matter, that a discussion of the voluntary demands *some* view of deliberation and its proper relations to action. This is for the following reason.

Defects of action are properties possessed by some actions and not by others. Just as somnambulism and hypnotism offer examples of defects of action as such, so defects of deliberative action are incontestably displayed by cases of extreme incident passion and by some of the cases classed as *akrasia*. But with some other cases where the relation of action to deliberation is peculiar, it will beg important questions to classify the actions as defective, since it is possible to 'place' deliberation itself. Both individuals and cultures have differed on the question of the extent to which actions in which deliberation was suppressed (at least) might not be entirely appropriate.

Some thinkers, on the other hand, have held – some seemingly do now – that the ideal of action is deliberated action. (One wonders what they may seem like to their sexual partners – not because they regard their immediately sexual behaviour as no exception to their doctrine, but because they regard it as the only exception.) There are some actions that, in virtue of their peculiar relations to deliberation, should be seen as embodying defects of action, as falling short of what action by a deliberating agent should be, but we need to be aware of the evaluational territory into which this category may rapidly move. The evaluational territory can be restricted, at this point of the argument, in one important way. The question whether an action displays a defect in this respect may be relativized to the dispositional activities and motivations of the particular agent. At this level, it is relative to the agent's expectations of himself or herself that the absence of deliberation will be counted a defect, or the emphasis on some matters rather than others in a deliberation will count as a skewing of it. It is not yet a question whether the agent should have deliberative dispositions that he or she does not have.

We shall have to move out of that relativity later. But even at this level, we have to be aware that relativizing the question to a particular agent does not answer all the questions. If there is a lack of fit between the outcome of an action and some deliberation that the agent made before the event, this does not imply that even from the agent's perspective the action is necessarily what is defective. He may conclude that he went in for unrealistic, self-deceiving or priggish deliberations.[5] There is something wrong in his deliberative economy, and it lies in the relation of its parts, but it does not follow that the action has the defect.

A particular application of this general point lies in the theory of *akrasia*. Some very extreme cases are naturally classed with defects of deliberated action as a purely psychological phenomenon: they unqualifiedly display lack of control. But consider the only too well-known case of a man who wants to be loyal to one woman and resolves to stop seeing another. He sees her all the same. If he finally goes back to the first woman he may classify these episodes as akratic, *i.e.* as cases of his doing other than what at the time he thought he had most reason to do. But if he finally leaves the first woman to live with the second, he may not see the episodes in this light, but rather identify them as the first steps in the recognition of what he had most reason to do. It was not a psychological defect that he could not achieve that recognition in full synchronous consciousness; perhaps it could not be achieved in any way other than that in which it actually came about.

Such an identification seems essentially retrospective. It is not clear, in the light of this, how far *akrasia* is altogether a psychological category: beyond a certain point, it is ineliminably an ethical category, as Aristotle, for different reasons, thought that it was.[6] This touches on some matters that will be of concern later; now, we are concerned just with making the point that there are evaluative limits to the notion of a deliberative defect of action. Let us say, at any rate, that there are actions that suffer from 'inherent or deliberative defect'. The phrase is deliberately wide-ranging, grouping several different kinds of defect, and it is also vague, in shading off into cases in which it is unclear, sometimes for evaluative reasons, whether there is a defect of action. But it is enough to distinguish this from another familiar dimension of the subject, the unintentional.

I take it as common ground now that 'being unintentional' is not a property of an action.[7] 'Falling under some description under which it is not intended' is a property of an action, but it is a property of every action. What is not a property of every action, fortunately, is 'falling under some description under which it is not intended and is regretted by the agent'; but it is manifestly not possible to eliminate actions that have that property. An action may, in a special case, be regretted under an unintended description because it possesses some inherent or deliberative defect, but being so regretted is not in itself an inherent or deliberative defect. You could not, so to speak, by inspecting the conditions of action discover that there was something peculiar about it as an action.

What we have so far are actions of agents capable of knowledge, belief, desire, passion, and intentions, and which are in some cases the results of those agents' deliberations; we have inherent and deliberative defects of actions; we have descriptions under which actions may be intended or not intended; and we have ways in which the actions may fail to relate to aims or desires of the agents, which are longer-term in the sense both of being held over a longer time and relating to a longer time.

What is the voluntary? We might say: an agent does X fully voluntarily if X-ing is an intentional aspect of an action he does, which has no inherent or deliberative defect. This idea of a voluntary act is, basically, a concept in the theory of action.[8] It is, roughly, the concept of an action that is intentional in the relevant respect and that, to the extent the agent deliberated, is the appropriate product of that deliberation. We now have to ask what the ethical use of this concept might be.

The Aristotle–Irwin theory

Should this concept be turned to ethical use and, if so, how? A familiar suggestion is that fully voluntary actions are all and only the actions for which an agent is (fully) responsible; and this has been traditionally expressed by saying that such actions are those that appropriately attract reactions such as praise and blame (many problems are concealed in the phrase 'such as'). This is, very roughly indeed, Aristotle's proposal. It must be said at once that it does not accord with practice, even if we consider only the dimension of the intentional, and if we stick with the far from perspicuous reaction of blame. An agent can be blamed for some unintended aspect of what he did, even though he would not have done it if he had known, and indeed would have wanted not to do it if he had known. He can be blamed, for instance, because he ought to have known. But this is not the only case. If some distinguished person, opening a nuclear power station, idly turned a handle, releasing dangerous radiation, he would be blamed (and not just for turning the handle, but for releasing the radiation), although he did not know; and this would not be because he ought to have known, but because he ought not to have done it granted he did not know – that is, he ought to have known better.

Such cases show that you can be blamed for things you do non-voluntarily. But my aim here is to press the connection between responsibility and voluntary action in the opposite direction. The question is whether performing a voluntary act is a sufficient condition of being responsible for that act – in particular, in a sense of 'responsible for it' in which only responsible agents are responsible for their actions. We can usefully approach this by considering an ancient criticism of Aristotle, and a development of Aristotle's view which has been advanced against that criticism by Professor T. H. Irwin.[9]

Aristotle said that children and animals were capable of voluntary actions, and also that they were not responsible for what they did, and this, together with what (roughly) has been ascribed to him, yields a contradiction, as Aquinas and others noted. I shall leave aside animals; and I do doubt that children cannot be held responsible for particular actions. But there is clearly a problem here: one can hold that children are not responsible agents, in some sense, without thinking that they never perform a voluntary action.

Irwin's aim is to work up to a notion of 'responsible for a given voluntary act' by developing first a notion of 'responsible agent'. The theory that yields these notions goes beyond Aristotle's but is claimed not just to be a present to him either: it is developed in Aristotle's spirit from Aristotelian materials. Putting it in the terms that I used in my account of voluntary actions (which is not quite the same as Irwin's) it requires not just that whatever deliberation the agent makes is effective, but that the agent does indeed deliberate, and is open to deliberative considerations. This makes the agent a rational agent. But in addition to this, Irwin requires that the agent does not merely reason in the service of desire, but has rational desires, a kind of desire that 'results from someone's deliberation about what it would be best to do in the light of all his aims'. The rational agent 'deliberates about [his] final good'. 'We normally suppose that a responsible person can do something about the desire he acts on – that it is not compulsively strong but is responsive to his reason and deliberation.'[10]

This gives us 'responsible agent', and we have 'voluntary act'. The aim of the strategy is to arrive at 'act for which the agent is responsible'. This is not simply equivalent to 'voluntary act of a responsible agent'; the responsible character of the agent needs, so to speak, to be focussed on to the particular act. Irwin's own proposal is that A is responsible for doing X if and only if (a) A does X voluntarily[11] and (b) A is capable of deliberating effectively about X (where X is a particular); and (b) means 'there is some deliberative argument about X which if presented to A would be effective about A's doing X'.

I shall not consider the details of this proposal. I shall take up three more general questions. I shall consider first a well-known difficulty in such an account of what it is to be a responsible agent; I shall then raise the question of what motivates this kind of account of that notion – as I shall call it, an *ideal-bearing* account; and, last, I shall ask what reasons there may be for explaining 'responsible for doing X' in terms of such an ideal-bearing account of the responsible agent. First, the only too well-known difficulty.

Responsible agents and the ideal-bearing account

Since character is itself constituted in part by patterns of desire, the idea that if one's desires are rational, then, quite generally, reason must not be in the service of desire but must be productive of it, implies that one can deliberate about one's character, indeed about one's character as a whole. Irwin, as I understand him, accepts this consequence, one even stronger than that accepted by Aristotle.

Aristotle thought that people voluntarily had their characters because they originally brought them about by what they voluntarily did: 'thus it was open at the beginning to the unjust and the self-indulgent man not to become like that, and so they are voluntarily as they are: but when they have become so, it is no longer possible for them not to be so'.[12] This account is hopeless, in part because it just shifts the question back; and even if bad character were a kind of addiction brought about by voluntary action, it would not follow that the addiction was voluntary: the agents might not have known that their actions would lead to the addiction. If, moreover, the doctrine is motivated by considerations of fairness, it offers very rough justice. Why should the feckless acts of long ago lead to blame for everything we now do as a result? Some of these problems will be avoided if, as Irwin's account seems to imply, we retain the power to reshape our characters by reason. But in avoiding some of Aristotle's difficulties, this type of account loses his psychological realism. The ideal of total deliberative control of all one's dispositions is, for more than one reason, a hopeless fantasy.

However, we may be able to reshape the requirement to some degree. If we drop the ideal of total deliberation, we may still recognize a picture of how an agent should desirably be, a picture that has been offered in various forms by writers other than Irwin, such as Frankfurt and Charles Taylor.[13] This agent has evaluative attitudes that apply to other of his or her desires; his or her attitudes are effective in controlling desire; we might say, too – though this is not the formulation of all these writers – that the agent tries to make sense of his or her life.

This type of picture occupies the same space as Irwin's picture of the responsible agent. However, in order not to beg some later questions, I am not going to call this, now, the idea of a responsible agent, but rather of a *mature agent*. There are many hesitations and divergences among these writers in formulating a description of what I am calling 'the mature agent', and these illustrate the important point that there is no one picture of such a person. This is not merely because there are basic ethical differences here and it is hard to choose between different formulations. It is also that there are basic difficulties in what is to be formulated. They go back in particular to the problems I mentioned earlier when I discussed, in relation to voluntary action, the placing of deliberation itself. If there are questions about the proper relations between deliberation and particular actions, they meet up with questions about the role of deliberation in life more generally. Another way of putting the point is this: if we dispense with the fantasy of global deliberative control, what exactly are we left with? How does one deal with the fact that the life that best honours the proper role of deliberation is likely to be one that is not too meticulously deliberated? How does one react to the terrible Socratic over-simplification – or, to put it more plainly, falsehood – that the unexamined life is not worth living? What marks are there that distinguish the deliberation that helps insight from the deliberation that is a further elaboration of evasion?

These are real and surely unanswered questions – unanswered, at least, at any general level. But, happily, it is not necessary to answer them to make some progress with the present question. For, whatever conception of a mature agent we may have or may develop, it is quite plain that it will be an *ideal-bearing* conception – it will represent an aspiration for human growth. But this leads to the question, how could *that* be the conception lying behind the everyday notion: *he was responsible for this action*? How could the purposes for which we need that notion harmonize with these ideals of maturity?

We may say that we have two starting points, and we are considering the idea that from these two starting points, we can arrive at the same place. One is the notion: *responsible for this action*; the other is an ideal of maturity. The idea that these two routes coincide seems to be based on the conception that they both deploy the same idea of freedom. What is involved in being fully responsible for an action is freedom in the sense, most primitively, of control, but going beyond that. Maturity turns out also essentially to involve freedom, in a sense that yields responsibility for self.

Responsibility for self implies also that the person has a certain under-standing of himself or herself. The ideal need not involve many of the things that moralists have supposed it to involve, such as a lot of long-term diachronic deliberation or life planning; or the necessary supremacy of values over desires – you may be able to modify your values in the light of your desires as well as conversely; or an inability to have desires that surprise you. The ideal may also not be found just in a certain kind of life, but rather in a certain way or condition of living, which may indeed vary at different points in a life. Granted all this, it may be claimed that the ideal represents, in a fuller state of development, something that has to be true, in a minimal form, of anyone who is capable of deliberation and sustained control at all – that is to say, of anyone who is a non-defective and grown-up person. Anyone who deliberates at all requires a sense of reality, and hence some insight into the place of one desire or another in his or her internal economy.

Such is the line of thought that suggests that the requirements of the ideal of maturity (the second starting point) coincide with those of responsibility for an action (the first starting point). Do they really coin-cide? Is the idea of a responsible agent that is implied just by one's being responsible for one's acts the same as that involved in the ideal of maturity as responsibility for self? I think not. The interests of that first starting point of course involve the minimal requirements of a person capable of deliberation and sustained control. But it does not follow from this, nor do I think it is true, that those interests must also be concerned with an ideal of maturity, even if that ideal is understood, to some extent, as a fuller development of those requirements. There are, of course, many relations between people for which such an ideal is relevant – if you want to share close relations with them, for instance. But if we are addressing the ideas of being held responsible or regarded as a responsible agent, it is not clear why such an ideal should be relevant. The ideas of responsibility developed from the first starting point are rather a matter of what is involved in a set of persons, not necessarily known to each other or specially important to one another, living under a common system of justice.

These people do not, just from this perspective, have any great interest in one another's powers of self-understanding – that is to say, in the ideal of maturity. They do have an interest in others' having powers of self-control and enough deliberative foresight to avoid unnecessary colli-sions with the law or with each other. Already at this level, the level of persons subject to the law, there is a model of people understanding the requirements of society, and an interest in whether their general set is to conform or not, and this brings into play a certain notion of a responsible

29

agent, one that does not go far beyond the minimum requirement of an adult, non-defective person. Only with slaves, persons treated as things, would questions of responsibility be reduced simply to causal questions of what they have brought about and of what would be the most effective way of influencing their behaviour.

In the case of relations that are supposedly between equals, more elaborate concerns may be added to those implicit in persons being responsible to the law, more sophisticated forms of assessment, interpretation, and recrimination. The model then is not just of people subject to the law, but of people capable of deliberating together about what the law should be. In those circumstances, there might be an interest at the public level not just in whether a person broke the law, for instance, and whether he broke it deliberately, but in his reasons for breaking it – the principles, for instance, that he might be expressing in doing so.

Three kinds of politics

Corresponding to these distinctions, we may identify three levels of political and social conceptions. The levels are cumulative, each higher level requiring some application of the lower as well.

There is a politics of mere *control*: this corresponds simply to 'he did it'. If there is this and no more, the people involved are slaves.

There is a politics of *acknowledgement*. This corresponds to 'he voluntarily did it'; there is a concern with whether the agent was in normal control of the act, what he meant to do, and his or her capacity dispositionally to shape his actions to social expectations. If there is this and no more, the people involved are *subjects*.

There is a politics of *communal deliberation*. There is a concern with whether an agent has the general capacity to engage in long-term practical thinking, consider the relations of his life to that of others, and so forth. Under this, people are regarded by each other as *citizens*.

At the first level, there is no notion of a responsible agent, and the sense in which someone is responsible for his actions is basically that he is responsible for an outcome – he is the cause of it. (This is not to say that there is any polity in which people are only treated in this way; the model represents rather a schematic type of the most limited and manipulative public attitude to individual behaviour.) At the second level, people are responsible for their actions, and are responsible agents, in the sense of being able reliably to accommodate their actions to public requirements (which does not exclude their having reasons for not doing so). This is, roughly, the notion already mentioned, of an adult, non-defective person.

The third level is more ambitious than that (and even less definite) in what it might hope for from people in the polity. The idea here is of one who could responsibly play a part in sharing a political life with others, and depending on how ambitiously that aspiration itself is taken, it will make further demands on what the agents may be like. It may be thought that, at this level, the idea of a responsible agent does finally coincide with the ideal of maturity. We must bear in mind that, even if this were so, it would still not be right to suppose that this ideal coincided with what is implicit in 'responsibility for one's actions' without qualification. Under actual circumstances, and to a considerable degree under any imaginable circumstances, the use of that notion will be that appropriate to the second level. But even beyond that, when one considers the kind of character that might be looked for, not just in a responsible agent who is a subject, but in a responsible citizen, it still seems wrong to identify this with the ideal of a mature agent.

The ideal of the mature agent is of a different character from any of the political conceptions, even the third, and it is a mistake to suppose that it merely represents a higher version of what one needs if one makes increasingly demanding claims on a free polity. In its most popular form, the ideal involves the self-reflexive application of virtue to control desire. The conception that the ideal in that form coincides with what you arrive at from ideas of citizenship seems to me a version of a familiar and suspect device of reconciliation, designed to show that what society can reasonably hope its citizens will be like coincides with what they would ideally want to be like: that freedom, rationality, virtue, citizenship, and individuality can ultimately coincide.

As I have already suggested, we may reasonably move the ideal of maturity away somewhat from a necessary engagement with the supremacy of co-operative virtue. But it still remains an open question how far the politics of citizens does require them to pursue these ideals of maturity. There may be a strain, however happy the circumstances, between the expectations of civic responsibility and some expressions, at least, of the ideals of maturity. The point is not that there will necessarily be such a strain, but that it is a substantive question whether there will be, and this substantive question is merely concealed, and not resolved, by forcing the aspirations of the ideal notion onto the notion of responsibility, even in the more ambitious interpretations of that, let alone in the minimum interpretation of it that is required in order to make sense of 'responsible for what he did'.

There is more than one reason, I think, why we should remain sceptical about the extent to which ideals of maturity and self-development should be involved in, or assimilated to, the politics of control and of mutual acknowledgement, or even those of communal deliberation. The maturity or self-understanding of the well-formed agent never attains a necessary claim on the attention of the public, in the way that a person's intentions may have on it in a system of mutual acknowledgement, or his mere identity as an agent will in any system of justice at all, however rudimentary. Certainly his character and maturity may be of public interest if, for instance, he is running for office, but they can never make claims parallel to those other claims, which are claims of justice. Even if there were, in a sense, a politics of individual maturity – that is to say, a politics that valued it, encouraged it, and respected it – that could never be a substitute for, or even simply an extension of, the politics of justice.

There is a converse reason as well. The mature agent, when that idea has been freed from the false idea of global deliberative control, will recognize his relation to his acts in their undeliberated, and also in their unforeseen and unintended aspects. He recognizes that his identity as an agent is constituted by more than his deliberative self. This may remind us of the difficulties in identifying the ideal of maturity, and also, earlier, in saying what counted as a deliberatively defective action. The agent lives with the truth that his character, what he is, is neither a deliberative construct of his, nor fully expressed in his deliberations. Indeed, he lives from that truth. But that does not mean that he cannot acknowledge actions that flow from it as his – in what way could they more be his? They will sometimes include instances of what we first identified as deliberative failure. Beyond this, he will be able to acknowledge more generally that he can be as responsible for some things that he did not intend as much as he is for things that he did intend, and in ways that have nothing to do with the law of negligence.[14] For him, to be responsible is not simply to be properly held responsible by others, by the institutions of control and cohesion, but to hold himself responsible. He acknowledges that in that sense, responsibility can reach beyond the voluntary (and not merely in the ways acknowledged in the law of negligence). In this sense, the ideal of maturity does not involve a restriction of the situations of responsibility, as the move from slavery to subjecthood does, but rather a broadening of them. No conception of public responsibility can match exactly an ideal of maturity because, among other reasons, to hold oneself responsible only when the public could rightfully hold one responsible is not a sign of maturity.

Notes

An earlier version of this chapter was given as the third Hart Lecture in Oxford in May 1987; it was a particular pleasure to give this lecture near the occasion of Professor Hart's 80th birthday. I am very grateful for comments made in a seminar after the lecture, particularly by Herbert Hart himself and by Philippa Foot. I gave a much modified version, nearer to the present text, as the Whitehead Lecture at Harvard in April 1989.

1 O'Shaughnessy, *The Will*, Vol. II, ch. 16.

2 *Macbeth* V, i.

3 Hypnosis, of course, also displays the feature that the action is under the control of someone else's intentions. This feature in itself is not part of this subject: the topic of coercion is not part of the theory of action, but of the theory of freedom – the kind of freedom, moreover, of which one can have more or less. See 'How free does the will need to be?', and *Shame and Necessity*, chapter 6.

4 Amelie Rorty, in several writings, has illuminatingly illustrated the point that it is quite a different question whether this phenomenon represents the triumph of the worse over the better: see now her *Mind in Action: essays in the philosophy of mind* (Beacon Press, 1991).

5 The important point that the seat of the trouble may lie in the deliberation is made by David Pears in *Motivated Irrationality* (Oxford: Oxford University Press, 1984).

6 For further discussion of this point, see now *Shame and Necessity*, pp. 44–6.

7 The fundamental work is that of Donald Davidson: see his *Essays on Actions and Events* (Oxford: Clarendon Press, 1980).

8 Not in the theory of freedom: in line with what was said earlier, an action can be fully voluntary in this sense, and yet be done under constraint. This is not a problem for the considerations about praise and blame that follow: actions done under constraint can be praised or blamed – it is merely that they may be praised or blamed on grounds different from those appropriate in other circumstances.

9 T. H. Irwin, 'Reason and responsibility in Aristotle', in Amelie Rorty (ed.), *Essays on Aristotle's Ethics* (Berkeley and Los Angeles: University of California Press, 1980).

10 *Ibid.*, pp. 128, 129 and 131. Irwin acknowledges a debt to H. G. Frankfurt, 'Freedom of the will and the concept of a person', *Journal of Philosophy* 68 (1971), 5-20, and to G. L. Watson, 'Free agency', *ibid*. 72 (1975), 205–20.

11 As I have already mentioned, he does not mean exactly the same by 'voluntary' as I do, but the differences do not affect the argument.

12 Aristotle *Nicomachean Ethics*, 1114 a19; cf. 1114 b30 seq. See on this subject M. F. Burnyeat, 'Aristotle on learning to be good', in Rorty (ed.), *Essays on Aristotle's Ethics*.

13 Frankfurt, 'Freedom of the will and the concept of a person'; Charles Taylor, 'What is human agency?' and 'Self-interpreting animals', both in his *Human Agency and Language* (Cambridge and New York: Cambridge University Press, 1985). Taylor is particularly clear that he is discussing an ethical ideal, an achievement: he speaks, for instance (*ibid.*, p. 67), of seeing 'ourselves and others more broadly, more objectively, more truly. One is a bigger person, with a broader, more serene vision, when one can act out of this higher standpoint.' Frankfurt, on the other hand, takes himself, in introducing

second-order desires, simply to be defining a person. However, he calls someone who lacks such desires 'a wanton', and talks about him as though he were a certain, undesirable, sort of person. For comment on Frankfurt, see Watson, 'Free agency'.

14 There is fuller discussion of this in *Shame and Necessity*, chapter 3.

Internal reasons and the obscurity of blame

Internal reasons

I have argued elsewhere[1] for a view that can be rather roughly expressed by saying: there are only internal reasons for action. A number of discussions has led me to think there is something about this view, or the ways I have so far found to express it, that easily leads to misunderstanding. Here I shall first try to explain, as well as I can, what the view is, and I shall then apply it to the question of blame.

What are the truth conditions for statements of the form 'A has a reason to φ', where A is a person and 'φ' is some verb of action? What are we saying when we say someone has a reason to do something? Consider the following formulation: A could reach the conclusion that he should φ (or a conclusion to φ) by a sound deliberative route from the motivations that he has in his actual motivational set – that is, the set of his desires, evaluations, attitudes, projects, and so on. (The agent's actual motivational set I shall label, as I have done elsewhere, with the unlovely abbreviation 'S'.) The internalist view of reasons for action is that this formulation provides at least a necessary condition of its being true that A has a reason to φ: A has a reason to φ only if he could reach the conclusion to φ by a sound deliberative route from the motivations he already has. The externalist view is that this is not a necessary condition, and that it can be true of A that he has a reason to φ even though A has no motivation in his motivational set that could, either directly or by some extension through sound deliberation, lead him to φ.

It is a further question whether the formulation provides a sufficient condition of an agent's having a reason to φ. I actually think that it provides a sufficient condition as well, but this is not an issue I shall consider here; I shall be concerned solely with the question of whether it provides a necessary condition.

An important part of the internalist account lies in the idea of there being a 'sound deliberative route' from the agent's existing S to his ϕ-ing. It is important that even on the internalist view a statement of the form 'A has reason to ϕ' has *normative force.* Unless a claim to the effect that an agent has a reason to ϕ can go beyond what that agent is already motivated to do – that is, go beyond his already being motivated to ϕ – then certainly the term will have too narrow a definition. 'A has a reason to ϕ' means more than 'A is presently disposed to ϕ'. One reason why it must do so is that it plays an important part in discussions about what people should become disposed to do. One example of this, which is uncontentiously related to questions raised by the internalist view, is given by advice in the 'if I were you ...' mode. Taking other people's perspective on a situation, we hope to be able to point out that they have reason to do things they did not think they had reason to do, or, perhaps, less reason to do certain things than they thought they had.

The claim that somebody can get to the conclusion that he should ϕ (or, the conclusion to ϕ) by a sound deliberative route involves, in my view, at least correcting any errors of fact and reasoning involved in the agent's view of the matter. Suppose, to take an example I have used elsewhere, the agent thinks that he has a reason to drink what is in a certain glass. He believes that he has reason to do this because he wants a drink of gin and tonic. He believes that this glass contains gin and tonic, but it does not – it contains petroleum set aside from some chemical experiment. I say, as any reasonable person would say, that he does not have reason to drink what is in the glass, though he thinks he has. This is because there is not a sound deliberative route from his motivational set to this glass of petroleum: what he wants is a drink of gin and tonic. We are allowed to change – that is, improve or correct – his beliefs of fact and his reasonings in saying what it is he has reason to do. That is already enough for the notion to be normative.

But if we are licensed to vary the agent's reasoning and assumptions of fact, it will be asked why we should not vary (for instance, insert) prudential and moral considerations as well. If we were allowed to adjust the agent's prudential and moral assumptions to some assumed normative standard, then obviously there would be no significant difference between the internalist and the externalist accounts. We would have incorporated into the notion of a 'sound deliberative route' anything the externalist could want. The internalist proposal sticks with its Humean origins to the extent of making correction of fact and reasoning part of the notion of 'a sound deliberative route to this act' but not, from outside, prudential and moral considerations. To the extent that the agent already has prudential or moral considerations in his S, of course, they will be involved in what he has a reason to do. They will contribute to an internal reason.

The grounds for making this general point about fact and reasoning, as distinct from prudential and moral considerations, are quite simple: any rational deliberative agent has in his S a general interest in being factually and rationally correctly informed. There could be a case of somebody who had an overwhelming need to be deceived; and if his relations to reality were so poorly negotiated that he actually needed to believe what was false, then perhaps he would have reason to acquire false beliefs – in that particular respect.[2] The basic point, however, is that on the internalist view there is already a reason for writing, in general, the requirements of correct information and reasoning into the notion of a sound deliberative route, but not a similar reason to write in the requirements of prudence and morality. Somebody may say that every rational deliberator is committed to constraints of morality as much as to the requirements of truth or sound reasoning. But if this is so, then the constraints of morality are part of everybody's S, and every correct moral reason will be an internal reason. But there has to be an argument for that conclusion.[3] Someone who claims the constraints of morality are themselves built into the notion of what it is to be a rational deliberator cannot get that conclusion for nothing. Merely to point out that we have a notion of a good reason that includes prudential and moral considerations as well as, for instance, getting the facts right, effects nothing. If we have that notion, it is no doubt because, among other things, we assume that, for most people we deal with, some kinds of moral reasons are internal reasons.

It would also be a misunderstanding to suppose the force of the internalist view disappears if one grants that some moral (or, as I should prefer to say, ethical) statements are themselves factual: that their application is 'world-guided'.[4] Internalism does not, despite its view of a 'sound deliberative route', depend on a distinction between fact and value. It may well be that 'thick' ethical concepts are, to an adequate degree, both 'world-guided' and 'action-guiding'. People who use a given concept of this sort will find their application of it guided by their experience, and also accept that it gives them reasons for or against various kinds of action. Then this disposition will figure in their S, in rather the same way as a disposition to avoid the poisonous or the disgusting may figure in it.

But this does not mean that a speaker who does use a given concept of this kind (*chastity* is an example that focuses the mind) can truly say that another agent who does not use the concept has a reason to avoid or pursue certain courses of action in virtue of that concept's application. To show this, the speaker would need to show that the agent *has reason to use that concept*, to structure his or her experience in those terms. That is a different, and larger, matter; all the work remains to be done. This point is typically concealed in discussions of this matter because it is simply assumed that all the agents involved belong to one 'community' or 'form of life' – that they can, in the relevant respects, all think of themselves as 'we'. To the extent that this is true of them the S of each resembles the S of others, and internalism correctly describes the situation. The difficulties arise when this situation does not obtain; but in that case, this view in itself neither supports externalism nor, alternatively, serves to overcome the distinction between internalism and externalism.

Leaving now the matter of what kinds of consideration contribute to the idea of a sound deliberative route, there is a question of the kinds of thinking that may be involved in it. The first thing to be said is negative: it does not merely involve perceiving means to an end that has already been formulated. There are many other possibilities, such as finding a specific form for a project that has been adopted in unspecific terms.[5] Another possibility lies in the invention of alternatives. One of the most important things deliberation does, rather than thinking of means to a fixed end, is to think of another line of conduct altogether, as when someone succeeds in breaking out of a dilemma. Yet another line of deliberative thought lies in the perception of unexpected similarities. Since there are many ways of deliberative thinking, it is not fully determinate in general, even for a given agent at a given time, what may count as 'a sound deliberative route'; and from this it follows that the question of what the agent has a reason to do is itself not fully determinate. It is sometimes held against the combination of the internalist view with this broad conception of deliberation that it leaves us with a vague concept of what an agent has a reason to do. But this is not a disadvantage of the position. It *is* often vague what one has a reason to do. For one thing, the lines between rationality and imagination are vague. If someone is good at thinking about what to do, he or she needs not just knowledge and experience and intelligence, but imagination; and it is impossible that it should be fully determinate what imagination might contribute to a deliberation. This is one reason why it may be indeterminate what exactly an agent has a reason to do. There is another reason as well, which I shall touch on later: that it may be indeterminate what the condition of the agent's S relevantly is.

There are two fundamental motivations of the internalist account. The first point is the interrelation of explanatory and normative reasons. It must be a mistake simply to separate explanatory and normative reasons. If it is true that A has a reason to φ, then it must be possible that he should φ for that reason; and if he does act for that reason, then that reason will be the explanation of his acting. So the claim that he has a reason to φ – that is, the normative statement 'He has a reason to φ' – introduces the possibility of that reason being an explanation; namely, if the agent accepts that claim (more precisely, if he accepts that he has more reason to φ than to do anything else). This is a basic connection. When the reason is an explanation of his action, then of course it will be, in some form, in his S, because certainly – and nobody denies this – what he actually does has to be explained by his S.

Internalist theory explains how it is that the agent's accepting the truth of 'There is a reason for you to φ' could lead to his so acting, and the reason would thus explain the action. It is obvious on the internalist view how this works. But suppose we take the externalist view, and so accept that it can be true that A has a reason to φ without there being any shadow or trace of that presently in his S. What is it the agent comes to believe when he comes to believe he has a reason to φ? If he becomes persuaded of this supposedly external truth, so that the reason does then enter his S, what is it that he has come to believe? This question presents a challenge to the externalist theorist.

The second motivation for the internalist view is based on what is, in a sense, another application of the same point. There are many things we can say to people who lack appropriate items in their S. Suppose, for instance, I think someone (I use 'ought' in an unspecific way here) ought to be nicer to his wife. I say, 'You have a reason to be nicer to her'. He says, 'What reason?' I say, 'Because she is your wife.' He says – and he is a very hard case – 'I don't care. Don't you understand? I really do not care.' I try various things on him, and try to involve him in this business; and I find that he really is a hard case: there is *nothing* in his motivational set that gives him a reason to be nicer to his wife as things are.

There are many things I can say about or to this man: that he is ungrateful, inconsiderate, hard, sexist, nasty, selfish, brutal, and many other disadvantageous things. I shall presumably say, whatever else I say, that it would be better if he were nicer to her. There is one specific thing the external reasons theorist wants me to say, that the man has a reason to be nicer. Or, rather, the external reasons theorist *may* want me to say this: one of the mysterious things about the denial of internalism lies precisely in the fact that it leaves it quite obscure when this form of words is thought to be appropriate. But if it is thought to be appropriate, what is supposed to make it appropriate, as opposed to (or in addition to) all those other things that may be said? The question is: what is the difference supposed to be between saying that the agent has a reason to act more considerately, and saying one of the many other things we can say to people whose behaviour does not accord with what we think it should be? As, for instance, that it would be better if they acted otherwise.

I do not believe, then, that the sense of external reason statements is in the least clear, and I very much doubt that any of them are true. I think the sense of a statement of the form 'A has a reason to ϕ' is given by the internalist model. I suspect what are *taken for* external reason statements are often, in fact, optimistic internal reason statements: we launch them and hope that somewhere in the agent is some motivation that by some deliberative route might issue in the action we seek.

Blame

In discussing blame, I am not considering it as just the causal, diagnostic notion that is deployed when we blame the valve for the failure of the rocket. I am concerned with blaming agents for specific acts or omissions,[6] what may be called the 'focussed' application of blame. This is often said to be a moral notion, but this requires a distinction. Focussed blame does not have to be blame for something that is an offence against morality. People can be blamed for missing their opportunities or making mistakes, and they can be blamed by non-moralizing people. For example, one partner to a bank robbery may ruin it by an idiotic mistake and be blamed by his companion for the fact that they are in jail. His companion is not invoking the system of morality and does not think that this was an offence against moral canons. Nevertheless, there is something in the idea that the failure that is being blamed has some kind of ethical dimension to it. When the failure is explained, it seems that for blame to be appropriate, there must be some generally reprehensible characteristic involved in the explanation: the agent must have been careless, or lazy, or self-serving, or something of the sort.

Focussed blame operates in the mode of 'ought to have', which has a famous necessary connection with 'could have'. Focussed blame will go by the board if 'could have' is absent. The reason for this seems to be connected with the following consideration: if 'ought to have' is appropriate afterwards in the modality of blame, then (roughly) 'ought to 'was appropriate at the time in the modality of advice.[7] Now 'ought to' in the modality of advice implies 'can', because advice aims to offer something as a candidate for a deliberative conclusion. If ϕ-ing is not available to the agent, 'You ought to ϕ' cannot function as a piece of advice about what he should now do; when it is a matter of what I am to do, manifestly 'I cannot' acts as a stopper.

If 'ought to have' in the mode of blame corresponds to 'ought to' in the mode of advice, this strongly suggests that what it refers to is the agent's having (having had) a reason: 'ought to have' will carry the thought that the agent had a reason to act in the desired way but failed to do so. But it may seem a rather obvious fact about blame that someone can be blamed even though his S does not contain anything that would lead to the appropriate motivation: we can blame a man (we may think) for neglecting his wife even though he has no motivation to be concerned about his wife.[8] So if blame is necessarily connected with reasons, it seems to be necessarily connected with external reasons. Therefore, if there are no such things as external reasons for action, there is something suspect about blame.

In what follows, I am going to assume, on the strength of the earlier considerations, that there are no external reasons for action. I am also going to assume, for the sake of the present discussion, that the parallelism between blame and advice does establish a close connection between focussed blame and the agent's reasons. It may be that the connection with reasons is not as close as the parallelism makes it seem; but I think it will shed light on the problem and on the operations of blame, if we make the strong assumption that there is a close connection. Making these assumptions, how should we understand the operations of focussed blame?

The first point is that blame is, much of the time, applied to people who do have some appropriate item in their S, and the person is blamed because it was not brought to bear in the right way on the particular case. In other cases, the agents may not have in their S the motivation to do just the kind of thing they failed to do on the occasion for which they are blamed. They may have other dispositions, however, in their S to which the blame, less directly, may relate. In particular, they may have a motivation to avoid the disapproval of other people – for instance, to avoid their blame. When a motivation of this kind takes a deeper form than merely the desire to avoid hostility, it can be the ethically important disposition that consists in a desire to be respected by people whom, in turn, one respects.[9] People who have such a disposition have in their S a motivation that may not have been strong enough, or may not have been mobilized in the right way, for them to have avoided this particular action; but they have a general desire to be ethically well related to people they respect, and the expression of blame serves to indicate the fact that in virtue of this, they have a reason to avoid these things they did not have enough reason to avoid up to now. In these circumstances, blame consists of, as it were, a proleptic invocation of a reason to do or not do a certain thing, which applies in virtue of a disposition to have the respect of other people. To blame someone in this way is, roughly, to tell him he had a reason to act otherwise, and in a direct sense this may not have been true. Yet in a way it has now become true, in virtue of his having a disposition to do things that people he respects expect of him, and in virtue of the recognition, which it is hoped that the blame will bring to him, of what those people expect.

A rather similar proleptic mechanism may be involved even when the agent did have in his S a more direct motivation to avoid the act for which he is later blamed. When we say that he ought to have acted otherwise, we may imply, in such a case, that he did indeed have a reason to act otherwise; but it would be rash of us to imply, simply given his S as it then was, that he had more reason to act in this way than to do anything else. What we are blaming him for may not be a failure to recognize what he then had most reason to do; even in the cases in which there is a directly appropriate motivation in the agent's S, not every failure to act appropriately is simply the product of deliberative failure. Our thought may rather be this: if he were to deliberate again and take into consideration all the reasons that might now come more vividly before him, we hope he would come to a different conclusion; and it is important that the reasons that might now come more vividly before him include this very blame and the concerns expressed in it. This kind of thought helps us to understand a sense in which focussed blame asks for acknowledgement.

A rather similar structure can apply to advice: the parallel between focussed blame and advice, from which I started, is sustained. For even when we are advising in the 'if I were you' mode, our claim that the agent has most reason to ϕ does not necessarily imply that simply given his S as it is, it already determines that ϕ-ing has priority over anything else. We are saying that the conclusion to ϕ, rather than to do something else, can be reached from his S by a sound deliberative route, and that is something that involves such things as the exercise of his imagination and the effective direction of his attention. But among the things that will affect his imagination and his attention, we hope, is our advice itself and how it represents things. This dimension of advice, the fact that it has to be understood, in part, in terms of its own intended effects, does not mean that it is insincere. The question of insincerity lies not in whether it changes the situation, but in what spirit it does so, and how far it reveals what it is trying to do. Blame, similarly, presents a consideration that contributes to what it is talking about; but it must be more obliquely related than advice to the agent's reasons at the time of action, since it presents its consideration only retrospectively.

Focussed blame, then, involves treating the person who is blamed like someone who had a reason to do the right thing but did not do it. It does not typically register simply a deliberative failure at the time, but rather, in varying strengths, the kinds of proleptic mechanism I have sketched. Of course, there are some hard cases, people who lie beyond any such mechanism; and it is a support for an account on these lines, that it is precisely people who are regarded as lacking any general disposition to respect the reactions of others that we cease to blame, and regard as hopeless or dangerous characters rather than thinking that blame is appropriate to them. This represents the absence from their S of anything that can be reached by these mechanisms, anything it might even be hoped could yield recognition.

Between the hard case, to whom blame is admitted to be inappropriate, and the cases this internalist account can describe, there will be many in which it will be merely unclear what, if anything, blame is effecting: unclear, in particular, whether it is appropriate in a focussed form, as opposed to its acting as a broader instrument of correction and disapproval. This is bound to be so, above all because it must very often be obscure to those who are blaming, and quite probably indeterminate in itself, what the motivational state is of the person being blamed. The inherent obscurity of focussed blame and its operation are closely related to the vagueness, which I discussed earlier, of 'A has a reason to φ'; but it goes beyond that, because it adds to this a further obscurity about the ways in which blame may be relying on the proleptic mechanisms. In both the cases, of an agent's having a reason for action and of the operation of focussed blame, the vagueness or indeterminacy that follows from the internalist account matches, as it seems to me, a vagueness or indeterminacy that is a genuine feature of our practice and experience; and this is an advantage of the internalist account. Equally, it is a disadvantage of the externalist account that it cannot place these phenomena, and has nothing to say about the ways in which the presence of deliberative reasons, or, again, the appropriateness of focussed blame, *fall off* in one or another direction. The externalist account does not mirror a genuine obscurity in the phenomena – it is merely obscure what account it gives of the phenomena.

It seemed at first glance an advantage of an externalist account that it could directly pursue the hints given by the parallelism between the 'ought to have' of focussed blame and the 'ought to' of deliberative advice: just because it allowed for external reasons, it could quite readily accept that focussed blame was to be understood in terms of the agent's reasons. But just as externalism is uninformative about the conditions of saying that A has a reason to act in some desired way, as opposed to the other things that may be said to or about A, and, correspondingly, it leaves it quite unclear what it is for an agent to come to act for a given reason: so, equally, if focussed blame is understood in terms of the agent's reasons, externalism has nothing interesting to say about it, because it offers no route to a concrete psychological understanding of the relations between the agent's reasons, his failure to act in the desired way, and the content of blame.

Externalism is indeed external, and the image of blame that can be derived from its account of reasons, in failing to provide any way to engage with an agent's actual motivations, leaves us also without ethical resources. It gives us no way of understanding the difference between a blame that might hope to achieve recognition, and the blame that hopes by mere force to focus on the agent's reasons a judgement that represents in fact only a rejection (perhaps an entirely justified rejection) of what he has done. It leaves us, that is to say, in the condition of moralism.

The proleptic mechanism I have sketched is not merely an accommodation to fit the internalist view. Rather, this mechanism, or some other on these lines, is likely to prove essential to an intelligible account of how focussed blame is a distinctive ethical reaction (just as internalism in general claims to show that it is a distinctive claim about A and his not ϕ-ing, that A has a reason to ϕ). To show, in psychologically realistic terms, how focussed blame can be a distinctive ethical reaction is important, moreover, to showing that it is something rather than nothing at all. The intelligible obscurity or indeterminacy of blame's operations replaces the unintelligible mystery that surrounds it on less naturalistic accounts; a mystery that, unless it can be dispelled, will only promote the belief that focussed blame is through and through suspect, and rests on nothing more than the fictions of the morality system.[10]

Notes

This chapter is based on a lecture given to the conference on Reason and Moral Judgment at Santa Clara University, April 1989; I am grateful to Leo van Munching for help in reconstituting the chapter from the lecture.

1 'Internal and external reasons', reprinted in *Moral Luck*. Since the present article appeared, I have written some more about this question, defending my view against criticisms made by John McDowell. McDowell's paper, and my reply, are to be found in a collection of essays on my work, *World, Mind and Ethics: essays on the ethical philosophy of Bernard Williams*, ed. T. R. Harrison and J. E. J. Altham (Cambridge: Cambridge University Press, 1995).

2 This leads to well-known paradoxes that belong with the general theory of self-deception. The agent has to have true beliefs about where to go in order to acquire the false beliefs he needs on the other subject; at the same time, he cannot be too clear that that is what he is doing.

3 In this respect, I have no basic disagreement with Christine Korsgaard's excellent paper 'Skepticism about practical reason', *Journal of Philosophy* 83 (1986).

4 I have in mind the Wittgensteinian position expressed by Sabina Lovibond in *Reason and Imagination in Ethics* (Minneapolis: University of Minnesota Press, 1983), and in work by John McDowell. For discussion of such a position and of the consequences of accepting some version of it for 'thick' ethical concepts, see *ELP*, chapters 8 and 9.

5 Such possibilities for deliberation have been explored by David Wiggins, 'Deliberation and practical reason', in *Needs, Values, Truth*, and elsewhere.

6 It is relevant to the present subject that the notion of a *specific* action or (still more) omission is, in some ways, quite obscure.

7 It is important, in exploring these connections, that we are indeed concerned with the modality of blame. In the case of an error that is not blamed, for instance because it was due to unforeseeable circumstances, 'ought to have' may mean, at most, 'could have; and it would have been better if he had'.

8 Though, as we shall recall later, there comes a point at which the case is hard enough for it to be beyond blame.

9 I have discussed this form of disposition in connection with the operations of shame, in *Shame and Necessity*, chapter 4.

10 For the morality system, see *ELP*, in particular chapter 10. The general lesson, that our ideas of blame and responsibility are answerable to an adequate psychology (rather than to generic worries about determinism), is argued in 'How free does the will need to be?' In addition to the mechanisms sketched here, blame certainly has some less benign aspects, particularly related to the metaphysics and psychology of the morality system. This side of it gets more attention in 'Nietzsche's minimalist moral psychology'.

4

Moral incapacity

I am not concerned with an incapacity to engage or be engaged in moral life, but, on the contrary, with incapacities that are themselves an expression of the moral life[1]: the kind of incapacity that is in question when we say of someone, usually in commendation of him, that he could not act or was not capable of acting in certain ways.

There are first-personal and third-personal aspects of this question, and one of my concerns will be to relate them to one another. Just for that reason, it may be helpful to mention at the beginning, chiefly to get it out of the way, a kind of case in which the first-personal aspect cannot come up: the kind of case in which A could not have done a certain (kind of) thing because he could not have thought of it, that it would never enter his head. A remark to this effect does not have to be a compliment, but it can be. However, the question whether it is a compliment or not is less important than the question whether the incapacity is related to what sort of person the agent is: as we may say, to his character. This will be true of other, more central, examples as well. The difference between an incapacity's being a matter of character and its not being so is, in itself, neutral between the favourable and the unfavourable. Being incapable of a certain course of conduct, in the relevant sense, and more particularly being incapable of thinking of it, may indeed be a virtue, but it can also be a failing, for instance a kind of feebleness.

In some cases where a certain course of action could not occur to someone, the explanation may be historical or sociological. I do not mean the obvious sense in which Alexander the Great could not have thought of building a nuclear power station, but rather the sense in which (as seems to me to be true) it was historically impossible that Alexander the Great should think of cancelling the expedition to the East in order to give the money to the poor. Such a project was not, for cultural reasons,

on his moral map. By contrast with this, it may be a distinctive characteristic of a particular individual that he could not think of a certain course
of action, or, if it crossed his mind or was mentioned to him, he would
never for a moment consider it. This is one form that moral incapacity can
take. However, having mentioned this quite significant sort of case, I am
not going to address it from now on. For the rest of this chapter, I am
concerned with a more complex type of moral incapacity that does not
take this form.

I claim that remarks about moral incapacities, about what people
cannot or could not do in this sense, are what they seem. These are
indeed incapacities, and they are connected with prediction and understanding in some of the ways that physical, and other psychological,
incapacities are. In particular, they sustain inferences of the form *esse ad
posse* and, significantly, *non posse ad non esse*. At the same time, they are
special incapacities, which differ from others. These differences are particularly related to the idea, which I have already mentioned, that the
incapacities in question are expressive of, or grounded in, the agent's
character or personal dispositions.

I do not intend the notion of 'character' itself to be explanatory in this
discussion; it helps, if at all, in locating what has to be explained. It, itself,
stretches beyond the matter of incapacities and brings in ideas not just of
what an agent can or cannot do, but of what he is typically eager or
reluctant to do for certain kinds of reasons. Indeed, it might well be a
mark of someone's character that there was nothing that in this sense he
was incapable of doing. So 'character' does not contribute much to the
explanation of moral incapacity; perhaps, rather, if we can shed light on
moral incapacity we can shed some light on the idea of 'character'.

There is of course scepticism – some of it justified – about the idea of
character. It is a prime target of scepticism about a 'fixed' or 'substantial'
self or subject, when that is not merely scepticism directed at Carte-
sianism. But that point need not undermine the present discussion. The
sceptic about character should consider the status of these incapacities;
considerations about the incapacities can focus questions about the
reality of character.

In the third-person cases, there are connections between 'he can't' and
'he won't', and between 'he couldn't have' and 'he didn't'. Prima facie
these function as with other kinds of incapacity, as I suggested when I
mentioned the *esse ad posse* inferences. There is also a first-personal 'I
can't', which is concerned with the same kind of subject matter as
third-person ascriptions of moral incapacity, and is related to deliberation. The 'I can't' may express the conclusion of a deliberation: my
practical question has been whether to ϕ, and after rehearsing the moral

and other reasons I come to the conclusion that I cannot φ – as I may equally say, it is not something I can do, it is ruled out, it is impossible. When I am considering more broadly what to do in a given situation, and not just whether to φ, 'I can't' may express a subconclusion of my deliberation; ruling out one line of action, it leads me to the conclusion that I will or must do something else.

When the conclusion is 'I must', this may simply be a consequence of 'I can't' – I had only two alternatives, and the other is ruled out. In other cases, slightly differently, 'I must' is the primary thought, and 'I can't' represents the ruling out of all the alternatives to what (I have concluded) I must do. When Luther famously said 'hier steh' ich, ich kann nicht anders', he meant that having reached this position, there were indefinitely many things he could now not do. I shall ignore from now on these various refinements, and for the most part just refer to 'I can't' in the deliberative context as expressing conclusions.

When 'I can't' expresses a deliberative conclusion, it is tempting to think that it (and the other related modal expressions) have some different, normative sense; that they are particularly emphatic members of the family of 'should' and 'ought', and, indeed, do not represent incapacities at all. This suggestion is fortified by a number of assumptions, which focus on such points as that 'can't' and 'must' as deliberative conclusions are alternatives to 'should not' and 'should'; since these latter are not predictive, the argument may go, neither are the former. Again, it may be argued that a deliberative conclusion is a decision and a decision is not a discovery. The deliberative conclusion is based, as decisions indeed are, on considerations of the good, the useful, the obligatory and so on, and not on psychological information about myself, which is presumably what I would need in order to have a basis for ascribing an incapacity to myself.

Some real questions are raised by these considerations, and I shall come to some of them later, but I am going to suggest that their conclusion is basically a mistake. 'Can't' is, once again, 'can't', and it has the same sort of implications as it does in third-person cases for the question whether the world will contain my doing the thing in question. It is indeed true, and important, that as expressing a deliberative conclusion, it rests on considerations of the good and the useful and so on, and not just (if at all) on psychological information that the deliberator has about himself. I am going to suggest that, when we understand better what kind of incapacity is in question here, we shall see that this is what we should expect.

A moral incapacity belongs to the species: incapacity to do a certain thing knowingly. With a straightforward physical incapacity, by contrast, if I cannot φ, then there is no event that the world will contain that will be a φ-ing by me.² If Rambo cannot lift a 500 lb weight, then he will not lift it, period. If it turns out that he does lift it when hypnotized, or when excited by the presence of the enemy, then it is not true he cannot lift it; he can lift it, under those conditions. This absoluteness applies to many psychological incapacities as well. If I cannot, in my head, work out in ten seconds the product of two numbers, each of which consists of five different digits, then that is something I shall not be doing, however the task is represented to me and whatever the conditions under which I am invited to do it.

Other incapacities, however, take the form of one's being unable to φ if one knows that one is φ-ing. These might include such things as walking a narrow plank over the Avon gorge; having a relaxed and friendly conversation with the lover of one's spouse; and eating roast rat. (This phenomenon must be distinguished from another, that of being unable to φ if one is thinking about one's φ-ing. In many cases of which that is true, it may still be the case that I need to know that I am φ-ing. The trick is to combine knowing what I am doing with not thinking about it, and the kinds of techniques discussed in *Zen and the Art of Archery*, for instance, are directed to just that end.) Where my incapacity to φ is the incapacity to φ knowingly, it does not follow, of course, from my having the incapacity that the world will not contain any instance of my φ-ing, but only that it will not contain any instance of my φ-ing while knowing that this is what I am doing.

None of the examples of this sort I have mentioned so far is yet a moral incapacity. The incapacity to have a friendly and relaxed conversation with the lover of one's spouse could be a moral incapacity, if, very roughly, it were grounded in the agent's thinking that such a thing would be a shaming, dishonest, lax, or grotty thing to do. But it is not a moral incapacity if, thinking no such thing, the agent finds, or knows that he or she would find, that he or she would be too angry or embarrassed to carry it off.

This suggests a basis of the difference. In this last kind of case – and the same is manifestly true of the Avon gorge and the roast rat – if I have this incapacity, then if I were to try to do the thing in question, I would fail. But in the pure case of moral incapacity – I say 'pure', because there are certainly, and importantly, mixed cases – it is not necessarily true that if I tried I would fail. If I tried, I might well succeed. The moral incapacity is revealed in the fact that for the appropriate kinds of reasons, I will never try.

This point might lead, in turn, to a suggestion: that moral incapacity consists in the agent's not being able (even) to try. Or, again, it might be suggested that what such an agent cannot do is choose to do the things in question. But this does not offer any account of the distinction between moral incapacities and other incapacities to φ knowingly. A preliminary point is that in the formulation

A cannot choose/try to φ,

'φ' has to occur intensionally (the action is not specified as in 'Hobbes spent years trying to do something mathematically impossible.') But the states reported in such formulations need no more be moral incapacities than those introduced originally in 'A cannot φ'. The dizzy, squeamish, or embarrassed agents who were the subjects of the last examples might equally be incapable of trying to do the acts which, for these reasons, they cannot perform; and since they may know this, they may not be able to choose them either. Of course, it is true that the way in which vertigo or embarrassment excludes trying is different from the way in which the reasons associated with moral incapacity rule it out. But that is simply the difference we have noticed already and which we are trying to explain; it is not explained by shifting the incapacity from doing to trying.

To understand moral incapacity, we have to consider more closely the way in which the incapacity is connected with the agent's reasons. The distinctions we need are not caught simply by the idea that in the different cases different considerations are present to the agent. We have explanations, or elucidations, of the following kinds:

He cannot eat rat because he finds it disgusting

He cannot walk the plank across the gorge because he is subject to vertigo

and these are not merely extended by examples such as

He could not gossip to reporters about his wife's problems (would be incapable of doing so) because he would find it disloyal, shabby, etc.

In a general way, of course, they are all alike. In all the examples, the explanation connects the incapacity to a mode in which the action, or an attempt at the action, or the mere idea of the action, presents itself to the agent. Equally, in all these cases, it may be through imagining φ-ing, or trying to imagine φ-ing, or imagining trying to φ, that the agent discovers that he cannot φ. Again, the similarities between them enable them all to be used in similar ways in third-personal explanations and inferences. But there is a difference between moral incapacity and the others, which is to be found in the way in which the agent's incapacity is connected to the mode in which the action presents itself to him; there is a corresponding difference in the way in which he discovers that he cannot φ 'through' imagining φ-ing.

In the cases of vertigo or disgust the incapacity presents itself to the agent through an imagined encounter. It may do so also in the case of moral incapacity, but if it does so, it is as part of a more complex process. I imagine the act as I might in deliberating whether to do it. It is the process of deliberation that actually bears the weight here, and it is at the centre of the moral incapacity. For the same reason, the fact that an act would be (in my view) disloyal or shabby is a consideration *for me* in deciding not to do it. The fact that an act would disgust me can be such a consideration. But where the act is so disgusting that I cannot do it, then the fact that it is disgusting does not function in that way: the question of deciding not to do it does not come up, or is cut off; or, if I do decide to try, the incapacity will make me fail. (This is the difference that we noticed earlier, in discussing the relations between incapacity and trying.) In the case of moral incapacity, my deliberative conclusion not to do the act, reached on the basis of these totally decisive considerations, just is the conclusion that I cannot do it.

Another way of putting the difference is that other kinds of incapacity, if known to me, are inputs *into* decision. They constitute the limits within which I decide: if I know I cannot φ, then φ-ing is not one of the courses that can enter my deliberative field of choice. For a given deliberation, a particular moral incapacity can function in that way: as I remarked earlier 'I cannot do that' can function as an excluder, on the way to the conclusion of what I should do. But wherever this is so, it introduces the idea of a deliberation upstream from that one, of which the 'I can't' corresponding to that moral incapacity would itself be the conclusion. So far from the deliberative 'I can't' representing something different from an incapacity, its role as a conclusion provides the best understanding of the distinctiveness of moral incapacity.

Of course this does not mean that for every such incapacity that we can rightly ascribe to an agent, he must have deliberated in such terms; indeed, in the case of incapacity through the silence of certain courses of action, which I mentioned at the beginning, it could not be so. But, beyond those cases, the idea of a possible deliberation by the agent in such terms gives us the best picture of what the incapacity is. Indeed, it may even give us knowledge or well-grounded belief; if we want to know what exactly an agent can and cannot do in this sense, we need to know how that agent would deliberate in given circumstances. It is a summary of the differences between moral and other kinds of incapacity that it should be this way round. We understand the agent's moral incapacity just because we understand how 'I can't' could be the conclusion of his deliberation; in the other cases, it is the other way round, and we conclude from our knowledge of his incapacities how he will deliberate. This explains, too, how moral incapacity can be to an indefinite degree fine-grained. If we know an agent well, we may be more certain that he could not do this very specific thing, than that he could not do anything of a certain general character; or, even if we are clear that he could not do anything that he saw as having that character – that it was disloyal, for instance – we may be clearer that he will see this particular act as having that character, and will deliberate accordingly, than we are about any more general class of acts that he could not do for this reason.

All this comes about because the dispositions that are the ground of the agent's incapacities are focussed on to a particular case through the ways in which the features of the case impress themselves on the agent – ways that are best represented by a deliberation, even though the deliberation need not consciously occur. It is because of this, too, that when there is a conscious deliberation, which issues in 'I can't', that conclusion can present itself to the agent at once as a decision, and as a discovery. It is a decision, as being indeed the conclusion of a deliberation whether to do that thing. But it presents itself to the agent also as a discovery, because the underlying dispositions have not before been focussed through and on to that very conjunction of features. The incapacity to do this thing is an expression of those dispositions as applied to this situation *through this very deliberation*. In one sense, the highly specific incapacity comes about through the deliberation: indeed, in some cases, it might not be true that the agent could not φ, if he had not deliberated. But this is not always so, and even when it is, it is not unequivocally true that the incapacity comes about through the deliberation: if the deliberation is sound and convincing, it is so because it is the best expression of dispositions that were there already. In creating an application, the deliberation reveals a potentiality.

Of course there is also room here for scepticism. On a more sceptical reading, we may say, rather, that in *seeming* convincing, a deliberation of this kind *seems* to yield a discovery. There is no doubt that, sometimes, this is what we should say; it also explains the first-personal facts. But there are limits to that kind of scepticism, because it does not explain our correctness, so far as it exists, in the third-personal mode. If we can know that this is how this agent will decide (and it may not be a case of a mechanical or simple application of a disposition), then there was something to be discovered by the agent in concluding that (as we knew) he could not do the thing in question.

We have been tracking correspondences between the agent's deliberative conclusion, 'I can't', and the ascription to that agent by someone else of a moral incapacity. The correspondences are based on the point that the other person recognizes the incapacity because he or she understands the agent's dispositions and the way in which they might be focussed on such an action, for instance through just such a deliberation. In this sense, 'he can't' is the third-personal analogue of the deliberative conclusion 'I can't'.

However, perhaps we should not say without qualification that this use of 'he can't' is the third-personal analogue of the first-personal deliberative conclusion. There is another claimant for that role, a normative 'he can't' that is something like a stronger version of 'he shouldn't'. The construction is familiar, too, in the second person, as when we say 'you can't do that', meaning that the relevant reasons tell overwhelmingly against the action. The mark of these uses will be that *non posse ad non esse* does not apply: from 'he can't ϕ', in the sense that there are overwhelming reasons against his ϕ-ing, it does not follow that he will not ϕ. He may not share the speaker's conception of what reasons are overwhelming; or he may share that conception, but not see that the reasons are so in this case.

The normative sense of 'he can't' or 'you can't' certainly exists. The important point, however, is that in the second and third persons there is room for a split between the normative and the predictive that cannot occur in the first person. My account is that the agent's 'I can't' has the force of both a deliberative conclusion drawn from reasons, and a statement about what the world will contain in the way of actions intentionally done by him. In this respect 'I can't' contrasts with 'I should not'. If the agent concludes 'I should not ϕ' and nevertheless does ϕ, that does not show his conclusion to have been a mistake; if his conclusion was 'I can't ϕ', then he must recognize this as a mistake if he, in fact, knowingly ϕ's. 'I can't' recognizes an incapacity in the light of deliberative reasons. 'He can't', in the sense in which it has predictive force, ascribes the same thing, and in this sense it is the third-personal analogue. At the same time it is clear why there should be in the third and second persons a sense for which there is no room in the first person, one in which the other person conducts the agent's deliberation for him and possibly arrives at a different conclusion.

Moral incapacities have relations to impossibility, but those relations are limited. In this they are like all other capacities and incapacities. If A cannot lift 100 lb weights, this does not mean that it is impossible that he should have been able to, or that it is impossible that he will ever be able to. There are many incapacities, of various kinds, for which it need not be true that there is no possible world in which the agent does the thing in question; the agent may indeed do that thing at some time in the future – if, that is to say, he loses his incapacity. The same is true for moral incapacity. The agent cannot, of course, lose the incapacity at will: but that is not because it is peculiarly moral incapacity, but just because nothing one can lose at will is an incapacity. Moral incapacity is explained through the will, as I have tried to show, but it is not subject to the will.

In these respects there is a difference between moral and other incapacities, but it follows simply from their character as it has already been described. With other incapacities, while the agent cannot remove them at will, he may coherently set about trying to remove or overcome them, but with a moral incapacity he cannot do this, because a fundamental way in which a moral incapacity expresses itself is in the refusal to undertake any such project. A moral incapacity in the sense under discussion is one with which the agent is identified. Of course an agent may come to see a moral incapacity of his as something with which he is no longer identified, and try to overcome it. But so soon as this is really his state of mind – as opposed to the familiar phenomenon of merely occurrent resentment at one's moral identity – then he has already lost the moral incapacity: not necessarily in the sense that he can now do the thing in question, but in the sense that if he cannot, it is no longer a moral incapacity, but rather one that is merely psychological.

These might be called questions of the *endurance* of a moral incapacity. They are not easy to answer, but the problems are for the most part no different from those that arise with other kinds of incapacity. A different question concerns a moral incapacity's *scope*. What I have in mind are the limits of the agent's endurance that may be met by any of his moral characteristics under threat or other extreme circumstances. It is plausible to say, with the pessimist, that if having a moral incapacity implies that there are no circumstances at all in which the agent would knowingly do the thing in question, then there are no moral incapacities. Ingenious coercion or brutal extremity can always produce such circumstances. We do not have to say with the cynic that the same holds for rewards. The truth seems to be that moral incapacities are meant to be proof against rewards; and if an agent is not proof against rewards, then we may not be amazed, but we do say that, after all, we were wrong to ascribe the incapacity to him. He is one who, after all, could act in that way, because, faced with that reward, he did do so. If, however, an agent does under coercion what we said he could not do, this does not necessarily show that we were wrong in ascribing the incapacity to him: *esse ad posse* does not apply without qualification.

If this is a reasonable view of the way things are, the explanation will lie, once more, in the basic connections between moral incapacity and deliberation. All the considerations to which agents attach importance, which matter to them, and which figure in their deliberations, have their limits under extreme coercion: there comes a point at which the agents' normal deliberative priorities are suspended. This is not because they become incapable of deliberation. That may be true, but if it is true, their actions will have a different character, and there will be another kind of reason why those actions do not count, for instance in relation to moral incapacities. The point is rather that no-one, familiarly enough, is expected to resist certain ultimate kinds of coercion, though what degree of resistance should be shown to what kinds of coercion of course varies, and that point itself applies to the assessment of moral incapacity. If I say of a certain secret agent, for instance, that he is incapable of going over to the enemy, it would count against what I say if he were to go over to the enemy as soon as they threatened him. The moral incapacities of secret agents have to apply, up to a point, in situations in which they are threatened; if that were not so, those incapacities would not determine as much as they have to determine. In more domesticated cases, however, if a threat (in itself, perhaps, similar to that applied to the secret agent) elicits the actions that the agent was supposed to be incapable of doing, that may not falsify the claim of his incapacity. The scope of moral incapacity, as with all considerations of deliberative priority and of character, is limited by a sense of the boundaries of terror beyond which human beings cannot be expected to lead their moral lives at all.

Notes

1 I use the term 'moral' throughout, and the discussion applies to the character-istics that people do, if vaguely, call 'moral'. There are, indeed, some familiar conceptions central to morality which imply that there cannot be such a thing as a moral *incapacity* at all: I have ignored those issues. I have also ignored the much more interesting consideration that a lot of what is said applies to dispositions that are not in a narrow sense 'moral' at all.
2 So long as I retain the incapacity, of course: see below.

5

Acts and omissions, doing and not doing

1 Preliminaries

In a famous and strongly argued essay,[1] Philippa Foot sought to explain a range of widely held moral beliefs, including some about abortion, partly in terms of a distinction between doing and allowing. Her article was not primarily directed to the analysis or explication of the distinction itself, though she was careful to separate it from some other distinctions that resemble it and perhaps overlap with it; she was concerned, rather, with organizing moral beliefs around it. In the enormous literature on these subjects, there is a rough distinction between writers who have been mainly concerned with the ethical application of such distinctions, and others who have been more interested in them as part of an attempt to understand the structure of action and action-ascriptions. Few writings fall unequivocally, of course, into one of these classes or the other. Many of them belong to what might be called 'applicable philosophy' – the kind of analysis that treats distinctions in the philosophy of mind or action for their own interest, but keeps in mind their ethical relevance. This chapter is intended to be of that sort. Since distinctions do not exist in a vacuum, it may well be the potential moral interest of a distinction that motivates the attempt to make it out, but 'applicable' philosophy of action does stand a step further away from the exchange of moral intuitions than the other type of discussion does.

There is more than one kind of ethical relevance, and this is one reason why even the less directly ethical discussions of these notions may be ethically relevant. The first question is whether a distinction can even be coherently formulated; there is then another question, whether, even if it can be coherently formulated, it makes a moral difference. Corresponding to this distinction there are, for instance, two different criticisms of the doctrine of the Double Effect. One claims that the distinction on which the doctrine relies, between two different causal structures relating outcome to action, is arbitrary or excessively sensitive to redescription.[2] The other criticism admits that the distinction can be made out, but denies that it corresponds to reasonable ethical discriminations.

It is worth insisting, further, that it makes sense to say that a certain distinction makes a moral difference in some cases and not in others. This has been denied, in any interesting sense, by Jonathan Bennett.[3] Bennett himself makes the point that, with respect to the distinction between bringing something about and letting something happen, the fact that an example of the second may be just as bad as an example of the first does not in itself prove that the distinction has no moral force. He thinks that someone who defends the intrinsic moral relevance of the distinction will see this phenomenon as a case of the distinction's having force in the particular case, but the force's being overcome by stronger influences. This belongs with a general additive model of moral considerations or reasons in terms of the resolution of forces: if a type of consideration (for instance, this distinction) ever in itself exerts an influence, then it always exerts an influence, and the method of agreement and difference can be used to isolate the influence it exerts. I see no necessity to accept this idea; there are surely many examples of non-moral practical reasoning, and also of aesthetic judgement, that tell against it.

2 Doing and not doing

'A is not doing anything' is, literally taken, hardly ever true; at least if A is conscious. Indeed, granted that A is conscious, it is hardly ever true even if 'doing' is confined to 'intentionally doing' (which I shall take for the purposes of this discussion to be equivalent to performing an action).[4] There is, however, a comprehensible sense in which it can be true, that is to be found, for instance, in a holiday postcard. If my friend writes to say that he is having an excellent time doing nothing, he means something to the effect that there is no Z such that he is Z-ing, and Z-ing is noteworthy, what he would do professionally, or whatever. This gives us the basic idea of *not doing*: 'not doing' is *not doing anything of the Z sort*, for some stated or implied Z.

The central point for the present discussion concerns the *causal powers of not doing*. Consider the formula

[I] A brought about S by doing nothing.

Though it may seem paradoxical, what is very often true when [I] is true is that some doing – and usually some action – of A's was causally relevant to the happening of S. This follows from the conjunction of two things:

(a) [I] implies that A exists, is an agent, etc. This distinguishes [I] from 'no action of A's brought about S': that is true of me and the sinking of the Titanic.

(b) A is, as already stated, (more or less) always doing something if conscious, and usually doing some action. [I] can of course be true in virtue of A's being unconscious at the relevant time, but, if we leave this aside, it will standardly be the case that if [I] is true, then:

[N] there is some time span of the life of A, T, which stands in an appropriate relation to S, such that T contains one set of actions, X, and if it had contained in place of X other actions, Z, which A might have done, then (other things being equal) S would not have happened.

[N] is not sufficient for [I], for at least two reasons:

(i) 'Brought about' is stronger than 'made a causal contribution to', and in particular, stronger than 'made a negative causal contribution to', which is what [N] offers. [I] requires, in addition to [N], that there should be something that makes the fact reported in [N] salient with regard to the explanation of S and/or our dealings with A.[5] It is important that in the first instance this is a (familiar) point about cause, not a point specifically about action. But there are cases where salience arises from considerations specially connected with agency, as we shall see below, in connection with omissions.

(ii) Even granted salience, the relation between Z and X (we may call it the 'relevant replacement relation', or 'RRR') is not enough for [I]. We must add, further, that A did not intend X to prevent S; if he did have this intention, then it was not his doing nothing, but his poorly conceived, ineffective, or unlucky action that brought S about. However, we do not have to say that A did not intend to prevent S *tout court*. He may even have acted at some other time unsuccessfully to prevent it, but even if he did it will still be true, given [N], that his doing nothing *at* T brought about S.

[N], and so [I], contain the notion of actions that A *might* have done. What this means depends, among other things, on what use is being made of [I]. If [I] is involved in blaming A, it is usual to say that 'might have' should imply 'could have'. If it is a matter just of historical explanation, perhaps it does not. The question is one of what range of counterfactuals is intelligible in relation to the matter in hand, and of their (usually very obscure) truth conditions.

Two comments on the literature may be appropriate here.[6] First, even [N] can satisfy Warren Quinn's condition for harmful positive agency ('the agent's most direct contribution to the harm is an action'), if A's doings at T constitute the nearest that A gets to S. This suggests that

Quinn's condition for that notion is too weak. Second, Bennett has been much impressed by a typical feature of the RRR, that for given X and S, there are few values of Z for which [N] is true and many for which it is false. But as Quinn and others have pointed out, this is not necessary. The important point is that the causal relevance of X is essentially explained by the RRR, i.e. through X's not being Z.

3 Two further developments

It follows from the possibility of [I] that there is such a thing as acting at T by not doing anything at T. This possibility goes beyond the *causal* structure deployed in [I].[7] A particularly important example is conventional actions, where there is a specific agreement, a general explicit understanding, or a readily inferred convention that A's 'doing nothing' will count as, e.g., agreeing, or voting, or bidding at an auction. There are other questions, of course, about what counts as an action: e.g. whether dropping out of the bidding is one. But the present point is that there are cases in which A has certainly done an action Y at T; by doing X; where what makes X a doing of Y at T is that it is (one of many things that are) not Z, where Z is a contrary conventional action. (He bid for the Miro because he stared at his programme or whispered to his neighbour, and did not shake his head, which is what, by prior agreement, would have counted as his not bidding for it.) Actions of this kind can in some cases be done unintentionally: whether this is possible turns on the conventions.

On the present account, the much discussed distinction between doing and allowing seems not to be a distinction at all. Allowing is best understood as an action, and it is usually an intentional action; whether it is allowing someone to do something, or allowing things to take their course. As Philippa Foot pointed out in her original article, it is an action that may be performed by doing something. Thus it may be a conventional act of giving permission; or it may be the act of preventing someone from intervening, as when the doctor stops the nurse from giving emergency resuscitation. It may equally be done by not doing anything (in the [I] sense), as in Bennett's example of the person who by sitting still and quiet allows a blind or inadvertent man to walk off the cliff: that is indeed something this person, A, did, though of course it is not the same thing as if A had made him, or encouraged him, or induced him to walk off the cliff; or if A had pushed him.

No doubt there are more and less restrictive accounts of what might count as 'allowing' something to happen. What we must guard against are the two ideas: (a) that there are two different relations to S's coming about – one, that of bringing about that this happens, and one, of allowing this to happen; and (b) that the first of these represents an action while the second does not. The first pair, first of all, are not exclusive of one another; moreover, allowing something to happen is, typically, itself an action, though it is one that, like some other kinds of action, can be performed by not doing anything.

It may be that there are some sound moral distinctions that correspond to distinctions between certain actions and certain allowings. But if so, it is not because the first are actions and the second are not. Rather, they are (typically) different actions.

4 Omissions

I take it that the omission of an action, Z, may be either intentional or unintentional. In either case it is a non-doing of Z which possesses a particular kind of salience, derived from normative expectations on the agent.

I take it that 'normative expectation' is not pleonastic. On the day that Kant did not take his habitual walk (because he was so intent on reading Rousseau), perhaps a citizen of Koenigsberg, relying on the regular occurrence of Kant's walk, missed an appointment. But it would be an understatement to say that Kant was not *guilty* of an omission – there is nothing that was his omission. (This is not to deny the general point that some normative expectations may be created just by giving rise to expectations; it is a broader question when this is so, and a notoriously controversial one.)

The salience, derived from a normative expectation, can arise at two different points in the structure. It may be the salience mentioned in consideration (i) of section 2, in connection with strengthening [N] to get [I]. This is the relevant point when we say that by omission he brought about the (presumably bad) situation S: it selects one causal contribution from others as the cause. However, not all omissions produce bad, or any specifically interesting, results. If it is A's job to Z, then his non-Z-ing (i.e. the fact that the relevant T contains some, different, X in place of Z) counts as an omission even if it has no distinctive effects at all. Here the point lies just in the identification of the RRR: X-ing is identified as what was done at T *instead of Z* just because of the expectations on A, derived from his job.

This second point in fact presents the more basic consideration. The question with an omission always is the introduction of the RRR: the identification of X at T, probably otherwise uninteresting, as an omission of Z. However, the distinction between the two kinds of salience is not irrelevant. We can get directly to the RRR when we have expectations of a specific kind, and the *effects* of the agent's not doing Z will then come into the question, not in identifying an omission, but in judging the gravity of his omission, and so forth. However, in other cases, the introduction of the RRR in the first place – that is to say, the identification of what the agent did at T as an *omission* at all – can depend on the occurrence of certain effects. This may well be so with expectations based on duties of general care, and more generally with expectations that are grounded in general human relations and responsibilities rather than in such things as specific job descriptions.

5 Omissions and bringing about

These considerations about two kinds of salience are relevant to a familiar kind of moral dispute (or, at any rate, a dispute over moral description). I end with some rather general remarks about this.

Suppose I spend $100 on some luxury purchase; that I could have given $100 to a relief agency, and did not; and that if the relief agency had received an extra $100, then, everything else being equal, some extra person in Ethiopia would not have died of starvation. The last claim may be hard to establish, but that is not the point on which to take up the argument.

The following are among the things that might be said:

(a) I omitted to give $100 to Ethiopian relief;
(b) that omission caused someone's death in Ethiopia;
(c) I brought about the death of someone in Ethiopia;
(d) I killed someone in Ethiopia.

There is a further possible remark:

(e) I allowed someone in Ethiopia to die.

(e) perhaps implies, more strongly than (a), that I knew the relevant facts. Beyond that, I will leave (e); nothing in what I have to say, so far as I can see, provides materials for denying it.

Some would deny even (a); viz. those who deny any normative expectation on people to assist famine relief (though they may say that it is nice of people if they go in for it). Others would suggest that anyone living at a Western standard of life is guilty of such omissions. I suggested an indeterminately middle position when I supplied the information that it was a luxury purchase.

Many of those who accept (a) would resist (c) and (d). Various reasons for this may be suggested. Some of the reasons may be compatible with accepting (b), though I find it hard to see why (b) should not imply (c). At any rate, if one rejects (b), this will be enough for one to resist (c) and (d). Can we reject (b)? This turns in good part on the answer to the question: when does the salience that identifies an act as an omission also identify it as a cause?

Sometimes, clearly, it does: inattentive lifeguards cause deaths from drowning. Someone who is merely a lazy sunbather resting on the beach may, equally, cause a death from drowning if he omits to save, but he will be thought to have caused the death only if he is very saliently related to the drowning in terms of proximity, capacity to save, obviousness of what has gone wrong, and so on. The conditions for identifying the lazy person's inaction as an omission are weaker than this: weaker, that is to say, than for identifying this person's inaction as the cause of the drowning, or (as it might also and revealingly be put) for identifying his or her omission as the cause of the drowning.

In the case of the lifeguard the situation is clear. If he is inattentive, he is guilty of an omission even if there is no disaster (if, for instance, he fails to notice a swimmer who might easily have got into difficulties). When there is a disaster his inattention is a salient part of the explanation, because his attentiveness is part of a system of prevention, and it is the part that failed. The general structure of informal obligations to assistance, not based on specific duties – a structure to which (roughly) everyone belongs – can also be seen in an extended sense as a system of prevention; but it is only if quite strong conditions are satisfied that a person's failure to act will count as the cause of a given bad outcome. Even when those strong conditions are not satisfied, however, his failure to act may still count as an omission. To claim that he is guilty of an omission is to say something about the agent, who falls under a normative expectation of how we would hope he would conduct himself in such circumstances. (We may hesitate to say 'in such circumstances' here, or 'in the consciousness of such circumstances', because one thing that is indeterminate in these general cases is the degree to which people are required to find out about potential disasters that are not immediately obvious.)

The distinction between an omission which is a cause of a disaster and one that is not (even though there was a disaster, and the disaster would not have happened without the omission) helps to focus reproach by distinguishing from one another different things that may be said about the agent. The distinction rests on the point that the causal explanation of the disaster may not rest saliently on the failure of the agent, even though that failure is, in terms of his character and habits, reproachable. Utilitarians tend not to make such distinctions, and that is why they move easily in the present case from (a) to (d). Thinking that there is only one thing needed of agents, they also think that there can be only one thing wrong with them, and hence one reproach to them.

This is an area in which Utilitarians remain fully participating adherents of the morality system. Besides their consequentialist interest in systems for securing desirable outcomes, they remain attached to notions of guilt, shame, and responsibility grounded in the idea of what an individual person has done or might have done, and there is an uneasy join between the two.[8]

Notes

1 Philippa Foot, 'The problem of abortion and the doctrine of the double effect', *Oxford Review* 5 (1967), reprinted in *Virtues and Vices* (Berkeley, CA: University of California Press, 1978); see also 'Euthanasia', *Philosophy and Public Affairs* 6 (1977), reprinted in the same volume; and for a more restricted account of the moral application of the doing/allowing distinction, 'Morality, action and outcome', in Honderich (ed.), *Morality and Objectivity*. This chapter offers a structure that I hope may be useful in thinking about these issues, without relating it properly to the many useful contributions to these questions that have been made in the subsequent literature, or defending it against alternative proposals. I should have preferred to do those things, but I have not been able to do so, and rather than offer a gesture towards adequacy in this respect I have confined myself to one or two relevant references.

2 As the late Warren Quinn pointed out in 'Actions, intentions and consequences: the doctrine of doing and allowing', *Philosophical Review* 98 (1989), coherence in a distinction does not require that there are no marginal, ambiguous, or indeterminate cases. What matters is that it should be clear why a case is indeterminate, and that the explanation should be comprehensibly connected to the purpose of the distinction. (See also his 'Actions, intentions and consequences: the doctrine of the Double Effect', *Philosophy and Public Affairs* 18 (1989).) In the same article Quinn also made the point which follows, about 'making a difference sometimes', and drew attention to the aesthetic analogy.

3 Jonathan Bennett, 'Positive and negative relevance', *American Philosophical Quarterly* 20 (1983); the 'equally bad' point in '"Whatever the consequences"', *Analysis* 26 (1965/6), on p. 93.

4 This is to follow Donald Davidson's usage; a Davidsonian understanding of actions as events can also be assumed for the discussion, though nothing important, I think, turns on it for present purposes.

5 [N] seems equivalent to what Bennett calls A's behaviour being 'negatively relevant' to the outcome: Bennett, 'Positive and negative relevance'.

6 Quinn, 'The doctrine of doing and allowing'; Bennett, '"Whatever the consequences"', and elsewhere.

7 It may thus go beyond what some writers have called 'negative agency', but I am not clear exactly what this expression is taken to cover.

8 For the basic character of notions connecting agency with guilt and shame, and the relations of all this to 'moral responsibility', see *Shame and Necessity*, especially chapters 3 and 4. For the morality system and Utilitarianism's relations to it, see *ELP* chapter 10.

6

Nietzsche's minimalist moral psychology

Nietzsche, Wittgenstein and the extraction of theory

Nietzsche is not a source of philosophical theories. At some level the point is obvious, but it may be less obvious how deep it goes. In this respect, there is a contrast with Wittgenstein. Wittgenstein said repeatedly, and not only in his later work, that he was not to be read as offering philosophical theory, because there could be no such thing as philosophical theory. But his work was less well prepared than Nietzsche's was to sustain that position posthumously. There is more than one reason for this.[1] Wittgenstein thought that his work demanded not only the end of philosophical theory but the end of philosophy – something associated, for him, with the end of his demands on himself to do philosophy. That association, of the end of philosophical theory with the end of philosophy, does not deny the idea that if there is to be philosophy, it will take the form of theory; indeed, it readily reinforces that idea. Moreover, the topics on which Wittgenstein wanted there to be no more philosophy – the topics, for him, of philosophy – were traditional topics of academic philosophy. It is not surprising that those who continue theoretical work on those topics still look for elements in Wittgenstein's work itself from which to construct it.

No doubt many who do this lack a suitable irony about what they do to Wittgenstein's texts, but their attitude is not in any important sense a betrayal: less so, in fact, than the attitude of those who think that Wittgenstein did bring to an end philosophical theory on those topics, and themselves sustain an academic activity that consists of reiterating that very thing. Among those who think that there is room for ongoing philosophical theory on those topics, and that Wittgenstein contributed to it, someone owes Wittgenstein an account of why he had ceased to see that this was so. But such an account might be given, and we might come to understand that if Wittgenstein could no longer see the edifice of an intellectual subject, his sightlessness was not that of Samson, but rather that of Oedipus at Colonus, whose disappearance left behind healing waters.

Wittgenstein's posthumous texts, though not designed to express or encourage theory, are not actually mined against its extraction. With Nietzsche, by contrast, the resistance to the continuation of philosophy by ordinary means is built into the text, which is booby-trapped not only against recovering theory from it, but, in many cases, against any systematic exegesis that assimilates it to theory. His writing achieves this partly by its choice of subject matter, partly by its manner and the attitudes it expresses. These features stand against a mere exegesis of Nietzsche, or the incorporation of Nietzsche into the history of philosophy as a source of theories. Some think that these features stand against the incorporation of Nietzsche into philosophy as an academic enterprise altogether, but if that is meant to imply the unimportance of Nietzsche for philosophy, it must be wrong. In insisting on the importance of Nietzsche for philosophy, I mean something that cannot be evaded by a definition of 'philosophy'. In particular, it cannot be evaded by invoking some contrast between 'analytic' and 'continental' philosophy. This classification always involved a quite bizarre conflation of the methodological and the topographical, as though one classified cars into front-wheel drive and Japanese, but besides that and other absurdities of the distinction, there is the more immediate point that no such classification can evade the insistent continuities between Nietzsche's work and the business of what anyone calls philosophy. At least in moral philosophy, to ignore them is not simply to adopt a style, but to duck a problem.

I agree with a remark made by Michel Foucault in a late interview, that there is no single Nietzscheism, and that the right question to ask is 'what serious use can Nietzsche be put to?' One serious use is to help us with issues that press on any serious philosophy (in particular, moral philosophy) that does not beg the most basic of its own questions. Nietzsche will not help if he is taken to impose some one method on us. I have already said that I find his texts securely defended against exegesis by the extraction of theory; but it does not follow, and it is important that it does not follow, that when we are trying to put him to serious use our philosophy should contain no theory. This is because the insistent continuities between his questions and our business run in both directions. Some of the concerns to which he speaks are going to be better met – that is to say, met in a way in which we can better make something of them –

by quite other styles of thought, and perhaps by some theory that comes from elsewhere; certainly not by theoretical, or again anti-theoretical, incantations supposedly recovered from Nietzsche himself.

Naturalism and realism in moral psychology

There is some measure of agreement that we need a 'naturalistic' moral psychology, where this means something to the effect that our view of moral capacities should be consistent with, even perhaps in the spirit of, our understanding of human beings as part of nature. A demand expressed in such terms is perhaps accepted by most philosophers, apart from some *anciens combattants* of the wars of freewill. The trouble with this happy and extensive consensus, however, and no doubt the condition of it, is that no-one knows what it involves. Formulations of the position tend to rule out too much or too little. The position rules out too much if it tries reductively to ignore culture and convention; this is misguided even on a scientific basis, in the sense that to live under culture is a basic part of the ethology of this species.[2] It rules out too little if it includes many things that have been part of the self-image of morality, such as certain conceptions of moral cognition; a theory will scarcely further the cause of naturalism in this sense if it accepts as a basic feature of human nature the capacity to intuit the structure of moral reality. It is tempting to say that a naturalistic moral psychology explains moral capacities in terms of psychological structures that are not distinctively moral. But so much turns on what counts as explanation here, and what it is for a psychological element to be distinctively moral, that it remains persistently unclear whether the formula should be taken to be blandly accommodating, or fiercely reductive, or something in between.

The difficulty is systematic. If a 'naturalistic' moral psychology has to characterise moral activity in a vocabulary that can be applied equally to every other part of nature, then it is committed to a physicalistic reductionism that is clearly hopeless. If it is to describe moral activity in terms that can be applied to something else, but not everything else, we have not much idea what those terms may be, or how 'special' moral activity is allowed to be, consonantly with naturalism. If we are allowed to describe moral activity in whatever terms moral activity may seem to invite, naturalism excludes nothing, and we are back at the beginning. The trouble is that the very term 'naturalism' invokes a top-down approach, under which we are supposed already to know what terms are needed to describe any 'natural' phenomenon, and we are invited to apply those terms to moral activity. But we do not know what those terms may be, unless they are (uselessly) the terms of physics, and this leads to the difficulty.

In this quandary, we can find in Nietzsche both a general attitude, and some particular suggestions, that can be a great help.[3] I shall say something later about what I take some of his suggestions to be. The general attitude has two relevant aspects, which have to be taken together. First, to the question 'how much should our accounts of distinctively moral activity add to our accounts of other human activity?' it replies 'as little as possible', and the more that some moral understanding of human beings seems to call on materials that specially serve the purposes of morality – certain conceptions of the will, for instance – the more reason we have to ask whether there may not be a more illuminating account that rests only on conceptions that we use anyway elsewhere. This demand for moral psychological minimalism is not, however, just an application of an Occamist desire for economy, and this is the second aspect of the Nietzschean general attitude. Without some guiding sense of what materials we should use in giving our economical explanations, such an attitude will simply fall back into the difficulties we have already met. Nietzsche's approach is to identify an excess of moral content in psychology by appealing first to what an experienced, honest, subtle, and unoptimistic interpreter might make of human behaviour elsewhere. Such an interpreter might be said to be – using an unashamedly evaluative expression – 'realistic', and we might say that what this approach leads us towards is a realistic, rather than a naturalistic, moral psychology. What is at issue is not the application of an already defined scientific programme, but rather an informed interpretation of some human experiences and activities in relation to others.

Such an approach can indeed be said to involve, in Paul Ricoeur's well-known phrase, a 'hermeneutics of suspicion'. As such, it cannot compel demonstratively, and does not attempt to do so. It invites one into a perspective, and to some extent a tradition (one marked by such figures as Thucydides, for instance, or Stendhal, or the British psychologists of morals whom Nietzsche described as 'old frogs'), in which what seems to demand more moral material makes sense in terms of what demands less. The enterprise can work, however, only to the extent that the suspicion it summons up is not a suspicion of everything. Writers on Nietzsche typically pay most attention to his claims, or what appear to be his claims, that every belief about the relations of human beings to reality are open to suspicion, that everything is, for instance, an interpretation. Whatever may need to be said at that level, it is equally important that when he says that there are no moral phenomena, only moral interpretations,[4] a *special* point is being made about morality. This does not mean that we should simply forget, even in these connections, the larger claims. We need to get a deeper understanding of where these points of particular suspicion are to be found, and it may be helpful to work through larger claims on a path to getting a grasp on more limited claims. This is particularly so if we bear in mind that 'claim', for Nietzsche, is in fact rarely the right word. It is not only too weak for some things he says and too strong for others; we can usefully remember, too, (or perhaps pretend) that even when he sounds insistently or shrilly expository, he is not necessarily telling us something, but urging us to ask something.

In the rest of this chapter, I shall try to assemble some of Nietzsche's suggestions about a supposed psychological phenomenon, that of willing. I shall leave aside many interesting things that Nietzsche says about this concept, in particular about its history. My aim is to illustrate, through a schematic treatment of this central example, the way in which a method of suspicion – the search, one might almost say, for a culprit – can help us to achieve a reduced and more realistic moral psychology.

Illusions of the self

Speaking seriously, there are good reasons why all philosophical dogmatiz-ing, however, solemn and definitive its airs used to be, may nevertheless have been no more than a noble childishness and tyronism. And perhaps the time is at hand when it will be comprehended again and again *how little* used to be sufficient to furnish the cornerstone for such sublime and unconditional philosophers' edifices as the dogmatists have built so far; any old popular superstition from time immemorial (like the soul superstition which, in the form of the subject and ego superstition, has not even yet ceased to do mischief): some play on words perhaps, a seduction by grammar, or an audacious generalization of very narrow, very personal, very human, all too human facts.[5]

The general point that Nietzsche makes here (one shared with Wittgen-stein, and indeed J. L. Austin, about the extraordinary lightness of philo-sophical theories) is directed to a particular idea, that the ego or self is some kind of fiction. Later in the same book he follows Lichtenberg in criticising the *cogito* as the product of grammatical habit. Elsewhere, he makes a similar point more specifically about action. He quotes a sceptic:

'I do not in the least know what I am doing. I do not in the least know what I ought to do.' You are right, but be sure of this: *you are being done* [*du wirst getan*], in every moment. Mankind at all times has mistaken the passive for the active: it is their constant grammatical mistake.[6]

Many ideas might be drawn from this complex, some of them uninvit-ing; for instance, that we never really do anything, that no events are actions. More interestingly, Nietzsche can be read as saying that *action* is a serviceable category of interpretation, but a local or dispensible one; this seems to me hardly less implausible, but some have accepted it.[7] If people perform actions, then they perform them because they think or perceive certain things, and this is enough to dispose, further, of a crude epiphenomenalism that might be found in some of Nietzsche's sayings – perhaps in his suggestion that all action is like willing the sun to rise when the sun is just about to rise.

Nietzsche's doubts about action are more usefully understood, I suggest, as doubts not about the very idea of anyone's doing anything, but rather about a morally significant interpretation of action, in terms of the will. The belief in the will involves, for him, two ideas in particular: that the will seems something simple when it is not; and that what seems simple also seems to be a peculiar, imperative, kind of cause.

> Philosophers are accustomed to speak of the will as if it were the best-known thing in the world ... But ... [w]illing seems to me to be above all something *complicated*, something that is a unit only as a word – and it is precisely in this one word that the popular prejudice lurks, which has defeated the always inadequate caution of philosophers.[8]

He goes on to explain that what is called 'willing' is a complex of sensations, thinking, and an affect of command. He points to the consequences of our being both the commanding and the obeying party, and of our 'disregarding this duality'.

> Since in the great majority of cases there has been an exercise of will only when the effect of the command – that is, obedience; that is, the action – was to be *expected*, the appearance has translated itself into the feeling, as if there were a *necessity of effect*. In short, he who wills believes with a fair amount of certainty that will and action are somehow one; he ascribes the success, the carrying out of the willing, to the will itself, and thereby enjoys an increase of the sensation of power that accompanies all success.

What exactly is the illusion that Nietzsche claims to expose here? It is not the idea that a certain experience is a sufficient cause of an action. He does indeed think that the experiences involved in 'willing' do not reveal, and may conceal, the shifting complex of psychological and physiological forces that lies behind any action, the constant, unknown, craving movements that make us, as he puts it, a kind of polyp.[9] But it is not that the experience sets itself up as the cause. Rather, the experience seems to reveal a different kind of cause, and suggests that the cause does not lie in any event or state of affairs – whether an experience of mine or otherwise – but in something that I refer to as 'I'. Such a cause seems to be related to the outcome only in the mode of prescription, through an imperative;

and since this stands in no relation to any causal set of events, it can seem to bring about its outcome *ex nihilo.*

Of course, any sensible theory of action, which allows that there is indeed action, and that thoughts are not merely epiphenomenal in relation to it, will have to allow that my consciousness of acting is not the same as a consciousness that a state of mine causes a certain outcome. This follows merely from the point that the first-personal consciousness which one has when involved in action cannot at the same time be a third-personal consciousness of that very involvement. But the first-personal consciousness which an agent necessarily has does not in itself have to lead to the kind of picture that Nietzsche attacks; action does not necessarily involve this understanding of itself.[10] The picture is a special one, particularly associated with a notion such as 'willing', and when it is present, it is not merely a philosophical theory of action, but can accompany many of our thoughts and moral reactions. So where does it come from, and what does it do?

Part of Nietzsche's own explanation is to be found in the course of one of his most famous passages:

> For just as the popular mind separates the lightning from its flash, and takes the latter for an *action*, for the operation of a subject called lightning, so popular morality also separates strength from expressions of strength, as if there were a neutral substratum behind the strong man, which was *free* to express strength or not to do so. But there is no such substratum; there is no 'being' behind doing, effecting, becoming; 'the doer' is merely a fiction added to the deed – the deed is everything. The popular mind in fact doubles the deed; when it sees the lightning flash, it is the deed of a deed: it posits the same event first as cause and then a second time as its effect.[11]

There are two helpful ideas in this account. One is that the picture under attack involves a kind of double counting. The self or I that is the cause is ingenuously introduced as the cause *of an action.* If my agent-self produces only a set of events, it may seem that I shall not have enough for my involvement in the action: I shall be at best the 'pilot in a ship' to which Descartes referred. The doubling of action also follows from the idea that the mode of causation is that of command. Obedience to a command consists of an action; but commanding is itself an action. The self can act (at one time rather than another, now rather than earlier) only by doing something – the thing it does, willing; but, for more than one reason, what it brings about in this way seems itself to be an action. In making action into something that introduces an agent-cause, the account has a powerful tendency to produce two actions.

The second helpful thought to be recovered from Nietzsche is that such a peculiar account must have a purpose, and that the purpose is a moral one.

The target of blame

The purpose of the account can be read from the way in which it associates two ideas, which contribute to its incoherence and together compound it. One idea is that there is a metaphysically special unit, a real action, unlike anything else that can be individuated among the world's processes. The other is that this stands in an unmediated relationship – something like being an effect *ex nihilo* – to something of quite a different kind, again unique – a person, or self, or agent. There is an idea that needs items standing in just such a relation: it is a certain purified conception of blame.

Blame needs an occasion – an action – and a target – the person who did the action and who goes on from the action to meet the blame. That is its nature; as one might say, its conceptual form. In the real world, it does not need these things in the pure and isolated form implied by the account of the will. The Homeric Greeks blamed people for doing things, and whatever exactly went into their doing so, it was not all this. Rather, this version of the occasion and the target will be demanded by a very purified conception of blame, a conception seemingly demanded by moral justice. It is important that the mere idea of just compensation does not make this demand, nor every idea of responsibility. If A has been damaged by B's careless action, B may be held responsible for the loss and reasonably required to compensate A, though the loss to A formed no part of what B willed. A very exact concentration on B's will, and the purely focussed conception of blame that goes with it, are demanded not merely by responsibility or demands in justice for compensation, but by something more specific.

It is not hard to find an explanation of the more specific demand. It lies in the seeming requirement of justice that the agent should be blamed for no more and no less than what was in his power. What the agent brought about (and for which, in the usual order of things, he may be asked to provide compensation) may very well be a matter of luck, but what he may be strictly (as these conceptions say, 'morally') blamed for cannot be a matter of luck, and must depend in a strict and isolable sense on his will. It is appropriately said that what depends on his will is what is strictly *in his power*: it is with regard to what he wills that the agent himself has the sense of power in action to which Nietzsche refers. As agents, and also as blamers under justice, we have an interest in this picture.

The needs, demands, and invitations of the morality system are enough to explain the peculiar psychology of the will. But there is more that needs to be said about the basis of that system itself. Nietzsche himself famously suggested that a specific source for it was to be found in the sentiment of ressentiment – a sentiment which itself had a historical origin, though hardly one that he locates very precisely. I shall not pick up the historical aspect, but I think it is worth suggesting a brief specu- lation about the phenomenology of focussed blame, which is a close enough relation to Nietzsche's 'genealogy', perhaps, to be a version of it.[12]

If there is a victim with a complaint for a loss, there is an agent who is to blame, and an act of that agent which brought about the loss. The anger of the victim travels from the loss to the act to the agent; and compen- sation or recompense given by the agent will acknowledge both the loss and the fact that he was the cause of the loss. Suppose the agent brings about a harm to the victim, and does so intentionally and voluntarily; where 'intentionally and voluntarily' is not supposed to invoke the special mechanisms of the will, but merely means that the agent knew what he was doing, wanted to do it, and was in a normal state of mind when he did it. Suppose that the agent is not disposed to give compen- sation or reparation, and that the victim has no power to extract any such thing from him. In refusing reparation, the agent refuses to acknowledge the victim or his loss; it is a peculiarly vivid demonstration of the victim's powerlessness.

These circumstances can give rise, in the victim or in someone else on behalf of the victim, to a very special fantasy of retrospective prevention. As victim, I have a fantasy of inserting into the agent an acknowledge- ment of me, to take the place of exactly the act that harmed me. I want to think that he might have acknowledged me, that he might have been prevented from harming me. But the idea cannot be that I might in some empirical way have prevented him: that idea presents only a regret that it was not actually so and, in these circumstances, a reminder of humili- ation. The idea has to be, rather, that I, now, might change the agent from one who did not acknowledge me to one who did. This fantasied, magical, change does not involve actually changing anything, and it therefore has nothing to do with what, if anything, might actually have changed things. It requires simply the idea of the agent at the moment of the action, of the action that harmed me, and of the refusal of that action, all isolated from the network of circumstances in which his action was actually embedded. It involves precisely the picture of the will that has already been uncovered.

Much can grow from this basic feeling. It lays the foundation for the purest and simplest construction of punishment, and it is very significant how the language of retribution naturally deploys teleological notions of conversion, education, or improvement ('teaching him a lesson', 'showing him') while insisting at the same time that its gaze is entirely retrospective and that, inasmuch as it is purely retributive, it does not look to actual reform.[13] But the construction is at least as much at work when it is not a question of any actual punishment, but only of the purely moral conceptions of guilt and blame, and it then involves a further abstraction; it introduces not only retribution's idea of retrospective causation, but morality's idea of an authoritative but sanctionless law, of a judgement that carries no power besides that judgement itself.

Conclusion

This is, of course, only a sketch of a possible account, drawn (fairly directly) from Nietzschean materials. The most important feature of it, for the present purpose, is its structure. We start with a supposed psychological phenomenon, willing, associated with the conception of the self in action. The phenomenon seems recognizable in experience, and it seems also to have a certain authority. Its description already presents difficulties and obscurities, but proposals merely to explain it away or to ignore it seem typically to have ignored something important, even to leave out the essence of action. Reminded both that different pictures of action have been held in other cultures and that the notion of action itself is less than transparent, we can be helped to see that the integrity of action, the agent's genuine presence in it, can be preserved without this picture of the will – indeed, can only be preserved without it. The process by which we can come to see this may be complex and painful enough for us to feel, not just that we have learned a truth, but that we have been relieved of a burden.

Since the picture is neither coherent nor universal, yet has this authority, we need to ask where it comes from and what it does. It is not itself manifestly tied to morality, offering rather a picture of voluntary action in general, but there is a moral phenomenon, a certain conception of blame, which it directly fits. This conception, again, is not universal, but is rather part of a special complex of ethical ideas which has other, and related, peculiar features. The fit between the special psychological conception and the demands of morality enables us to see that this piece of psychology is itself a moral conception, and one that shares notably doubtful features of that particular morality itself. In addition to this, we may be able to supply some further psychological conceptions which help us to understand the motivations of this particular form of the ethical. Those conceptions, as presented by Nietzsche under the name of ressentiment, certainly lead out of the ethical altogether, into the categories of anger and power, and it cannot be a matter simply for philosophy to decide how much those categories will explain. Other explanations may be needed, and it may be that they will prove to be more basically linked to notions of fairness, for instance. But in laying such explanations against one another, and in diagnosing the psychology of willing as a demand of the morality system itself, we shall be following a distinctively Nietzschean route towards the naturalisation of moral psychology.

Notes

1 Even when we leave aside the point that there is only one work by Nietzsche (*The Will to Power*) that is not a work by Nietzsche, whereas the later works of Wittgenstein are, as whole books, very variably his.

2 I discuss this point at greater length in 'Making sense of humanity'.

3 It will be obvious that Nietzsche's interest is located by the present discussion mostly in terms of his more 'sceptical' works, rather than in (for instance) his ideas of self-overcoming. This is not to deny that they, too, can have their uses. In any case, there is no hope of getting anything from his redemptive aspirations without setting them against his accounts of familiar morality.

4 Nietzsche, *Beyond Good and Evil*, translated by Walter Kaufmann (New York, 1966), 108.

5 *ibid.*, Preface. The reference to Lichtenberg, below, is at section 17.

6 Nietzsche, *Daybreak*, translated by R. J. Hollingdale (Cambridge: Cambridge University Press, 1982), 120. The passage about the sunrise, mentioned below, is also from *Daybreak*, 124.

7 E.g. Frithjof Bergmann, 'Nietzsche's critique of morality'. Bergmann includes 'individual agency' (along with such items as selfhood, freedom, and guilt) in a list of concepts allegedly special to our morality; he takes himself (wrongly, I think) to be following Clifford Geertz in the claim that it was not known in traditional Bali. Similar errors have been made about the outlook of Homeric Greece: see below, note 10. The idea that *action*, in our ordinary understanding of it, is a dispensable and indeed mistaken conception is shared by a very different kind of philosophy, eliminative materialism; in that case for scientistic reasons.

8 Nietzsche, *Beyond Good and Evil*, 19. The whole section is relevant.

9 Nietzsche, *Daybreak*, 119.

10 This is clearly illustrated by the treatment accorded by some scholars to the Homeric conception of action; not finding in Homer this picture of action, they have thought that the archaic Greeks either had no idea of action, or had an imperfect one, lacking the concept of the will. I discuss this and related misconceptions in *Shame and Necessity*: see in particular chapter 2.

11 Nietzsche, *The Genealogy of Morals*, translated by Walter Kaufmann and R. J. Hollingdale (New York, 1967), First Essay, section 13.

12 A Nietzschean genealogy typically combines, in a way that analytical

philosophy finds embarrassing, history, phenomenology, 'realistic' psychology, and conceptual interpretation. The historical stories, moreover, strikingly vary from one context to another. Some of Nietzsche's procedures are to be seen specifically in the light of Hegel's Phenomenology, and of his recurrent amazement that there could have been such a thing as Christianity. Some are certainly less helpful than others. But the mere idea that we need such elements to work together is surely right. We need to understand what parts of our conceptual scheme are, in what degree, culturally local. We understand this best when we understand an actual human scheme that differs from ours in certain respects. One, very important, way of locating such a scheme is finding it in history, in particular in the history of our own scheme. In order to understand that other scheme, and to understand why there should be this difference between those people and ourselves, we need to understand it as a human scheme; this is to understand the differences in terms of similarities, which calls on psychological interpretation. Very roughly speaking indeed, a Nietzschean genealogy can be seen now as starting from Davidson plus history.

13 A particularly illuminating example is Robert Nozick's discussion of retributive punishment in *Philosophical Explanations* (Oxford: Oxford University Press, 1984) pp. 363ff. His heroic attempt to express what pure retribution tries to *achieve* (as opposed to what, in actual fact, it does) reveals, it seems to me, that there is no logical space for it to succeed.

II

Philosophy, evolution, and the human sciences

7

Making sense of humanity

Are we animals? Are we machines? Those two questions are often asked, but they are not satisfactory. For one thing, they do not, from all the relevant points of view, present alternatives: those who think that we are machines think that other animals are machines, too. In addition, the questions are too easily answered. We are, straightforwardly, animals, but we are not, straightforwardly, machines. We are a distinctive kind of animal but not any distinctive kind of machine. We are a kind of animal in the same way that any other species is a kind of animal – we are, for instance, a kind of primate.

Ethology and culture

Since we are a kind of animal, there are answers in our case to the question that can be asked about any animal, 'How does it live?' Some of these answers are more or less the same for all human beings wherever and whenever they live, and of those universal answers, some are distinctively true of human beings and do not apply to other animals. There are other answers to the question, how human beings live, that vary strikingly from place to place and, still more significantly, from time to time. Some other species, too, display behaviour that varies regionally – the calls of certain birds are an example – but the degree of such variation in human beings is of a quite different order of magnitude. Moreover, and more fundamentally, these variations essentially depend on the use of language and, associated with that, the non-genetic transmission of information between generations, features that are, of course, themselves among the most important universal characteristics distinctive of human beings. This variation in the ways that human beings live is cultural variation, and it is an ethological fact that human beings live under culture (a fact represented in the ancient doctrine that their nature is to live by convention).

With human beings, if you specify the ethological in detail, you are inevitably led to the cultural. For example, human beings typically live in dwellings. So, in a sense, do termites, but in the case of human beings the description opens into a series of cultural specifications. Some human beings live in a dwelling made by themselves, some in one made by other human beings. Some who make dwellings are constrained to make them, others are rewarded for doing so; in either case, they act in groups with a division of labour, and so on. If one is to describe any of these activities adequately and so explain what these animals are up to, one has to ascribe to them the complex intentions involved in sharing a culture.

There are other dimensions of culture and further types of complex intention. Some of the dwellings systematically vary in form – being four-bedroom Victorians, for instance, or in the Palladian style – and those descriptions have to be used in explaining the variations. Such styles and traditions involve kinds of intentions that are not merely complex but self-referential: the intentions refer to the tradition, and at the same time it is the existence of such intentions that constitutes the tradition. Traditions of this kind display another feature that they share with many other cultural phenomena: they imply a consciousness of past time, historical or mythical. This consciousness itself has become more reflexive and complex in the course of human development, above all with the introduction of literacy. All human beings live under culture; many live with an idea of their collective past; some live with the idea of such an idea.

All of this is ethology, or an extension of ethology; if one is going to understand a species that lives under culture, one has to understand its cultures. But it is not all biology. So how much is biology? And what does that question mean? I shall suggest a line of thought about similarities and differences.

The story so far implies that some differences in the behaviour of human groups are explained in terms of their different cultures and not in biological terms. This may encourage the idea that culture explains differences and biology explains similarities. But this is not necessarily so. Indeed, in more than one respect, the question is not well posed. First, there is the absolutely general point that a genetic influence will express itself in a particular way only granted a certain sort of environment. A striking example of such an interaction is provided by turtles' eggs, which if they are exposed to a temperature below 30 degrees Celsius at a certain point in development yield a female turtle but if to a higher temperature, a male one. Moreover, the possible interactions are complex, and many cases cannot be characterized merely by adding together different influences or, again, just in terms of triggering.[1] Changes in the environment may depend on the activities of the animals themselves. In the case of human beings, the environment and changes in it may well require cultural description.

Granted these complexities, it may not be clear what is meant by ascribing some similarity or difference between different groups of human beings to a biological rather than a cultural influence. But insofar as it makes sense to say anything of this sort, it can be appropriate to ascribe a *difference* in human behaviour to a biological factor. Thus, the notable differences in the fertility rates of human societies at different times (a phenomenon that defies simple explanation) may be connected to a differential perception of risk.[2] This would provide a strong analogy to differences in the reproductive behaviour in groups of other species, and in this sense, it would suggest a biological explanation. But many features of the situation would demand cultural description, such as the reproductive behaviours so affected, the ways in which risks are appreciated, and, of course, what events counted as dangerous (e.g., war).

In the opposite direction, it has been a pervasive error of sociobiology to suppose that if some practice of human culture is analogous to a pattern of behaviour in other species, then it is all the more likely to be explained biologically if it is (more or less) universal among human beings. If this follows at all, it does so in a very weak sense. Suppose (what is untrue) that the subordinate role of women were a cultural universal. This might nevertheless depend on other cultural universals and their conditions, for example, the absence up to now of certain kinds of technology; it could turn out to be biologically determined at most to this extent, that if roles related to gender were to be assigned in those cultural contexts, biology favoured this assignation.

We cannot be in a position to give a biological explanation of any phenomenon that has a cultural dimension, however widespread the phenomenon is, unless we are also in a position to interpret it culturally. This is simply an application, to the very special case of human beings, of the general truth that one cannot explain animal behaviour biologically (in particular, genetically) unless one understands it ethologically.

Cognitive science and folk psychology

The claim that we are animals is straightforwardly true. The claim that we are machines, however, needs a determinate interpretation if it is to mean anything. What some people mean by it (despite the existence of machines capable of random behaviour) is merely that we, like other

81

large things, can be deterministically characterized, to some acceptable approximation, in terms of physics. This seems to me probably true and certainly uninteresting for the present discussion. Any more interesting version must claim that we are *each* a machine; and I take the contemporary content of this to be that we are each best understood in terms of an information-processing device. This, in turn, represents a belief in a research programme, that of psychology as cognitive science. However, the claim that human beings are in this sense machines involves more than the claim that human beings are such that cognitive science is a good programme for psychology. It must also imply that psychology provides an adequate programme for understanding human beings; this is a point I shall come back to.

To some extent the claim that human beings can be understood in terms of psychology as cognitive science must surely be an empirical one, to be tested in the success of the research programme. For an empirical claim, however, it has attracted a surprising amount of a priori criticism, designed to show that the undertaking is mistaken in principle. Less extreme, obviously, than either the comprehensive research programme or the comprehensive refutation of it is the modest suggestion that this kind of model will be valuable for understanding human beings in some respects but not others. The suggestion is initially attractive but at the same time very indeterminate, and of course it may turn out that, like some other compromises, it is attractive only because it is indeterminate. I should like to raise the question of how the compromise might be made more determinate.

Those who want to produce a comprehensive refutation of the programme sometimes make the objection that only a living thing can have a psychology. This can mean two different things. One is that psychological processes, of whatever kind, could be realized only in a biological system; that a mind could only be secreted by a brain.[3] This, if true, would certainly put the research programme out of business, since whatever other refinements it receives, its central idea must be that psychological processes could in principle be realized by any system with an adequate information-theoretical capacity. However, I see no reason why in this form the objection should be true: that mind is essentially biochemical seems a no more appealing belief than that it is essentially immaterial.

A more interesting version of the objection that only a living thing can have a psychology takes the form of saying that a human psychology, at least, can be possessed only by a creature that *has a life*, where this implies, among other things, that its experience has a meaning for it and that features of its environment display salience, relevance, and so on, particularly in the light of what it sees as valuable. This seems to me much more likely to be true, and it has a discouraging consequence for the research programme in its more ambitious forms, because the experience described in these terms is so strongly holistic. An example is provided by complex emotions such as shame, contempt, or admiration, where an agent's appreciation of the situation, and his or her self-reflection, are closely related to one another and also draw on an indefinitely wide range of other experiences, memories, social expectations, and so on. There is no reason to suppose that one could understand, still less reproduce, these experiences in terms of any system that did not already embody the complex interconnections of an equally complex existence.[4]

Another example is worth mentioning particularly because it has so often appeared in the rhetoric of arguments about such questions. This is creativity. An information-processing device might be a creative problem solver, and it might come up with what it, itself, could 'recognize' as fruitful solutions to problems in mathematics or chess (wagers on this being impossible were always ill-advised). But it could not display a similar creativity in some less formalized intellectual domain or in the arts. This is not (repeat, *not*) because such creativity is magical or a resplendent counter-example to the laws of nature.[5] It is simply that what we call creativity is a characteristic that yields not merely something new or unlikely but something new that strikes us as meaningful and interesting; and what makes it meaningful and interesting to us can lie in an indeterminately wide range of associations and connections built up in our existence, most of them unconscious. The associations are associations *for us*: the creative idea must strike a bell that we can hear. In the sense that a device can be programmed to be a problem solver, there may be, in creative connections, no antecedent problem. (Diaghilev, asking Cocteau for a new ballet, memorably said, '*Etonne-moi, Jean.*') None of this is to deny that there may be a description in physical terms of what goes on when a human being comes up with something new and interesting. The difficulty for the research programme is that there is no reason to expect that in these connections, at least, there will be an explanatory psychological account at the level that it wants, lying between the physical account, on the one hand, and a fully interpretive account that itself uses notions such as meaning, on the other.

The activities and experiences that I have mentioned as providing a difficulty for the research programme are all specifically human. Although it may sometimes have been argued that some such holistic features must belong to any mentality at all, the most convincing account of the problem connects them with special features of human consciousness and culture. The question on these issues that I should like to leave for consideration is the following: if we grant this much, what follows for activities and, particularly, abilities that human beings do prima facie share with other creatures? If we grant what has just been suggested, there will not be an adequate cognitive-scientific account of what it is to feel embarrassment, or of recognizing a scene as embarrassing, or (perhaps) of seeing that a picture is a Watteau. But there could be, and perhaps is, such an account of seeing that something is a cylinder or of recognizing something as a rabbit. Other animals have abilities that can be described in these terms, but are they just the same abilities in human beings and in other animals? (Consider, for instance, the relations, in the human case, between being able to recognize a rabbit and being able to recognize a rabbit in many different styles of picture.) What does seem clear, at the very least, is that a cognitive-scientific programme for rabbit recognition, and a human being skilled in recognizing rabbits, would not be disposed to make quite the same mistakes. What we shall need here, if this kind of research programme is to help us in understanding human beings, is an effective notion of a *fragment* of human capacities. There is no reason to think that there cannot be such a notion, but we need more thoughts about how it may work.

The cognitive science research programme and the hopes that may be reasonably entertained for it are a very different matter from the ambitions that some people entertain on the basis of a metaphysics of the cognitive science programme – that the concepts of such a science will eventually replace, in serious and literal discourse, those of 'folk psychology'. The main difficulty in assessing this idea is that the boundaries of 'folk psychology' are vague. Sometimes it is taken to include such conceptions as Cartesian dualism or the idea that the mental must be immediately known. These conceptions are indeed unsound, but if you attend to what 'the folk' regularly say and do rather than to what they may rehearse when asked theoretical questions, it is far from clear that they have these conceptions in their psychology. If they do, it does not need cognitive science to remove them, but, if anything, reflection: that is to say, philosophy.

In any case, the interesting claims do not concern such doctrines but rather the basic materials of 'folk psychology', notions such as belief, desire, intention, decision, and action. These really are used by 'the folk' in understanding their own and other people's psychology. These, too, the metaphysicians of cognitive science expect to be replaced, in educated thought, by other, scientific, conceptions.[6] In part, this stance may depend on confusing two different questions, whether a given concept belongs to a particular science and whether it can coexist with that science, as opposed to being eliminated by it. 'Golf ball' is not a concept of dynamics, but this is quite consistent with the truth that among the things to which dynamics applies are golf balls.[7] It may be said here that the situation with concepts such as *belief, desire,* and *intention* is different, because they, unlike the concept of a golf ball, have explanatory ambitions, and 'folk psychology', correspondingly, is in the same line of business as the theory, call it cognitive science, that will produce more developed explanations. But this is to presuppose that cognitive science does not need such concepts to characterize what it has to explain. No science can eliminate what has to exist if there is to be anything for it to explain: Newton's theory of gravitation could not show that there are no falling bodies, or Marr's theory of vision, that there is no such thing as vision.

The metaphysicians perhaps assume that there is a neutral item that cognitive science and 'folk psychology' are alike in the business of explaining, and that is behaviour. But to suppose that there could be an adequate sense of 'behaviour' that did not already involve concepts of 'folk psychology' – the idea of an intention, in particular – is to fall back into a basic error of behaviourism. Cognitive science rightly prides itself on having left the errors of behaviourism behind; but this should mean not merely that it has given up black box theorizing but, connectedly, that it recognizes that the kinds of phenomena to be explained cannot be brought together by purely non-psychological criteria, as, for instance, classes of displacements of limbs.[8]

Humanity and the human sciences

The claim that we are machines was the claim, I said earlier, that we are each a machine, and this, as I paraphrased it, entailed the idea that psychology is adequate for the understanding of human beings. What I have particularly in mind here relates to the much-discussed idea that for most purposes, at least, of explaining what human beings do, we can adopt the posture of what is called methodological solipsism and think of these creatures, in principle, as each existing with its own mental set-up, either alone or in relation to a physical environment not itself characterized in terms of any human science. This approach has been criticized in any case for reasons in the theory of meaning.[9] My concern here, however, is not with those issues but with the point that to make sense of the individual's psychology, it may well be necessary to describe the environment in terms that are the concern of other human sciences. It may be helpful, in this connection, to see how the false conception of methodological solipsism differs from another idea, which is correct. The correct idea is inoffensive to the point of triviality; I label it 'formal individualism',[10] and it states that there are ultimately no actions that are not the actions of individual agents. One may add to this the truth that the actions of an individual are explained in the first place by the psychology of that individual: this means, for instance, that to the extent those actions are intentional, they are explained in the first place by the individual's intentions.

The simple truths of formal individualism are enough to rule some things out. They imply, for instance, that if some structural force brings about results in society, it must do so in ways that issue in actions produced by the intentions of individuals, though those intentions, of course, will not adequately express or represent those forces. It also follows (unsurprisingly, I hope) that if Germany declared war, then some individuals did things that, in the particular circumstances, constituted this happening. But none of this requires that such things as Germany's declaring war are logically reducible to individual actions. (Germany embarked on war in 1914 and again in 1939, but the types of individual action that occurred were different: for one thing, Germany had different constitutions in these years.) Nor is it implied that the concepts that occur in individuals' intentions and in the descriptions of their actions can necessarily be reduced to individualist terms; in the course of Germany's declaring war on some occasion, someone no doubt acted *in the capacity of Chancellor*, and there is no credible unpacking of that conception in purely individualist terms. Again, it is a matter not only of the content of agents' intentions but of their causes. Some of the intentions that agents have may well require explanation in irreducibly social terms. Thus, some intentions of the person who is German Chancellor will have to be explained in terms of his being German Chancellor.[11]

What is true is that each action is explained, in the first place, by an individual's psychology; what is not true is that the individual's psychology is entirely explained by psychology. There are human sciences other than psychology, and there is not the slightest reason to suppose that one can understand humanity without them.

How the human sciences are related to one another – indeed, what exactly the human sciences are – as a much-discussed question that I shall not try to take up. I hope that if we are able to take a correct approach to the whole issue, this will make it less alarming than some obviously find it to accept that the human sciences should essentially deploy notions of intention and meaning and that they should flow into and out of studies such as history, philosophy, literary criticism, and the history of art which are labelled 'the humanities' and perhaps are not called 'sciences' at all. If it is an ethological truth that human beings live under culture, and if that fact makes it intelligible that they should live with ideas of the past and with increasingly complex conceptions of the ideas that they themselves have, then it is no insult to the scientific spirit that a study of them should require an insight into those cultures, into their products, and into their real and imagined histories.

Some resistance to identifying the human sciences in such terms – 'humanistic' terms, as we might say – comes, no doubt, simply from vulgar scientism and a refusal to accept the truth, at once powerful and limiting, that there is no physics but physics. But there are other reasons as well, to be found closer to the human sciences themselves. I have suggested so far that biology, here as elsewhere, requires ethology and that the ethology of the human involves the study of human cultures. Looking in a different direction, I have suggested that psychology as cognitive science, whatever place of its own it may turn out to have, should not have universalist and autonomous aspirations. But there is a different kind of challenge to the humane study of humanity, which comes from cultural studies themselves. I cannot in this context do much more than mention it, but it should be mentioned, since it raises real questions, sometimes takes the form of extravagantly deconstructive ambitions, and often elicits unhelpfully conservative defences.

This challenge is directed to the role of the humanities now. It is based not on any scientific considerations, or on any general characteristics of human life, but on certain features of the modern – or perhaps, in one sense of that multipurpose expression, post-modern – world. The claim is that this world is liberated from, or at least floating free from, the past, and that in this world, history is kitsch. Above all, it is a world in which particular cultural formations are of declining importance and are becoming objects of an interest that is merely nostalgic or concerned with the picturesque – that is to say, a commercial interest.

If applied to our need for historical understanding, such a view is surely self-defeating, because the ideas of modernity and post-modernity are themselves historical categories; they embody an interpretation of the past. This would be true even if the conception of a general modernity completely transcending local and cultural variation were correct. But it remains to be seen whether that conception is even correct. There is no reason at the moment, as I understand the situation, to suppose that patterns of development are independent of history and culture; South Korea and Victorian England are by no means the same place. But however that may be, these are indisputably matters for historical and cultural understanding.

What is more problematic is our relation in the modern world to the literature and art of the past. Our historical interest in it – our interest in it as, for instance, evidence of the past – raises no special question, but the study of the humanities has always gone beyond this, in encouraging and informing an interest in certain works, picked out both by their quality and their relation to a particular tradition, as cultural objects for us, as formative of our experience. There is obviously a great deal to be said about this and about such phenomena as the interest shown by all developing countries in the canon of European painting and music. Some of what needs to be said is obviously negative, and it is a real question whether certain famous artworks can survive – a few of them physically, all of them aesthetically – their international marketing. But the conversion of works of art into commodities is one thing, and their internationalization is another, even if the two things have up to now coincided, and we simply do not yet know, as it seems to me, what depth of experience of how much of the art of the past will be available to the human race if its cultural divergences are in fact diminished. However, it is worth recalling the number of cultural transitions that have already been effected by the works of the past in arriving even where they now are in our consciousness. What was there in classical antiquity itself, or in the complex history of its transmission and its influence, that might have led us to expect that as objects of serious study seven plays of Sophocles should now be alive and well and living in California?

'Humanity' is, of course, a name not merely for a species but for a quality, and it may be that the deepest contemporary reasons for distrusting a humanistic account of the human sciences are associated with a distrust of that quality, with despair for its prospects, or, quite often, with a hatred of it. Some legatees of the universalistic tendencies of the Enlightenment lack an interest in any specific cultural formation or other typically human expression, and at the limit urge us to rise above the local preoccupations of 'speciesism'. Others, within the areas of human culture, have emphasized the role of structural forces to a point at which human beings disappear from the scene. There are other well-known tendencies with similar effects. But the more that cultural diversity within the human race declines, and the more the world as a whole is shaped by structures characteristic of modernity, the more we need not to forget but to remind ourselves what a human life is, has been, and can be. This requires a proper understanding of the human sciences, and that requires us to take seriously humanity, in both senses of the term.

Notes

1 See Patrick Bateson, 'Biological approaches to the study of behavioural development', *International Journal of Behavioural Development* 10 (1987), to which I owe the example of the turtles' eggs.

2 See Richard M. Smith, 'Transfer incomes, risk and security: the roles of the family and the collectivity in recent theories of fertility change', in David Coleman and Roger Schofield (eds.), *The State of Population Theory: forward from Malthus* (Oxford: Blackwell, 1986).

3 John Searle suggested this in *Minds, Brains and Science* (Cambridge, MA: Harvard University Press, 1985), though I believe he no longer holds the view.

4 This argument has been forcefully developed by Charles Taylor in articles collected in his *Human Agency and Language*.

5 Advocates of this kind of research often claim that the only alternative to their programme lies in superstition and mystification; Marvin Minsky's book *The Society of Mind* (New York: Simon and Schuster, 1986) provides some (relatively mild) examples of this rhetoric.

6 The most extreme of these believers are Paul Churchland and Patricia Churchland, who once said that 'folk' psychology 'is a stagnant or degenerating research programme, and has been for millennia'. An extended statement may be found in Patricia Churchland, *Neurophilosophy* (Cambridge, MA: MIT Press, 1986). A more moderate line is taken by Stephen Stich in his book *From Folk Psychology to Cognitive Science* (Cambridge, MA: MIT Press, 1983). It is unfortunate that the phrase 'folk psychology' has caught on even with people who do not believe in the eliminativist programme. It is harmless if 'folk' is read as representing an objective genitive (as in 'child psychology'), but it is quite hard to hear the expression in this way, and to free it from the suggestions of populist incompetence or fraud with which it started out.

7 A related point is central to Donald Davidson's treatment of causality; see his *Essays on Actions and Events*.

8 A detailed and very effective argument is provided by Jennifer Hornsby's 'Physicalist thinking and concepts of behaviour', in Philip Pettit and John McDowell (eds.), *Subject, Thought and Context* (Oxford: Clarendon Press, 1986).

9 Recent discussion has been shaped by Hilary Putnam's important article, 'The meaning of "meaning"', reprinted in his *Mind, Language and Reality* (Cambridge: Cambridge University Press, 1975). The issues are set out in the introduction to Pettit and McDowell, *Subject, Thought and Context*.

10 The doctrine is weaker than several that could be expressed in those words. I have given some account of it in 'Formal and substantial individualism'.

11 Arguments on these points are well deployed in David Hillel Ruben, *The Metaphysics of the Social World* (London: Routledge and Kegan Paul, 1985).

8

Evolutionary theory and epistemology

If you consider theories in general, you usually find that if they are capable of very powerful explanatory applications, it is quite hard to apply them vacuously; while if they are easy to apply vacuously, it is hard to make them yield powerful explanations elsewhere. The power to explain, and the possibility of vacuity, are usually related to each other inversely. Particle physics maximizes the first and minimizes the second, while with systems theory, for instance, it is the other way round.

The theory of evolution by natural selection is untypical in this respect. It can be applied in such a way as to yield extremely powerful explanations, but it is also very susceptible to vacuous applications, which explain nothing and barely provide an interesting description of the matters in question. The reason that both these things are possible lies in this, that the basic pattern of explanation that the theory uses is extremely simple and familiar, and it can be applied where it is not obvious – that is why it is powerful – but its strength is very sensitive to certain conditions on the structure of the situation, which control the application of the theory, and it may easily look as though those conditions are satisfied when they are not.

In these remarks I shall consider some applications of evolutionary ideas to the theory of knowledge. In this area, as in others that involve human culture, it is very important to distinguish two different questions. The distinction turns on the kinds of thing that are supposedly selected for by the evolutionary process introduced by the theory. The evolution in question may, first, simply be the evolution that has produced human beings, ordinary biological evolution, and the selection will have been exercised on various species and characters in the emergence of human beings. The question then is: what light can be thrown on human knowledge, belief, understanding, scientific theories, and so forth from our knowledge of the ways in which human beings have evolved? This is the primary emphasis of what has been called 'evolutionary epistemology', as represented notably by the work of Donald T. Campbell.[1] The second interpretation applies a selective model to other items, of a cultural kind, such as scientific theories. These are represented as being themselves selected for. This is the principal emphasis of the work of Karl Popper.

The first of these interpretations sees scientific theories (and so forth) as *affected by* natural selection, namely the natural selection of human beings; the second interpretation sees them as themselves subject to an analogy of natural selection. These two issues, which are very different, are sometimes confused. Thus Franz M. Wuketits has written: 'Since the human mind is a product of evolution ... the evolutionary approach can be extended to the *products* of mind, that is to say, to epistemic activities such as *science*' (his emphasis).[2] This simply runs the two matters together. The two approaches are compatible with one another, but they are different. The first approach will claim that certain cognitive capacities in human beings, relevant to science, are indeed the products of natural selection: if so, these capacities will have to be, in some sense, innate. But scientific theories themselves, the concern of the second approach, are not innate to those that hold them – here, the selective pressure is operating on the theories, not on the theorists.

Selection of theories?

Let us first look at the second approach. Here it is particularly important to make clear the conditions on the substantive application of an evolutionary theory, and to consider what is required by an interesting analogy to natural selection for cultural objects – in this case, scientific theories.

First, we set aside the distinction between phenotype and genotype.[3] In some cases of non-biological evolution, there may be some substantive analogy to this distinction, for instance in the case of firms and their products; but it is irrelevant here. Having taken this step, we then require analogies to three things:

(1) *Fitness* (Survival). Fitness is the probability of leaving offspring, so some analogy is needed in the cultural case to leaving offspring. This requires that there should be two 'populations', P_1 and P_2, P_2 later than P_1, and that there should be a given character F present in P_1, which can be present or absent in P_2 partly as a result of its presence in P_1.

(2) *Selection*. Features of the environment of P_1 and P_2 must empirically account for the likelihood of characters present in P_1 being present in P_2.

(3) *Mutation*. Something should count as the emergence of a new character.

Condition (1) is in general satisfied for such things as artefacts and other cultural items. Types of conveyance, for instance, once widely spread, at a later time have disappeared. There are further analogies to the biological case more complex than this: thus types otherwise extinct may survive in very special microenvironments. One has to be careful, though, in identifying such examples. Bugattis or Delahayes existing in a motor museum do not count, since they do not reproduce there, but are fossils; handmade shirts, on the other hand, are an example.

The problems in applying the analogy of natural selection to such things lie, rather, in the relations between (2) and (3). It is not inevitable that the evolutionary analogy will be fatally weakened at this point, but there is a danger of it. The emergence of some new character or type in the cultural field is usually to be traced to purposive thought by inventors, and so forth; but then the analogy to (3), *mutation*, is very weak, and the structure has low explanatory value. Alternatively an explanation may be found for the emergence of a new character which is nearer to random mutation; thus, for instance, producers often do not know what will succeed, but try out products to see what will succeed. In this case, the analogy to (2), *selection*, will lie in such things as taste: the product takes on, or it does not. But then a difficulty breaks out about the relations between (2) and (1): they are now, on this interpretation, too close to one another. The facts of survival, and the environmental cause of survival, are more or less the same, that these types of objects are preferred by the public, and the theory once more slides towards vacuity.

How are these analogies to be handled in the particular case of scientific theories?

(1) The relevant characters of theories presumably lie in what they assert, their conceptual features, and so forth. Their presence in a given population, and hence their survival, presumably lies in something like their *acceptance in the scientific community*. There are indeed serious questions about what that notion itself implies. Does it mean, for instance, merely that the theories are used operationally? Or that they are believed to be true?[4] But we will leave that problem to one side.

(2) For Popper, at least, the analogy to selection lies in theories being 'corroborated' or 'falsified'. These are, of course, for Popperian theory, *historical* properties, and so they must be if their impact is to

explain the survival that was introduced at (1), since that is itself a social characteristic. But, for the same reason, the fact that a theory has been falsified or corroborated is not in itself enough to explain the disappearance or the survival of that theory in the scientific community. Rather it has to be accepted by the scientific community that the theory has been falsified or, again, corroborated. There are several reasons for this. First of all, and obviously enough, the relevant experiments will have no effect on the scientific community if they are not known. Moreover, whether an observation or experiment is counted as a falsification is itself a function of theory. Moreover, as Kuhn has insisted, it is also a function of what, in terms of the evolutionary analogy, is the mutation rate – that is to say, the emergence of new theories: 'falsified' theories tend to stay around if there is no better alternative available.

What is the result of combining these various interpretations and concessions? It seems to be, more or less, the claim that theories do not stay accepted in the scientific community if the scientific community has agreed that they are to be rejected. But if this is the outcome, then (1) and (2) are, in this case also, too close to one another, and the account is vacuous.

It is important that on these interpretations the 'selective pressure' and the 'mutation rate' are up to us: they are a matter of what theories are invented, how many experiments are conducted, and so forth. However, nothing in the model could lead to Popper's normative conclusion that we *should* keep up the selective pressure and the mutation rate. (Obviously nothing can be added here by the purely verbal point that it is part of what we call 'science' that these things should be sustained: the question, of course, is about the rationality of what we call 'science'.) If there is a temptation to believe that this normative conclusion does follow from the model of natural selection of scientific theories, or is closely associated with that model, then I think it is due to the error, familiar in the biological field, of supposing that 'fitness' means *more* than the probability of survival or of leaving offspring. The idea will be that the surviving theory will be (also) the *best* theory: in particular, the true theory.

There are indeed many questions about what is meant by the truth of theories. (It is the problem that arose under (1) in connection with the scientific community's 'accepting' theories. It arises, obviously enough, also in relation to (2).) But even if we do move from considering merely the 'survival' of theories as a social fact about the scientific community, to questions of such theories being in some further sense true, it remains quite hard to say anything very illuminating about the effects of selective pressure on the chances of our theories being true. We can certainly say that if we base our beliefs on directed experiment and observation, use the methods of scientific communication, and so forth, we are more likely to end up with true beliefs than if our impressions come from casual observation, hearsay, and similar sources. This is true, and I suspect that, granted that the game against nature is not a two-person game, it is necessarily true. Some things will follow from this about how scientific enquiry should be conducted. But not much will follow from it to encourage specific proposals in favour of vigorous scientific competition, repeated attempts to falsify accepted theories, and so forth. Whether these strategies are appropriate, will depend on empirical sociological claims about the effects on the scientific community of different kinds of motivation and styles of scientific culture: to take one example, whether a vigorously competitive atmosphere in science is more likely to lead to honest experiment, rather than to fudging and premature publication. These are well-known and substantive issues, but I do not think that much help with them is to be gained from the natural selection analogy itself. This seems to be a typical case of the phenomenon that I referred to at the beginning of these remarks, that there is only a very narrow area, if any at all, between conclusions that do follow from the analogy, but are merely vacuous, and conclusions that do not follow from the analogy at all.

Science and the evolutionary history of human beings

I now turn back to the first of the two interpretations that were distinguished earlier. Here the evolution in question is the actual biological evolution of human beings. 'Evolutionary epistemology', in a sense appropriate to this interest, emphasizes the continuity of human beings' cognitive processes with those postulated for earlier stages of evolution. Such a theory insists that a theory of knowledge must be a naturalistic endeavour, which needs to be guided by what is known of human evolution. It emphasizes, in particular, that epistemology should be descriptive rather than justificatory, and, in particular, that it should not be foundationalist. A theory of knowledge, moreover, should not imply any 'transfusion of truths from outside'. As Donald Campbell rather colourfully puts it: 'We once saw as through the fumblings of a blind protozoon, and no revelation has been given to us since.'[5]

There is certainly much to be said on broader grounds for a 'naturalized epistemology'; the relation of this to any justificatory project in the theory of knowledge is largely beyond the present concern, though I shall touch on some questions of justification later. The present issue concerns the particular contribution made by evolutionary ideas to the broader enterprise of naturalized epistemology.

There is a certain tendency to equate all evolution with learning; in a famous phrase of Konrad Lorenz, 'Life itself is a process of cognition.' This idea is, in itself, the 'evolution of scientific theories' notion taken in the opposite direction: the staphylococcus has phylogenetically learned in developing immunity to a given antibiotic. But this extremely general idea is not the interesting one for evolutionary epistemology, which is concerned with a more specific matter, the capacities possessed by a member of a given species to acquire information about its environment and act directedly in virtue of that information. Neither these capacities, nor the states that they yield, are necessarily conscious. There are very considerable difficulties in distinguishing the required sense of 'acquiring information', from other causal processes that modify behaviour. I shall not try to discuss those difficulties here, but merely note what seems to me a necessary condition on regarding the state of an individual as being, in a sense relevant to these enquiries, a cognitive state: the state invoked in the explanation of behaviour should be the kind of state that can also be, in appropriate circumstances, false.

Campbell and other evolutionary epistemologists tell a hierarchical story, in which the most primitive capacities ('non-mnemonic problem solving') have had successively added to them 'vicarious locomotive devices' (the animal does not have to bang into an obstruction to recognize that it is there), visually and mnemonically supported thought, internalized experiments, cultural accumulation, and science. The effects of this process are, as things typically are in biology, largely cumulative, even though there are many specializations not shared by other genera in the family or order, such as the well-known sonic system of bats.

What can this picture tell us about our exercise of our cognitive capacities, in particular of our special cognitive capacities? One lesson is negative: that we carry with us what has been called in this literature 'a ratiomorphic apparatus', and this apparatus can mislead us. When we recognize this, we are led to a cognitive psychology of error, particularly with regard to probabilities.[6] There are also positive lessons to be learned, for instance in the psychology of perception. Since basic features of our visual system were laid down at an early stage of evolution, we should expect to find certain constant principles of information-processing. This suggests biological contributions to what are indeed biological questions, though they are questions that have complex relations to the judgements made by creatures that are capable of making judgements.

All this is admirable and useful, but it mostly stands at some distance from traditional questions of epistemology. Evolutionary considerations come closest to those questions when they are applied to principles of abstract cognition – when we come to the conceptualization of the world in terms of space, time, and causality, and hence to the general structure of scientific understanding. Evolutionary epistemologists have believed themselves to be making contact in this area with traditional problems such as that of innate knowledge, the a priori, and the status of empiricism. Indeed, one of the principal insights of evolutionary epistemology is said to be that 'what is ontogenetically *a priori* is phylogenetically *a posteriori*'. The individual learner does bring something to the world – otherwise he could learn nothing – but it is an inherited accumulation from the evolutionary process.

It is always a problem with these epistemological questions, even in their traditional form, to determine what kinds of properties of the mind are being considered. Wuketits offers as the first postulate of evolutionary epistemology: 'All organisms are equipped with a system of innate dispositions: no individual living system is initially a ... *tabula rasa*.'[7] The first half of this claim was accepted by classical empiricists who thought that the human mind *was* a *tabula rasa*; they posited at least a disposition to association, and Locke postulated several other mechanisms as well. His denial was that there were innate *propositions* or *ideas*. But that leaves a very severe problem of what counts as a disposition, a principle, a proposition, or an idea. Leibniz, an innatist who was opposed, if anyone was, to empiricism, actually agreed with the empiricists and their scholastic predecessors that there was nothing in the intellect that was not in the senses, but added the vital reservation, 'except the intellect itself'.

To distinguish innate from non-innate material in such terms now seems a hopeless task. The question seems to turn on how *specific* or, alternatively, topic-neutral, the innate material is conceived as being. Are human beings general learning machines, or systems with much more specific expectations and models? To give a definite content to the latter account seems to be the most promising and interesting contribution of the evolutionary line of thought to our understanding of human knowledge.[8]

Realism

Evolutionary thought about our cognitive capacities may well have a contribution to make to our understanding of scientific knowledge. But this possibility raises a deep problem. It is not so much a problem *for* evolutionary epistemology as a problem that evolutionary epistemology helps to identify – and it is a virtue of it that it should lead one to identify this problem.

Evolutionary epistemology, obviously enough, assumes the independent existence of a physical world, and tells us quite a lot about its properties, notably just those properties that are invoked in the explanation of how human beings and other species evolved. At the same time, one of the things that it seeks to explain is our conception of that world in those very terms. There is nothing wrong with this situation and, as many writers have recognized, there is no vicious circularity. There would be a circularity if these considerations were used to 'prove' the existence of the external world; that would be to desert the naturalistic stance of evolutionary epistemology for foundationalist or justificatory epistemology, and in doing that, it would beg the question.

Evolutionary epistemology is from the beginning a realist theory. The only question is why some of its adherents insist on calling it *hypothetical realism*. Its realism is certainly no more hypothetical than the acceptability of its own assertions. In this sense, as G. Wollmer[9] and others have said, naturalistic epistemology in general represents a true Copernican turn, as contrasted with Kant's.

It is certainly no objection to a theory that its truth is compatible with its own existence. It can even be an attraction of the theory that accepting its truth helps to explain its own existence, or at least the possibility of its existence. But that relationship does put some constraints on what the theory can say. Evolutionary epistemology assigns to various creatures various representations of the world, related to their evolutionary needs and specific natures. Some writers have used in this connection the concept of an *Umwelt*.[10] This concept has rather ambiguous relations to ideas of consciousness: the paramecium, for instance, has an *Umwelt*, but how are things *for* that creature? But, leaving aside the most general questions about the use of this notion, let us allow at least some rather unspecific conception of 'how it is for' a bat or for a cat, and a much less unspecific conception of 'how it is for' us. The theory offers a general scientific vocabulary for explaining these various *Umwelten*, including ours. But that description is our description, and what it expresses is our *Umwelt*. Does this generate scepticism? Might not the cat, from its *Umwelt*, generate in what Thomas Nagel has called its 'furry little mind' a different science?

The first point to make here is that it has not done so. This is a non-trivial fact, and evolutionary epistemology, with its hierarchical story of cognitive capacities, helps to explain why that is to be expected. But then speculation is likely to move to the possible science of possible other, non-terrestrial, advanced creatures. Reflection can, I believe, help to disentangle those elements of our representation of the world, that we have reason to believe are peculiar to us and perhaps to other terrestrial species, from those that are not. But it is important to emphasize that it will be necessary to do this if the realism implicit in evolutionary epistemology is to be adequately settled, and is not to be exposed to scepticism. Moreover, the resources of evolutionary epistemology cannot themselves do this, though they can contribute to it. Evolutionary epistemology must allow some autonomy to abstract scientific theory construction, beyond the local constraints of terrestrial evolution. Otherwise, scientific theory, including the evolutionary theory itself, cannot be anything more than a product of evolution, a contribution to the particularly fantasticated *Umwelt* of one terrestrial species. It is acceptable that it should be a product of evolution, and it is not refuted or shown to be meaningless by the fact that this is what it is; but it must allow for a reflective understanding of the ways in which it is not just peculiarly such a product. In accepting that there is some degree of autonomy to abstract scientific theory in this sense, theorists of evolutionary epistemology will have to recognize that there are limits on what can be achieved within their research programme; moreover, considerable weight is put on the question of how they see the relation of sophisticated scientific theory to evolutionarily more primitive cognitive processes. Those relations are still obscure, and I believe that they are the crux of the question.

Notes

1 Donald T. Campbell, 'Evolutionary epistemology', in P. A. Schilpp (ed.), *The Philosophy of Karl Popper* (Open Court, 1978), i., pp. 413–51.

2 Franz M. Wuketits (ed.), *Concepts and Approaches in Evolutionary Epistemology: towards an evolutionary theory of knowledge* (Dordrecht: Reidel, 1983), p. 8.

3 Equivalently, we treat the survival of the items in question as like the survival of a gene in Dawkins's model.

4 These questions are often obscured in discussions of the relations of 'our' science to the science of other times. What is it for a science to be 'ours'?

5 Campbell, 'Evolutionary epistemology', p. 414.

6 For important discussions, see D. Kahneman, P. Slovic, and A. Tversky (eds.), *Judgement under Uncertainty: Heuristics and Biases* (Cambridge: Cambridge University Press, 1982).

7 Wuketits, *Concepts and Approaches*, p. 5.

8 It is certainly more interesting than another line in evolutionary epistemology, which is that of trying to elicit very general principles of learning. These principles tend to be either vacuous or comically misleading. Thus the fourth hypothesis of Robert Kasper (in Wuketits, *Concepts and Approaches*) states: 'The probability that two or more things will serve the same purpose increases with the number of their common features.' Before one puts in the restrictions that

will eventually make this principle into a tautology, it seems to lead to the conclusion that if I can reach something with the help of a tall man, I am more likely to be able to reach it with the help of a short man than with a tall ladder.

9 Wuketits, *Concepts and Approaches*, p. 81.

10 Introduced, it seems, by Jakob von Uexküll, *Streifzüge durch die Umwelten von Tieren und Menschen* (1934). The term has been happily paraphrased as 'a cognitive niche'.

Evolution, ethics, and the representation problem

This chapter is concerned with culture and with evolution, but not with cultural evolution. It discusses the relations between biological evolution and the areas of human culture which may broadly be called 'ethical'. The concept of *cultural* evolution is problematical, and there are notorious difficulties about applying the notions of evolution and natural selection to cultural development.[1] That area, however, is not the concern of the present discussion.

There are two kinds of connection between evolutionary theory and ethics: one normative, and one explanatory. There is also a connection between these two, to which I shall come later. The first of these is older than the second, and has acquired a bad name; indeed, it acquired it fairly early, in some part from the monumental and unappealing system of Herbert Spencer. In fact, as John Burrow has shown (*Evolution and Society* (Cambridge: Cambridge University Press, 1966)) a lot of this material antedated *The Origin of Species*; the concept of 'the survival of the fittest' (Spencer's own phrase) was already implicit in earlier sociological work which Spencer derived from Malthus. Darwin himself had little sympathy for these ideas and not much, personally, for Spencer, though he did once say – I quote Burrow (p. 182) – 'in a moment of enthusiasm ... that Spencer's *Principles of Biology* made him feel that he "is about a dozen times my superior", and thought that Spencer might one day be regarded as the equal of Descartes and Leibniz, rather spoiling the effect by adding, "about whom, however, I know very little"'.

The bad normative applications of evolutionary theory to ethics which were made by Spencer and others also, of course, involved a lot of bad evolutionary theory: if normative lessons could be drawn from Darwinian theory, there is certainly no reason why they should take the form suggested by Social Darwinists. However, there is in addition a standard objection which holds that no such lessons can be drawn at all, at least in any directly logical way, since any project of deriving ethical content from premises of evolutionary theory commits the 'naturalistic fallacy', an error which is today often equated with that of trying to derive *ought* from *is*.[2]

Interesting questions about 'naturalism' in ethics in fact go beyond these purely logical issues. Naturalism in a broader sense consists in the attempt to lay down certain fundamental aspects of a good human life on the basis of considerations of human nature. If this project fails, it is not for purely logical reasons; it will rather be for the more interesting reason that the right sort of truths do not exist about human nature. I shall come back to this wider question at the end of this chapter.

The point about *ought* and *is*, so far as it goes, does have some force. It can be put in the following way. Suppose that considerations of evolutionary theory show that certain behaviour is in some sense appropriate for human beings. Either human beings can diverge from this pattern, or they cannot. If they can, then the biological considerations are not going to show that they ought not to; while, if they cannot so diverge, then there is no question of *ought*. This argument seems to me sound so far as it goes, but it does not go very far.

Implicit in this last argument is another logical relation which is more interesting for this question than that between *ought* and *is*: the relation, that is to say, between *ought* and *can*. This relationship underlies some important negative arguments which, by citing certain claims to the effect that human beings cannot, as they may suppose, live in a certain way, lead to the conclusion that certain ethical goals or ideals are unrealistic and should be revised. By arguments of this kind biological or similar arguments could coherently yield *constraints* on social goals, personal ideals, possible institutions and so forth.

To say that human beings cannot do certain things is, of course, an extremely vague form of statement. At one extreme, it may mean that the world will not contain an example of any single human being doing that thing; at the other end, it may merely mean that if a group of human beings adopts a norm requiring that behaviour, the norm will often be broken, its observance will give rise to a good deal of anxiety, those who comply without anxiety to the norm will be unusual in other respects, and so forth. This vagueness will not matter so long as one is clear about the level at which the formula of *'ought* implies *can'* is being applied: thus the latter, and weaker, kind of 'cannot' would be enough to provide a strong argument against the behaviour being made into a norm for a human society, but it would not be enough if the question concerned the adoption of a personal ideal in an individual case. Here, as so often, it is a centrally important question, who is supposedly being addressed by a given piece of ethical discourse. Granted that one is clear about that, the fact that relevant statements of what human beings can and cannot do come in various strengths is not so important. What is vitally important is the difficulty of knowing which of them, relevant to difficult ethical issues, are on biological grounds in fact true.

In this area there is an important connection, which I mentioned before, between what I called the normative and the explanatory interest. If some biological constraint can rule out, or make unrealistic, some normative practice or institution, then knowledge of this may not only encourage us to decline that practice if it is suggested, but may also contribute an explanation of why human communities do not in general display that practice or institution. Might biological considerations then go further and explain the human adoption of other practices, which are conformable to biological constraints?

This raises a general question which is central to these areas, and which I shall call *the representation problem*. It is a problem that comes up at various points in considering the relations between biology and human practices, and may be put in the following way: *how is a phenotypic character which would present itself in other species as a behavioural tendency represented in a species which has a culture, language, and conceptual thought?* It may be said that in some cases, at least, such a tendency will show up in that species merely as itself – that is to say, as a merely biological character of that species. But, in fact, virtually no behavioural tendency which constitutes genuine action can just show up in a cultural context 'as itself'. Where there is culture, it affects everything, and we should reject the crude view that culture is applied to an animal in a way which leaves its other characteristics unmodified. (Related to that view is the naive assumption of certain sociobiologists that sociobiology should expect to be more closely related to social anthropology than to other social sciences, because the 'primitive' peoples studied by social anthropology are nearer to nature than human beings who live in large industrialized societies.) None of this is to deny that there is a biological basis for elements in human behaviour which are culturally affected, moulded, and elaborated. It is not to deny that some culturally elaborated behaviour can usefully be explained from a biological perspective. It is simply to recall the fact that almost all human behaviour, at least that which deserves the name of 'action', is in fact culturally moulded and elaborated.

In accepting that there is a representation problem, I reject two views according to which there would be no such problem. First is a simple reductionist view, which would neglect the way in which culture not only shapes but constitutes the vast mass of human behaviour. When ancient Greek thought first discovered the opposition of 'nature' and 'convention', it also discovered that an essential part of human nature is to live by convention. The study of human nature *is*, in good part, the study of human conventions, and that is what it is from the strictest ethological point of view. That is how *this* species is. It is a claim additional to this, but one which I also believe to be true, that human conventions, at least beyond a certain state of elaboration, can be understood only with the help of history, and that the social sciences accordingly have an essential historical base. To pursue the question of whether that is so, would go beyond the limits of the present discussion,[3] but it is worth bearing in mind, when the relations are discussed of biology to the social sciences, that an essential social science is likely to prove to be history.

The second point of view which is excluded by taking seriously the representation problem is one that I am disposed to call 'the Wittgensteinian cop-out'. This is a view implicit in the idea that the central concept for gaining insight into human activities is that of a 'language game'. Since 'language' in this formulation is regarded both as the key to human convention, and also as something that human beings possess and animals do not, the phrase itself implies the lack of interesting explanatory or constraining connections between human and animal behaviour. It suggests an autonomy of the human, under a defining idea of linguistic and conceptual consciousness, which tends to put a stop to any interesting questions of the biological kind before they even start. It therefore does not give any help even in the areas, such as sex and hunger, where we most obviously need means of describing the relations between culture and the biological.

The feature of human culture and human activities that gives rise to the representation problem is above all that human communities embody *norms*, and it is this notion that I shall principally discuss. However, there are other ways, as well, of picking out differences between human activities and those of other animals. One is the very general feature that humans possess conceptual and reflexive consciousness; this, and the very large philosophical problems introduced by those three terms, I shall happily leave on one side. Another distinction between human and animal behaviour is that considerations of *motive* are appropriate to the assessment of human action. This is a matter that is worth some brief discussion, since it is closely connected with the fuss that has been made about the application of the term 'altruism' to animal as to human behaviour.

In other animals there is behaviour that benefits another individual, and moreover there is behaviour the end of which is to benefit another individual. (The sense of 'end' requires a lot of work to make clear, but it is uncontentiously illustrated by behaviour the end of which is that the animal should take in food.) In the human case, many more layers can be added, and other distinctions drawn. There are questions of intention, where this concerns what thoughts produce the action, and what features of the action are, relative to that thought, accidental. There are questions of underlying desire. Some actions which benefit others come from the desire just to benefit that particular person, while others flow from some more general disposition, while the desire to benefit a particular person or group may be accompanied by a variety of other desires, for instance to extract goodwill from them, or the possibility of a reward.

The cultural and psychological elaboration of these various motives of course raises difficulties for any simple relation of them to the biological. Some of those difficulties arise just from the general problem of applying biological models to a species that engages in intentional thought; to that extent there is no *special* problem about altruism and morality. People think that there is a special barrier here to the application of biological models, I believe, because they take 'altruism', in a 'properly moral' sense, to refer to some quite peculiarly pure motive, such as the intention to benefit others derived from impartial reflection on their interests and associated with no other desire whatsoever. But it is extremely unreasonable to suppose that all (perhaps any) human beings act from that motivation, either, and if morality is to be a generally human phenomenon, it is simply a mistake to equate it from the beginning with such exigently Kantian formulations, and it is a mistake even from the point of view of the distinctively human sciences. It is no doubt true that a biological perspective will make one more suspicious of extremely intellectualist or, again, very purist views of morality; but equally, so will a reasonable historical and psychological understanding of morality.

It is the notion of a *norm* that perhaps gives rise to the central representation problem. The main point is condensed in a question about the relation between an inhibition and a prohibition.[4] The most, it seems, that a genetically acquired character could yield would be an inhibition against behaviours of a certain kind; what relation could that have to a socially sanctioned prohibition? Indeed, if the inhibition exists, what *need* could there be for such a prohibition? If the prohibitory norm is to be part of the 'extended phenotype' of the species, how could we conceive, starting from an inhibition, that this might come about?

This is a central example of the problem, but it is not the only example even with respect to norms, and it will be helpful to distinguish various things that fall under the general heading of a 'norm'. Not everything that falls under this heading is a sanctioned prohibition. We can distinguish various items; I will represent them as *stacked*, in a way that is typical but not by any means universal.

(1) Behaviour which is normal. This does not just mean 'frequent': exceptions are perceived as 'odd', but are not necessarily disapproved of, sanctioned, etc.

(2) (1) together with an institution. This can be applied to the case of marriage, where there will of course be usually sanctions of varying degrees against behaviours that threaten marriage, and sexual activity outside marriage may be disapproved of, but this does not imply that merely not engaging in marriage is disapproved of, nor that an unmarried condition is sanctioned.

(3) Behaviour which lies outside (1) and (2), and to which in addition there may be strong personal disinclination: e.g. homosexuality as regarded in moderately enlightened circles.

(4) (3) together with rejection and disapproval of the deviant behaviour: e.g. homosexuality as regarded in less enlightened circles.

(5) (4) together with sanctions personal or legal: e.g. homosexuality in the least enlightened circles.

Among the cases in which the options are not stacked like this, is that in which sanctions and disapproval exist against behaviour which is in fact frequent and not the subject, perhaps, of any deep personal disinclination; this, at the limit, is pure humbug, like the old schoolmaster's attitude to masturbation.

(1) to (3) of course raise some difficulties for a biological approach, particularly with regard to institutions, and an adequate treatment of the representation problem will deal with all these levels. The question of inhibitions and prohibitions arises most clearly at levels (4) and (5). There is, moreover, a specially paradoxical version of it which arises from certain cases in which not only does extra conceptual content have to be introduced to characterize the human prohibition, but also the introduction of that content stands in conflict with the proposed biological explanation of it.

A clear example of this arises with the famous example of the incest taboo. There are of course many incest taboos, that is to say prohibitions on sexual relations between persons of various degrees of familial relation, and some of these are hardly even candidates for biological explanation. Moreover, there may well be some very severe doubts about the application of the biological model even to the favourite cases. The present discussion, is not, however, concerned with the factual merits of these explanations, but only with the shape that they take.

In other species, there are behavioural drives the function of which is to avoid inbreeding. Such a drive, however, has to be operationalized in some other way, since the animals do not have any direct knowledge of the matters relevant to inbreeding: the inhibition against mating has to be triggered by the recognition of or reaction to some property adequately correlated with the kin relationship, such as being an individual with which the animal has been brought up. It is *this* inhibition that is allegedly displayed, in the well-known case, by those brought up together in a kibbutz. But we have not yet reached any incest taboo. There are no sanctions against marrying those that one is brought up with (as such); the sanction is against marriages which would constitute close inbreeding. The conceptual content of the prohibition is thus different from the content that occurs in the description of the inhibition. It indeed relates to the suggested *function* of that inhibition, but that fact will not explain how the prohibition which is explicitly against in-breeding will have arisen. It certainly does not represent a mere 'raising to consciousness' of the inhibition. It can have come about, in fact, only given human knowledge of relevant facts – presumably, of the ill-effects of in-breeding. But once this is an essential step in the explanation, we no longer need the biological element in the explanation (of the prohibition, that is to say, rather than of the inhibition). It turns out that we have to appeal in any case to something like a rational collective agency, directed towards avoiding recognized and agreed evils, and that *already* provides an adequate explanation – a fairly traditional one – of the incest prohibition.

A similar paradox can arise with other norms supposedly based at a biological level, but there are cases that avoid it. Consider for instance the 'double standard' in sexual morality, traced by Symons (*The Evolution of Human Sexuality* (Oxford: Oxford University Press, 1979)) to the disparity between ovum and sperm. This account, though it applies much more widely, is essentially the same as an explanation of these social phenomena that goes back at least to Hume, who accounted for 'the artificial virtues of chastity and modesty in women' by referring to the naturally greater disposition of males to protect children whom they believe to be their own. Here again, there may be serious doubts about relevant anthropological facts, but the present point concerns the principle of the explanation, which involves an important difference from the incest case. Here, it *is* natural to think in terms of the institutionalization of a disposition which could be displayed in a simpler form pre-culturally. The conceptual content required in this case to describe the institution, though it involves a great deal of cultural elaboration, does not display the same kind of break between the pre-cultural and the cultural as is found in the incest case; and the biological pattern of explanation could recognizably run through such ideas as human beings finding certain institutions 'natural', an idea which does not require any appeal to a rational collective agency to understand the basic biological point, as is damagingly the case with the incest example. In fact, an explanation which went back to a biologically grounded disposition could in this case precisely avoid the invocation of rational collective agency, which is rather an intellectualist embarrassment to the story as Hume tells it. None of this implies that even if such biological elements did play some role in explaining these institutions, the institutions would then be necessary or unchangeable. Even if the explanation were true, this could still be a case in which becoming conscious of their rationale was a help in changing them.

In one of the two cases we have considered – incest – the prohibition is paradoxically related to pre-cultural dispositions: it expresses their function, but not their content. In the case just considered, social institutions could in principle be an expression of a pre-cultural disposition. In other cases, again, the existence of norms seems to be a *substitute* for a pre-cultural disposition. This might well be so with the control of aggression and of self-seeking behaviour; I shall make one or two remarks about this question without pursuing it at length.

In the work of Maynard Smith and others (see, for example, Maynard Smith, *Evolution and the Theory of Games* (Cambridge: Cambridge University Press, 1982)) games theory is applied to explaining selection for certain genetically based patterns of behaviour. Games theory can equally be applied to characterizing human norms which are instituted against aggression and other non-co-operative behaviour. (Ullmann-Margalit, in *The Emergence of Norms* (Oxford: Oxford University Press, 1977), gives a recent analysis, though the outlines of the idea that sanctioned norms represent a solution to the Prisoners' Dilemma can be found in Hobbes.) The principles of the two applications of games theory are in many ways the same, but their results point, in a sense, in opposite directions. If sanctioned norms are necessary in the human case, or socialization into rule-observing behaviour, this must be because constraints on human responses in these areas are not, or not significantly, genetically based. Within structures of the Prisoners' Dilemma type, co-operative behaviour can be secured only granted a certain level of assurance, and the need of norms (in particular of sanctioned norms) to produce that assurance shows that the assurance cannot be adequately delivered by genetically based signals. It is very tempting to suppose that the lack of any such reliable signals, and the perilously low level of

107

security often reached in human communities, must be connected with a high level of conceptual and, in particular, predictive thought, and with an associated capacity for deceit. This gives a special force to the Voltairean remark about the function of language being to conceal thought.

The previous remarks have raised some questions about the relations between human norms and possible underlying dispositions determined at a biological level. They represent some aspects of what I have called the representation problem, and it is only through further investigation of that problem, and by becoming clearer about how the various kinds of norm *could* relate to our biological inheritance, that we can come to see much about what biological constraints there might be, beyond the obvious ones, on social and ethical arrangements. I do not believe it to be excluded a priori that there could be some, and I do not believe that much is to be achieved by very general assertions or denials of the possibility. What is needed is more detailed analysis, not only anthropological but philosophical, of the demands that any explanations of this sort would have to meet.

It will be needed, above all, if we are to be able to read the historical record. It is only if we can read that record that we can discover some very important biological characteristics of human beings, since (to repeat an earlier point) it is through convention, convention which has a history, that human nature is expressed. It is not merely that without a hold on the representation problem we cannot discover the relevant content in the historical record; without understanding that problem, we cannot adequately control the idea that there is any relevant content at all. If a biologically grounded disposition showed up simply in the form of what human beings could not or would not do, then there would be no real problem of alternative behaviours. The alternatives will simply be absent from the record, and it is unlikely that anyone, except as the most extreme perversity, would want to undertake them. This, of course, is the area in which the *is/ought* argument scores its clear but uninteresting success. What is much more interesting, I have already suggested, is the idea that there could be patterns of behaviour which human beings are entirely capable of wanting and indeed, on an individual or limited scale, of achieving, but which for biological reasons are bound to be psychologically costly, or confined to a small group of otherwise unusual individuals, or otherwise bound to fail as *general* social institutions. To understand how this could be involves some understanding of the representation problem, and to decide that any given pattern of behaviour has this character of being, as one might put it, 'biologically discouraged' requires one to be able to read the historical record. It hardly needs emphasizing that on any question that is interesting, such as social roles of the sexes, we would have to be able to read the historical record better than we now can in order to arrive at any strong conclusions about what is biologically discouraged.

I come back finally to what I mentioned at the beginning as the area of 'naturalism' more broadly conceived: that is to say, the question of founding human ethics on considerations of human nature, in some way that goes beyond merely respecting the limits, biological or other, on what human beings are able to do. This is the project of thinking out, from what human beings are like, how they might best and most appropriately live.

Such a project continues to attract some philosophers. Its attractions are obvious. It does not, in any obvious way, require any supernatural warrant, while it is less arbitrary or relativistic than other secular ways of looking at the content of morality. It seems to offer some promise of being both well-founded and contentful.

It seems to me that a correct understanding of human evolution is very relevant to projects of this kind, but that the effect of that understanding is largely discouraging to them. This is for two different kinds of reason. The first is a reason at a more particular and factual level and is correspondingly more sensitive than the other to changes in hypotheses about the emergence of human beings. It is simply that the most plausible stories now available about that evolution, including its very recent date and also certain considerations about the physical characteristics of the species, suggests that human beings are to some degree a mess, and that the rapid and immense development of symbolic and cultural capacities has left humans as beings for which no form of life is likely to prove entirely satisfactory, either individually or socially. Many of course have come to that conclusion before, and those who have tried to reach a naturalistic morality which transcends it have had to read the historical record, or read beyond the historical record, in ways that seek to reveal a partly hidden human nature which is waiting to be realized or perfected. The evolutionary story, to the extent that it can now be understood (and to the much more modest extent to which I understand it myself) seems to me to give some support to the view that in this respect the historical story means much what it looks as though it means.

The second and more general reason lies not in the particular ways in which human beings may have evolved, but simply in the fact that they have evolved, and by natural selection. The idea of a naturalistic ethics was born of a deeply teleological outlook, and its best expression, in many ways, is still to be found in Aristotle's philosophy, a philosophy according to which there is inherent in each natural kind of thing an appropriate way for things of that kind to behave. On that view it must be the deepest desire – need? – purpose? – satisfaction? – of human beings to live in the way that is in this objective sense appropriate to them (the fact that modern words break up into these alternatives expresses the modern break-up of Aristotle's view). Other naturalistic views, Marxist and some which indeed call themselves 'evolutionary', have often proclaimed themselves free from any such picture, but it is basically very hard for them to avoid some appeal to an implicit teleology, an order in relation to which there could be an existence which would satisfy all the most basic human needs at once. The first and hardest lesson of Darwinism, that there is no such teleology at all, and that there is no orchestral score provided from anywhere according to which human beings have a special part to play, still has to find its way fully into ethical thought.

Notes

1 For some of these problems, see 'Evolutionary theory and epistemology'.
2 The conception of this 'fallacy' has been significantly extended since G. E. Moore introduced it in *Principia Ethica* (Cambridge: Cambridge University Press, 1903). I discuss this development and its presuppositions in *ELP*, chapter 7.
3 It is taken rather further in 'Making sense of humanity'.
4 See Bateson, 'Rules for changing the rules', in *Evolution from Molecules to Men*, edited by D. S. Bendall (Cambridge: Cambridge University Press, 1983), pp. 499ff.

10

Formal structures and social reality

In the first part of this chapter, I take up some analytical questions about the theory of games and its application to social reality. I emphasize the importance of thinking, not in terms of one-off games or even of repeated trials, but in terms of the general motivations or dispositions that exist in a society. In the second part, I consider some complications in the idea of a 'motivation to co-operate', and the relation of that idea to the idea of trust. In the third part, I offer some very general speculations about the motivations that might be necessary or sufficient to sustain a social framework of co-operation.

I

I start from some points about the classical Prisoners' Dilemma. If x_1 represents the situation in which a player X confesses, and x_0 that in which X does not confess, then the preference schedule of each player, A and B, in the standard game (PD) is as follows:

A: $a_1b_0 > a_0b_0 > a_1b_1 > a_0b_1$

(PD)

B: $a_0b_1 > a_0b_0 > a_1b_1 > a_1b_0$

These preferences, of course, lead to the well-known result: since for each player 1 strictly dominates 0, they both confess and each player gets no better than his third preference.

However, other preference schedules are possible. Consider those that define the *assurance game* (AG):

A: $a_0b_0 > a_1b_0 > a_1b_1 > a_0b_1$

(AG)

B: $a_0b_0 > a_0b_1 > a_1b_1 > a_1b_0$

Sen writes: 'A contract of mutual non-confession does not need any enforcement in the AG, whereas it is the crux of the matter in the PD' ('Choice, orderings and morality', in *Practical Reason*, edited by S. Körner (Oxford: Blackwell, 1974); reprinted in his *Choice, Welfare and Measurement* (Oxford: Blackwell, 1982)). However, this is a little misleading. It is true that in AG the players share a first preference for a_0b_0. But, as indeed Sen says, they do both need assurance, and the prospect of the enforcement of a contract might be how the assurance was secured. This points up an important difference in the possible role of sanctions, a difference relevant to political theory. The addition of sanctions may change the utilities for a basically egoistic agent, or they may provide assurance for an agent who is basically co-operative. The latter, a very important possibility, is connected to a point I shall consider later: that the disposition to co-operation is typically cost-sensitive.

There are other routes to assurance as well. The assurance needed is notoriously complex. Each needs to know that the other has the AG preference schedule. Moreover, each needs to know that the other knows that he (the first) has that preference schedule. If that is not so, each can conduct, and can replicate, reasoning that will lead him to believe that there is a risk that the other will defect, and hence he will defect himself, since each still has the preference

$$\text{self}_1 \text{ other}_1 \; > \; > \; \text{self}_0 \text{ other}_1.$$

Without this knowledge, or something that will stand in for it, the co-operation will unravel. In the standard theory of games, such knowledge is given a priori, since everyone is assumed to have complete relevant information and also the capacity to apply it with complete rationality.

Recent work has been more willing to weaken these assumptions. In real life there are several types of limitation, for instance:

(R1) (a) People are imperfectly informed, both about other people's preferences and about their assessment of probabilities.
    (b) Limitation (a) itself may be imperfectly understood.
    (c) The acquisition of such knowledge may be variously impossible, expensive, and so on. One particular difficulty is that any actual process of inquiry may itself change preferences, destroy information, raise more questions, and generally confuse the issue.
    (d) There is a very significant limit, for social as well as cognitive reasons, on the recursive complexity of possible calculations.

These real-life truths about the cognitive limitations of real agents I have labelled collectively (R1).

An impressive illustration of limitation (d), and of the way in which it can go beyond purely cognitive limitations, is provided by the history of conspiracy in post-war France (Williams, *Wars, Plots and Scandals in Post-war France* (Cambridge: Cambridge University Press, 1970)). The baroque structure of these intrigues, in which an agent might act to create the impression that a second agent was acting so as to create the impression that the first agent was engaged in a conspiracy (for instance, that one), must surely have resulted in a situation in which no one really understood what anyone was doing; and this lack of understanding will also have affected the situation to be understood. Since such a situation is structured by the agents' intentions, and their intentions are conditioned by their increasingly confused grasp of others' intentions, there comes a point at which there is no truth of the matter about what they are doing.

Sen refers to a third preference schedule, which he calls *other-regarding* (OR):

A: $a_0b_0 \ > \ a_0b_1 \ > \ a_1b_0 \ > \ a_1b_1$

$$(OR)$$

B: $a_0b_0 \ > \ a_1b_0 \ > \ a_0b_1 \ > \ a_1b_1$

As Sen remarks, with these preference schedules no player even needs assurance, since a_0 and b_0 are strictly dominant strategies for A and B respectively. But this helps us to see another kind of artificiality in the classical theory: that the structure implies either the one-off expression of a preference, or the repeated expression of one preference unaffected by learning. A second real-life truth is:

(R2) Preferences relevant to co-operation change, in particular under the impact of information about the reliability of different kinds of assurance.

Thus someone might start with the OR preference schedule and, finding that he frequently got his second preference, become discouraged.

When, in the classical theory of non-repeated (or only trivially repeated) games, we see the transactions as expressions of preferences, we are licensed to understand the preferences simply in terms of utilities attached to the outcomes. The outcomes are preferred simply as such, and while the preference schedules that characterize games such as PD, AG, or OR can be described as 'egoistic', 'co-operative', 'altruistic' or whatever, those descriptions merely provide some psychological scenery: the operative element is preference defined over a class of outcomes. In reality, however, preferences are expressions of actual psychological attitudes, notably of dispositions; and a given choice, such as the choice on a given occasion whether to co-operate with another agent, will be a function of several dispositions and attitudes – attitudes to risk, to co-operation, to this kind of enterprise, to this agent, to some group to which this agent belongs, and so on. These assorted facts about agents' dispositions will feature in other agents' beliefs, and affect their own decisions.

In these respects, Axelrod's competition between different strategies over repeated trials, important and interesting though it is, relates only indirectly to the question of human co-operation in society (*The Evolution of Co-operation* (New York: Basic Books, 1984)). All the competitors were playing PD, so they all had the same preference schedule. What differed were the strategies, aimed at maximising their scores as determined by that preference schedule. Moreover, the players were the strategies themselves, and the scores were allocated to those strategies. What the system therefore models is the survival or success of a conditional behaviour pattern, and the most natural interpretation of it is the intended one, in terms of evolutionary theory.[1] In the case of a human agent in social interaction, both his strategies and his preference schedule – the desire he has, for instance, for co-operation as such – may have conditional features, and also be modified by experience.

If an agent co-operates on a given occasion, this is not of course necessarily because he has an altruistic disposition to co-operate; as we have already noticed, and the literature only too often reminds us, a threat of sanctions applied to an egoistic agent can produce the same result. Besides that possibility, however, there are motives to co-operation that are not egoistic, but are more restricted than the kind of thing represented by the simplest psychological generalization of the preference schedule OR. There are general dispositions to co-operate which are conditional, and in particular are sensitive to costs: an agent will co-operate if it does not cost too much, but beyond this threshold he will not. The threshold may itself change over time. Moreover, failing perfect knowledge of the other agents' dispositions, he may take a risk on a co-operative initiative if the cost of being deceived falls below a certain threshold. In these various senses we have a third real-life truth:

(R3) A disposition to co-operate is cost-sensitive.

It is very important that the costs do not have to be egoistic. Indeed, an agent who had had some disappointing experiences might come to reject, for egoistic reasons, the simplest psychological generalization of OR (that is to say, the disposition that consists merely in the fact that he always orders such outcomes in the OR way). But a rejection of it could be expressed in terms of reasons that were not simply egoistic: by appealing to a right of self-defence, for instance (particularly when it is a matter of the kind of costs that are found unacceptable), or in the name of obligations to other groups, of family, friends, or whatever.

II

The previous discussion has referred often to motives (or, again, dispositions) to co-operate. Before moving on to consider, in the third part of this chapter, different sorts of motivations to co-operation, we should examine more closely what co-operation, and motives to co-operate, are. This will bring out some assumptions on which the discussion rests. I shall take it that:

Two agents *co-operate* when they engage in a joint venture for the outcome of which the actions of each are necessary, and where a necessary action by at least one of them is not under the immediate control of the other.

(The description can of course be generalized to cover co-operation by more than two agents; and one agent is said to co-operate, or to engage in co-operation, when there is someone with whom he co-operates.)

Under this definition, a situation in which two agents co-operate necessarily involves at least one of them *depending on* the other, or being, as I shall also put it, a *dependent party*. There are, of course, ventures that would naturally be called 'co-operation' but do not fall under this definition, because everyone in them is under the immediate control of everyone: if a party does not do his bit, this can be immediately detected. These are of no interest to the present discussion, which entirely concerns cases in which one party depends on another. (One important example of this is, of course, that in which one agent makes his essential contribution *before* the other makes his, but this need not be so, as the traditional PD itself illustrates.) They are the cases that lead us – though not quite directly – to the notion of trust.

Co-operation is a symmetrical relation: if X co-operates with Y, Y co-operates with X (if that seems unnatural, read 'co-operates' as 'engages in a co-operative venture with'). *Depends on*, however, is a non-symmetrical relation: if X depends on Y – in the sense that his getting what he wants out of the venture[2] depends on Y doing his part – it may or may not be the case that Y depends on X.

Within these definitions, we can distinguish significantly different kinds of motive that may be called 'motives to co-operate'. The phrase covers, most generally, any motive to enter a joint venture – that is to say, a situation in which one will be co-operating. But not all motives that lead agents to co-operate, on various occasions and in different circumstances, will produce the same results. In particular, some motives permit one to be a dependent party in some situations of co-operation, whereas others – though they are indeed motives to co-operate – will lead the agent to join in only if he is not the dependent party. One source of the Prisoners' Dilemma and similar problems of course lies in the fact that these various motives need not coincide.

The question for social theory is: what motivations do there need to be for there to be co-operation? That is the question to which the remarks in the third section are meant to contribute. One thing is immediately obvious: there will not be any co-operation if the only general motives there are for joining co-operative ventures are such that no one can (knowingly) be the dependent party.

This proposition, which is self-evident and about society, needs to be distinguished from another claim which is about individuals, and is true only under special circumstances. This is the claim that no individual agent can hope to enter co-operative ventures if he will not take a dependent position, or, again, if he usually defects when in a non-dependent position. This is no doubt often true in communities where agents and their dispositions are well known, but it need not be true in others. My question concerns what kinds of structure, in general, might serve to support co-operation. One possible *answer* to the question is that the only way to produce practices of co-operation is by confining them to persons whose dispositions and character are individually known to one another (they rely on what might be called 'thick trust'). This is a discouraging answer for modern life; the present point, however, is merely that it is one answer, among other possible answers, to the question of what motivations need to exist in society if people are to co-operate.

The obvious proposition was that if there are to be continuing practices of co-operation, then people must be motivated, one way or another, to enter into dependent positions. It is natural then to take two further steps. The first is to say that, in general, people will not do this unless they have some assurance that the other, non-dependent, party will not defect. This point, in a very abstract form, is of course central to the game-theoretical structures I have already discussed. This is also the place for the notion of trust. Co-operation requires trust in the sense that dependent parties need some degree of assurance that non-dependent parties will not defect: as I have already said, this need not take the form of 'thick' trust, individually based belief, but it must take some form or other. The next step after this is to claim that, in general, people will not trust others enough to bring about co-operation unless their assurance is to some extent well based: that is to say, unless in fact people are generally motivated, one way or another, not to defect if they are in a non-dependent position.

Both these steps involve empirical claims, and there are surely cases in which one or both of them might turn out false. But in their heavily qualified, 'for the most part', form, it is reasonable to take them as a basis for the discussion of trust and co-operation. I shall take these claims for granted in the way that I shall from now on discuss motivations to co-operate. I shall speak of motivations to co-operate, and their possible sources, sometimes to refer to motivations someone might have to become a dependent party, and sometimes to mean the motivations of non-dependent parties not to defect. They are two different sorts of thing. But once we leave the one-off case, and consider properly the implications of social practices of co-operation, and if we grant the empirical assumptions I have just mentioned, we are entitled to treat these two different things together, because they will, usually and for the most part, exist together – where 'together' means (as we have already seen) 'together in the same society', not necessarily 'together in the same person'.

The variety of dispositions that can lead an agent to co-operate or to withhold co-operation is very important in considering how various kinds of motivation and, correspondingly, various kinds of institution, may be effective or may unravel. In the third section I turn to some speculations on that question. They are extremely schematic, and designed to encourage lines of enquiry rather than to close the question.

III

I start with an axiom, which may be called *Hume's axiom*:

> Only motivations motivate.

This might be thought to be a tautology, and that is, just about, what I take it to be. Its content, relative to the question under discussion, is that if someone acts to further some collectively desirable outcome, then his doing so must be explained by some disposition or desire that he has (for instance, to do just that). His so acting cannot be explained merely by the fact that it furthers that outcome, or merely by his knowing that it does. It follows from this that if one wants people to pursue such outcomes, one will have to see that appropriate motivations do actually exist to produce that result. What kinds of motivation might serve to stabilize the possibility of co-operation?

It will be useful to introduce, first, a distinction between *macro-motivations* and *micro-motivations*. A general account of this distinction would involve a good deal of elaboration and qualification: I hope that what follows will be adequate to the present discussion. Suppose an agent regularly performs acts of co-operation, and that the co-operative

117

aspect of the acts is an intentional feature of them (he has not, for instance, carried out his side of a bargain by accident). We can explain these acts at various levels of generality. With some agents, the pattern of explanation will refer to a general motive to co-operate; the description of the acts as co-operative enters into the characterization of a motivation which he displays on all these occasions. This agent possesses a *macro-motivation* towards co-operation.

A co-operative macro-motivation does not have to be altruistic or ethical. There can be an *egoistic macro-motivation* to co-operation. This is the situation inside a Hobbesian structure. The motivation to co-operation is egoistic, since it lies essentially in the fear of the sanctions of the sovereign. However, the motivation to co-operation is also a macro-motivation, because what the sovereign's sanctions are designed to bring about (among other things) is a motivation, in general, to co-operate. It is not an accident that, from egoistic considerations, the agent on these various occasions co-operated: he knew that what he had egoistic reason to do was, precisely, to co-operate.

A *non-egoistic macro-motivation* will characteristically be found in some moral or ethical disposition, such as the recognition of a general duty of fidelity, or a duty to a state which requires co-operation. It could lie in the agent's relations to religious norms; though some crude religious moralities, couched purely in terms of reward and punishment, would return us to the egoistic option – the Hobbesian system with a divine sovereign.

A *micro-motivation* to co-operation is a motive to co-operate, on a given occasion or occasions, which does not imply any general motive to co-operate as such. A *non-egoistic micro-motivation* might consist in friendly relations towards a given person, the natural expression of which includes a willingness to co-operate with her. I may have, further, a disposition to enter into such friendly relations, and then I shall, in all those cases, be disposed to co-operate; but still I shall not have, in virtue of that, a macro-motivation towards co-operation, as opposed to a disposition to enter relationships in which I am motivated to co-operate.

An *egoistic micro-motivation*, lastly, is fairly self-explanatory: I have such a motivation to co-operate when, in those circumstances, I see it as in my egoistic interest to do so, but this is not because I am generally motivated, as in the Hobbesian system, to co-operate as such. This does not rule out the possibility that I may regularly find myself in such situations, or even that there may be some structure as a result of which I regularly find myself in such situations: to produce such a structure might be a triumph of the Invisible Hand. It will be a mark of this kind of motivation, however, in a pure form, that there will be no motivational momentum from one case of co-operation to the next. I may readily co-operate with X the next time, because I readily believe that it will suit my interest to co-operate with X next time, but there is no general disposition to co-operate, or even to co-operate with X, as such, and if the particular features of a given occasion do not make it in my interest to co-operate, I shall not do so.

If we now ask, in terms of these types of motivations, what a society needs in order to sustain structures of co-operation, a number of speculative conclusions seems to be plausible.

1 No macro-motivation by itself will do

(a) No *egoistic macro-motivation* by itself will do: it will be ineffective, or detestable, or both.

Since under this option the general motivation to co-operate is directly linked to the perception of self-interest, it is extremely sensitive to such things as the expectation of detection, and since this fact is itself common knowledge, there is (as in the classical PD case) a constant temptation to pre-emptive action. For such reasons, the system tends to unravel, and is prone to instability. The religious version might be thought to be more effective (though scarcely less detestable), if people could be brought to believe it, but the observed level of behaviour in societies which allegedly have believed it seems notably not to bear this out. (It may be that the certainty of a 100 per cent detection rate was offset by uncertainties about the practice of the court.)

(b) No *non-egoistic macro-motivation* by itself will do.

The purest form of such a disposition will be what I called earlier the simplest psychological generalization of the OR preference schedule, and this is unstable, particularly because of (R2) and (R3). As I have already remarked, that disposition can be conditionalized and made more complex: someone may think it right to co-operate if certain conditions are fulfilled, and not if not. But the need for these defences implies that the agent has other, in particular egoistic, motivations. Unless co-operation also, to some extent, serves those interests as well, the practices of co-operation will be unstable in the face of those other motivations. Another reason for the conclusion concerns not the potential enemies of co-operation, but the kinds of rewards it offers. Many cases of co-operation are satisfactory to the participants for reasons that imply co-operation but do not focus on it, and unless there are quite a lot of such cases, co-operation will not acquire much general attraction, and is likely to unravel in resentment. This is a particular danger for social arrangements based simply on egoism modified by a few moral principles such as the requirement to keep promises.

119

2 *Egoistic micro-motivation by itself will not do*

Without some general structure, egoistic micro-motivation merely returns us to the Prisoners' Dilemma. So if this kind of motivation is to do all the work, we need an Invisible Hand structure that will bring it about that a tendency to defect is offset by some other egoistic micro-motivation (and will also allow this to be adequately known, etc.) But one needs extraordinarily strong and implausible functionalist assumptions to believe that such structures could be self-regulating and self-preserving, and there is abundant evidence to hand, generated by a body of relentless social experiment, to show that they are not.

Conclusions 1(a) and 2 together imply:

3 *No egoistic motivation by itself will do*

Conclusions 1, 2, and 3 together imply that if anything will do by itself it will have to be non-egoistic micro-motivation. This will presumably have to be something like 'thick trust' – reliance on and between a group of persons in terms of their known dispositions, personal relations, and so on. It is not easy to see how this could be extended beyond a very small society. The only apparent way of taking it beyond this is to identify a particular set of people, a government or elite group, in whom thick trust is invested, and whose activities, example, or regulation serve to sustain co-operative activities throughout the society; but if this is conceivable at all, I find it impossible to see how such a structure could be the basis of our arrangements without an arrant degree of traditionalist or charismatic mystification. In fact, it seems to be obvious that:

4 *Non-egoistic micro-motivation will not do by itself, for us*

'We' are inhabitants of the modern world, involving vastly complex and complexly interrelated societies, which achieve an immense amount through impersonal relations. In particular, we achieve a lot by relying on egoistic micro-motivations, and it is a remarkable achievement of the modern world to have brought this about. Indeed, it is obvious beyond a certain level of social size and complexity that we must rely on such motivations, because of (R1): the kinds of mutual knowledge needed to stabilize egoistic micro-systems is easier to bring about in such circumstances than the kinds of knowledge involved in 'thick trust'. Moreover, this impersonality of modernity brings with it some well-known positive values that depend on mutual personal ignorance: freedom and the benefits of privacy – privacy not merely for the ego but for shared personal life which is genuinely personal.

If all of conclusions 1 to 4 are correct, then none of these kinds of motivation will do by itself. So should we look to some combination of them? Granted what has been said, the most promising combination, and one that has found favour, is one between egoistic micro-motivation and non-egoistic macro-motivations. One version of this, the combination of egoism and a few moral principles, I have already mentioned. The non-egoistic element might take some other, richer, form (this might, very recklessly, be called Durkheim's solution). But there is a notorious problem of how the non-egoistic motivation is to be encouraged and legitimated, when people are constantly and professedly expressing egoistic micro-motivations in much of their life; and there is a tendency for the required ideology to become ineffective humbug.

If that is right – and obviously each of these points needs proper discussion, which I cannot try to give them here – then in these terms there is no solution. But all that means is that there is no solution *at this level of generality*. The problem of co-operation cannot be solved merely at the level of decision theory, social psychology, or the general theory of social institutions. In fact, that there is no one problem of co-operation: the problem is always how a given set of people are to co-operate.

In a modern state, people are motivated by some version or degree of each of the sorts of motivations that have been distinguished, and their actions are often over-determined, quite often by all four. The right question to ask, at this level of generality, is not which of these simple models could be made to do all the work, but rather what combinations of such motivations make sense. How are they disposed to undermine one another? It will be particularly important here to ask what kinds of non-egoistic micro-motivation there are, and which of them might relate coherently (more coherently than national-level thick trust could) to both the egoistic micro-motivations and the large impersonal structures of a modern state. Asking such questions, we may be able to get some general perspective on the problems of co-operation in a given historically shaped society.[3]

Notes

1 See P. Bateson, 'The biological evolution of co-operation and trust', in *Trust*, edited by Diego Gambetta (Oxford: Blackwell, 1988). It has reasonably been found a reassuring feature of Axelrod's results that the successful strategies were all 'nice', in the sense that they never defected first.

2 'Getting what he wants' rather than the standard reference to his 'pay-off', to emphasize that an agent's aims in taking part in a co-operative venture need not be egoistic. An important case is that in which the agent's satisfaction from the venture necessarily implies the success of the venture – for instance, because what he wanted was *the venture to succeed*, not what he could get out of

the situation if it did not succeed. If all the participants want that kind of satisfaction, then indeed they all depend on each other. The existence of a society involves there being many situations of this kind.

3 It may be useful to add a comment on a remarkable misreading of this essay by Annette Baier ('Sustaining Trust', in Baier, *Moral Prejudices* (Cambridge, MA: Harvard University Press, 1994)). Among the claims I make here, according to Baier, are these: we have no good reason to depend on others, or 'at least none we can count on'; 'the would-be trusted will dependably sacrifice the good of the trusters to their own personal good, if it comes to a choice'; 'altruistic' micro-motivation only applies to special people, 'say Nietzsche's sovereign free spirits'; I am looking for a 'moral constraint' as a solution to these problems. I claim none of these things and clearly deny most of them. She also thinks that I need to be told that there is such a thing as thick trust, and that motivations are not divided into the egoistic and the altruistic ('non-egoistic' is in fact my term).

Some further simple, uninteresting, mistakes show that this was anyway not a very intent reading. But it can be so dramatically distorted, I think, only because some large preconceptions are at work. My guess is that they are, first, that anyone who uses a game-theoretical formulation in discussing trust (even in criticism of the standard theory?) must start from the assumptions of micro-economic egoism; and that if one sees problems about trust in a modern society, this must be because one is sceptical about trust as such. Both these assumptions are radically mistaken. I had hoped that the essay might itself help to make this clear.

11

Formal and substantial individualism

I

Most factual questions that I ask are not about me, but about something else that is the subject matter of the question.

> Is Lima the capital of Peru?

asked by me, in no way mentions me. It has reflective first-personal analogues, such as

> I wonder whether Lima is the capital of Peru,

and this stands to that question as the reflective analogue

> I believe that Wagner died in Venice

stands to the assertion of fact

> Wagner died in Venice.

Inasmuch as these first-personal forms are simply analogues of the questions or statements that do not mention me, I can be said to occur in them merely in the role of one who has this thought.

This should not lead us to say that *I* in these first-personal analogues does not mean me, the actual empirical person who, among other things, asks this question or makes this statement. We should not be led off to some other merely thought-having, or again potentially universal, *I*. This comes out clearly from the fact that I, the ordinary I, can occur in these contexts as a locus of evidence, as in

> From the ache in my knees, I expect it is going to rain.

It comes out also from the fact that in bringing my beliefs to mind, I can immediately make the step from a purely cognitive reflection to one that places me socially, as when I say 'I, for one, think ...' Every factual question that is actually asked has a first-personal reflective analogue, and that first-person indeed means the actual person who asks the question, but this does not imply that the question was really about the person.[1]

With practical questions, however, the form 'What should I do?' is primary.[2] The least personal, or most impersonal, form of practical question seems to be 'What is to be done?', but it cannot be seen as primary over 'What should I do?', as 'What is the case?' is primary over 'What should I believe?' First, and in strong contrast to the case of belief, there are many personal deliberative questions and conclusions that do not involve or stem from an impersonal question at all. An impersonal question often comes to be asked later, in order to place a proposed personal course of action in the context of others' projects or demands.

Even where the impersonal question 'What is to be done?' is asked in the first place, it will not have collected a complete answer until the question becomes a practical question for an agent or agents. Unless it does that, the question will not have been answered in terms of what is to be *done*, but, less specifically, in terms of what should come about. Suppose the answer to the question 'What is to be done?' is that A should do X. This still does not make it unambiguously clear that A is the person who, so to speak, puts into practice the conclusion of the original practical question. The answer might merely mean that what should happen is that A do X – for instance, involuntarily. Thus the plotters may answer their question 'What is to be done?' with the determination that a drugged or deluded Jones should shoot the President. But that will be a practical answer to a practical question only if they select someone who will bring *that* about, for instance by drugging or deluding Jones and pointing him in the right direction. Unless they do that, they will have got no further than concluding that it would be a nice idea if Jones, drugged or deluded, shot the President. An impersonal practical question that is genuinely a practical question requires a person or body of persons to be the agent of its answer.

Suppose that A is, now, the end-of-the-line agent of the answer. For him to be that, it has to be the case not merely that other deliberators think that A should do X, but that A thinks that he should do X, so he has to relate the project of doing X to his other reasons for action. Even if we assume that A has an overruling project of abiding by the answers to impersonal practical questions debated by this group of people, he will still have to reach various more specific practical conclusions, to the effect that he should do X now, for instance, rather than later, and such conclusions imply questions of the form 'What should I do?' So even the most impersonal practical questions necessarily issue, at the end of the line, in first-personal questions.

Not all first-personal practical questions are in the first-personal singular. 'What should we do?' is also a practical question. Here it is important that the plurality mentioned in the question can be identified only by reference to an individual, the speaker, and to that speaker's relations to a class of individuals. The ways in which the plural agency that is introduced by the question relates to that class of individuals are various. Thus some one person may eventually act as a representative of this group; or its members may each do X and so collectively do X (leave the room); or they may each do X and collectively do Y (elect the Chairman); or by each doing different things they may collectively do X (build a house): or they may collectively do X by most of them doing nothing at all, and so on. Moreover, the sense of the practical question is not determined on a given occasion by a particular mode of collective action, since 'What should we do?' can invite alternative answers which introduce various of these modes. This is quite an important point, showing that the notion of collective action is in one sense prior to the particular modes in which individual actions can constitute a collective action. But of course it does not show that a collective action could be altogether independent of individual actions.[3]

I take the points that have been made so far to add up to the truth that deliberative or practical questions are radically first-personal, where this means that they are individually first-personal. This is one of two truths that together constitute the position I shall call 'formal individualism'. The other is to the effect that what an individual does is often explained by the individual's deliberation, and, to the extent that his or her action is intentional, it can be explained in terms of a deliberation that the individual could have conducted. It follows from the two claims together that intentional action can always be explained by reference to a consciousness which the agent at least could have had and in many cases did have, and which refers to the agent.

II

Questions about individualism – at least as an issue in the social sciences – have often been understood to be questions about the possibility of reduction, but I take the interesting questions in that dimension to concern explanation rather than reduction.[4] Reduction in any demanding sense is so manifestly impossible that its failure leaves the important issues untouched. To put the point in very crude and extreme terms, it is surely consistent to claim both that references to institutional roles, and hence to institutions, are ineliminable in many cases from the descriptions of individual actions that go to make up social proceedings; and, at the same time, that the agents who fulfil those roles in every case freely and autonomously choose to do so. The second of those claims must surely – in this dimension at least – be enough for individualism, but the first is enough for the failure of reductionism.

While the notion of reducibility should not play any major role in questions of individualism, we cannot, all the same, forget about irreducibility. In emphasizing explanation, we shall be concerned with the extent to which individual actions receive social explanations, explanations in terms of social factors. We have some rough idea of what will count as social factors: matters, presumably, of class, social roles, political power, economic organization, and so forth. But the possible power and scope of explanations in such terms will bear significantly on the issues of individualism only if the social factors they deploy are themselves irreducibly social factors. I have already suggested that to demand this is not to demand much, but it is all the same to demand something.

What I have called 'formal individualism' roughly says that intentional action is individual, and that its explanation involves a consciousness, potential or actual, that refers to the agent. These claims might have been thought too limited to attract the label of any kind of individualism. But some opponents of individualism seem impelled to deny even this much, while on the other side some claims for individualism come to little more than a version of it. I think it is helpful to take this as a purely formal level of individualism, in order to ask how much more has to be asserted if anyone is to reach a substantial individualism in one or more of the several senses that have interested social and political theorists. This is not simply an expository device, to help in disentangling issues that have been confused in debates about individualism. It seems to me also the right place to start if one is to decide how much truth there is in individualism. To the extent, however, that questions about individualism are questions about explanation, they are unlikely to be answered entirely on philosophical grounds: it will be a matter of what social explanations can actually be achieved. I am not concerned here to speculate about this, but rather with questions of what would follow if strong social explanations of individual intentions were available. My concern with those questions, moreover, is not simply with an issue in the philosophy of the social sciences. Beliefs about these matters have characteristically been linked with disputes about individualism in what might be called a broad and ethical sense – a set of ideas, indeed unclear, about individual freedom and the significance of an individual life. I shall not try to define those ideas first and then join them up with the arguments about explanation; rather, in moving on from the questions about explanation, I shall try to give some more definition to those ideas.

According to formal individualism, it is true (indeed, unproblematically true) that intentional actions can be explained by reference to the intentional states of individuals. Substantial individualists and their opponents should be seen as differing on questions of how much that leaves to be said. Anti-individualists should concede formal individualism so far as it goes: their positions are to be put by saying that it goes neither very deep nor very far. On their view, it does not go very deep, because it says nothing about the explanation of those intentional states themselves; and it does not go very far, because it says something only about intentional actions, and nothing about the extent to which significant states of affairs may have nothing or little to do with intentional actions or, at any rate, with the distinctive actions of particular individuals. It is helpful to keep these kinds of issues distinct: I shall label them problems of *depth* and problems of *scope*.

III

The problems of depth are raised by theorists who claim for instance that all or most of the things that people do, or the things they do that are socially significant (whatever quite that may turn out to mean), can be explained by their position in the social structure: at the limit, that individuals act just as *Träger* or bearers of social roles, at (or as) the conjunctions of certain social practices. This I take to be a particularly ambitious form of anti-individualism, and I refer to it for that reason, not because it is the form most likely to be true. The point is that even this type of theory does not deny, or should not try to deny, that these actions can be explained by reference to the intentional states of the agents; what it offers is an account of those intentional states and their content, in terms of social structure.[5]

There are at least two reasons why the theorist should stick to this way of putting things. First, it represents the form that his explanations are going to take. If the social system has produced docile bearers of institutional roles who express those roles in their actions, then it has done it by socializing them appropriately and forming in them the appropriate intentions. It is important that someone whose actions were explained in this way might be entirely identified with his role: his role-governed behaviour might be entirely of a piece with his intentions, and his intentions with his dispositions.

This point leads to the second reason for describing things in this way: it preserves the superficial discriminations that relate to voluntariness. It fits the evident fact that there are relevant differences between ordinary intentional behaviour, somnambulistic or barely conscious behaviour, actions determined by short-term ignorance, actions determined by long-term general incapacities, and so on. We have good reason to preserve discriminations at this level, even though they will turn out not to have the significance that libertarians have hoped to attach to them. Our understanding of what intentional states are, and of how they stand to social and other kinds of explanation, will surely change, but no advance of the sciences is going to show that people do not have intentional states or that there is no difference between the kinds of behaviour that are expressions of their intentional states and those that are not.

The usefulness of the superficial distinctions of course does not end the question. It merely locates the starting point. We may still ask whether agents whose actions satisfy the conventional criteria for being expressions of their intentional states may not, for all that, be unfree or under an illusion. Anti-individualist theories have often suggested that agents are less free than they themselves, or individualists on their behalf, suppose, and those theories do not necessarily depend on neglecting the superficial distinctions. One way of exploring the problems they raise is to ask the following question: granted social explanations of an agent's intentional states, in what ways might we come to see the agent, in the light of those explanations, as deluded about his or her own actions, intentions, or powers?

There have of course been some libertarians who have suggested that if our actions are genuinely free and autonomous, then there can be no such adequate explanation at all. I do not know how far our society believes in this radical autonomy; the present state of belief on these matters is probably so confused that it is impossible to tell. At any rate it is not a sensible belief, and it is not a good place to rest anything we care about, such as (for almost all of us) a resistance to being exploited or manipulated, or (for some of us) a belief in a more substantial kind of individualism.

The important question is not whether an agent's intentional states can be explained, but how well the agent's understanding of them fits the explanation. There are several different ways in which it can fail to do so. It will be helpful to start with the case of neurotic behaviour. Some neurotic behaviour may be compulsive at the manifest level, and no intentional states recoverable by the agent explain it, except superficially ('I am going to wash my hands now'). More typically, however, and more relevantly, the neurotic's actions are explained, up to a point, by intentional states he has and knows he has, but the explanation of those states lies in other states that he cannot recognize. On many psychoanalytical accounts, there will be two different ways in which he cannot recognize them. He cannot, without help, come to recognize what they are, since they are repressed. Moreover, if he does come to know what they are, he cannot accept them into a deliberation – in particular, because they embody infantile wishes which cannot be satisfied in the real world.

For this to be the problem, the relation between the agent's known intentional states and the hidden material has to be specially intimate; the manifest has to be something like a disguised expression of the latent. By contrast with that, a man might be exclusively attracted to women of a certain character or appearance, and that fact might be explained by infantile fantasies or attachments, yet this in itself not present a difficulty. It cannot be a condition on people's affections that they would have had those affections even if they had had no infantile fantasies or attachments. If there is a difficulty in such cases, its source will not lie merely in there being an unconscious explanation of manifest intentionality; it will lie in the ways in which the explanation and the intentionality relate to one another. In particular, there is a problem when the intentionality is only an unsatisfactory symbolic expression of material that could not possibly be the content of manifest deliberation.

In the case of the social explanations that have particularly concerned individualism and its critics, the general point is the same, but it takes a rather different form. Here again, the agent cannot aspire to have only those attitudes he might have had if he had never been socialized at all. The objection, and the relevant kind of delusion, apply not simply to attitudes because they have been socially caused. They apply, rather, to attitudes that the agent could not acknowledge if he knew how they were caused. They arise when the agent – as in the case of neurosis, though for different reasons – cannot accept the attitudes, once they are properly understood, into a manifest deliberation. It is hard to see how this could turn out to be so, unless the attitudes, properly understood, were seen to be contrary to the agent's interests even as those interests are presently understood. The attitudes are legitimated by a myth, for instance, and when it is understood as a myth, the attitudes can be seen to stand in the way of what the agent already reasonably wants. In other cases, the explanations may show that the agent has a distorted picture of his or her interests; this possibility will of course make heavier demands on a theory of real interests.[6]

My aim here is not to pursue the large questions raised by that idea; in fact it does not directly matter to the present argument how far the notion of agents' (real) interests is extended beyond their perceived interests. The point is that the view one takes of the illusions from which agents may suffer in these respects, and one's views of their real interests, go together. If an agent's intentions can be socially explained; if the explanation shows that his intentions are contrary to his real interests; and if his intentions cannot accommodate his understanding those facts (his intentional state is such that he cannot merely recognise coercion or limitation in this respect), he is under a social illusion somewhat analogous to that suffered by the neurotic. Once again, it is the relation between the explanation and the agent's consciousness that matters, and not the mere fact that there is a social explanation of his intentions.

If there are convincing social explanations of people's intentional states, that is already a limitation to substantial individualism at the explanatory level. If, further, the explanations showed that people were under this kind of illusion, then that limitation would certainly have an ethical and political significance. Yet even this would not necessarily discredit all the aims of individualism in what I called the broad and ethical sense. So far as the account has gone up to now, it not only uses the idea of an individual's interests, but also leaves it open that the explanations might, as some radicals have hoped, help to provide means of affirming those individual interests.

Someone who is opposed to individualism in the broad and ethical sense will have to go further than this. He may try to distinguish, for instance, as two different things, the interests of the individual X, and X's interests as an individual, the latter being contrasted with the interests of other individuals. Thus the real interests mentioned in the explanatory framework might be class interests. The anti-individualist will then claim that the agent is under another and yet deeper illusion, to the effect that his interests as an individual are what matter; or that he individually matters; or that his thoughts and intentions and projects are importantly different or distinctive, when a true understanding of their causation will show that this is not so.

Such formulations have a lot to do with individualism in the broad or ethical sense, but it is not easy to see what they mean. A given agent's thoughts and projects certainly are to some extent different from those of other individuals. They may be more so in some cultures than in others – though it is of course a matter of the investigatory interest and its degree of resolution, what will count as different (it is notoriously only to strangers that the locals all look alike). The claim has to be that they are not *importantly* different, or that the differences do not matter. But to whom do they not matter? Even a numerical difference can matter to someone – to a monozygotic twin, for instance, who does not know which of two pills was poisoned, the one he swallowed or the one that was swallowed by his brother. I cannot see how an anti-individualist could show that if it matters to this twin whether he or his brother is subtracted from the world, he must be under a delusion. The anti-individualist must rather be saying that it does not matter much to the world, that individual people do not, as such, make much difference to the world.

On this showing, the central issues about individualism – in a broad sense, and not simply as a question in the theory of explanation – are not so much about the causes of intentional states as about their effects. So far I have been discussing what I called earlier the *depth* of intentional explanations of individual action; whether intentional states that explain action do or do not have social explanations, and, if they do, how that fact will bear on agents' conceptions of their own actions – in particular, whether it will show that agents are deluded about their own actions. The discussion has been admittedly very schematic, but its upshot, I suggest, is that even if individual intentional states turn out to be explained at the social level, and in ways that cannot be accounted for individualistically, this still need not upset the broader concerns of individualism, unless those are misguidedly identified with an extreme libertarianism. Various agents or classes of agents may indeed turn out, in the light of such explanations, to be deluded about their own interests, but there is nothing in the structure of social explanation as such to show that they must always be so. Moreover, the social explanation might help to give them power to improve their position.

IV

It now looks as though the interests of a broader individualism are affected not so much by the depth of intentional explanation as by its scope. What should the anti-individualist say about scope? He should certainly not claim that nothing is ever explained by action. He can, of course, point out that many things that are explained by action, and by the combination of actions, do not express the intentions of any of the agents. The social world is full of unintended consequences, and we may be able to explain how they come about. It is an important point that the explanation in such cases may itself be an individualist one – thus it may be couched entirely in terms of rational preference theory. It may, nevertheless, yield the conclusion that the system has properties that no-one desires; moreover, it may predict, for well-known reasons, that the system cannot be changed simply by appealing to individual agents to act more rationally (granted the system, they may already be acting rationally). These conclusions may stand opposed to some kinds of substantial individualism. But they do not capture a thought that in some sense individuals do not matter. They give us information about causal connections in society, and hence about what we can and cannot hope to do, but that is information which, once again, can coherently be used in the individual interests of individuals.

We get nearer to the anti-individualist thought with the idea that if effects are considered on a large enough scale, individuals do not make a difference. It is not that they do not effect anything, but they do not distinctively effect anything, and if a particular agent had not existed or had not acted in that way, someone else would have done something with similar effects. Individuals, in this perspective, are replaceable.

Someone who sustains this view must be talking about the large scale and the long run. But the large scale and the long run themselves cannot be identified simply by the number of people affected or the temporal and spatial scale over which effects are to be found. No remotely plausible view holds that if the person who wrote Shakespeare's works (say, Shakespeare) had not written them, someone else would have written them or something only trivially different from them; and they have certainly produced and still produce extensive effects involving many people. The claim must be that these are not the kinds of changes that are meant, but rather changes in social factors.

Even if we restrict attention to such factors, it would be a rash anti-individualist who claimed to know that no individual had ever made some large difference in a way that would not have existed if he or she had not existed (of course the changes will not accord very extensively with that person's intentions, but to ask that would be to ask a lot). Suppose there is such a figure, say Constantine or Alexander the Great.[7] The anti-individualist will of course point out a lot of truths about the explanation of this figure's intentional states, and the contribution made by historical circumstances to what happened. But he should not, and really need not, say that this figure cannot possibly have made a big difference, which was also distinctive (unlike the person who makes a big difference by starting an avalanche that would equally have been started by the next passer-by.) What he should say is that the difference is – perhaps in a rather special sense – uninteresting. It tells us nothing important about the ways in which history works.

A realistic anti-individualist, then, will be concerned with intentional action in the ordinary run of social and political events. He is not, once more, denying that at some micro-level it has some effects. He is denying that beyond a certain level of scale it has distinctive effects. Moreover, unlike the sceptical and possibly conservative person who might also say something like this, he bases it not on the view that human affairs are random and inscrutable, but on a theory about social states, that they are explained by other social states. A view of this kind would be opposed to substantial individualism, and not only on questions of explanation: it would extend its opposition recognizably to individualism in the broad or ethical sense. I know of no argument to show that such a view must be wrong, but I shall not try to discuss here what might be said directly for or against it. I shall merely mention, in concluding, a problem that arises about the ways in which we might use such a theory.

What the theory gives, in explaining the limitations on the scope of intentional explanations, is in effect an account of the realm of politics, and attempts at such theories are unsurprisingly taken as contributions to politics. But politics is in part a practical activity, and it is hard to accommodate such theories to that fact. It is hard to see how, if the theory comes to be known, it can fail to increase the efficacy of our interventions, even if it decreases their scope: unless – a further and real possibility – the theory ceases to hold in circumstances in which it is believed to be true and people start acting on it. And it follows merely from formal individualism that if it increases the efficacy of action, it increases the efficacy of individual action.

It is significant that one of the most insistent of such theorists should have called a famous political work 'What Is To Be Done?' On the account I gave at the beginning of this chapter, that question, the least personal of practical questions, issues at the end of the line in 'What should I do?' In this last perspective at least, though not in all the others that I have discussed, formal individualism turns out itself to be fairly substantial.[8]

Notes

1 This is opposed to the position of 'methodological solipsism', advanced by Jonathan Bennett, which holds that the basic intellectual question must be 'What should I think about X?' For criticism, see my *Descartes: the project of pure enquiry* (Harmondsworth: Penguin Books, 1978), p. 69, n. 13.

2 'Should' in this discussion has no special ethical implications. 'What should I do?' simply means 'What have I most reason to do?'

3 It is worth noticing the further point that collective actions, or actions by a non-individual agent, such as a corporation, nation, etc. may involve different modes of individual action even though they are, at the relevant level of description, the same action. Thus it was always an objection to the idea of logically reducing such actions to individual actions that the modes of individual action involved, for instance, in country X's declaring war, depend on the constitution and political arrangements of X at the given time. This is a different consideration from the more far-reaching point that in such a case any given account in terms of individual actions will itself involve references to institutional roles.

4 This point is well made by Susan James, *The Content of Social Explanation* (Cambridge: Cambridge University Press, 1984).

5 James, *The Content of Social Explanation*, is unclear on this point. She writes (p. 70): 'the claim that [actions] are autonomous can be interpreted as a summing up of the individualist view that they must be explained, at least in part, by appealing to the intentional properties of individuals'. This view is surely not adequate to the idea that actions are autonomous: this requires something like a claim that actions are explained by intentional states, and intentional states – unless they are cognitive, or (perhaps) irrational – are explained only by other intentional states. Elsewhere she admits formulations that at least allow for this point, e.g. p. 102: on Althusser's view, '[agents'] intentional properties are to be regarded as consequences rather than causes of social practice'.

6 For some further remarks on real interests and their definition, see *ELP*, pp. 40ff.

7 Though there is no reason to assume that the figure who makes a big difference must be well known or conspicuous.

8 I am indebted to G. A. Cohen for comments on an earlier draft of this chapter.

12

Saint-Just's illusion

In the first book that Marx and Engels wrote together, *The Holy Family*, there is a passage[1] about the Jacobin leader Saint-Just, who was famous not only for his ruthless conduct of the Terror, but for the intensity with which he urged ideals of civic virtue drawn from the ancient world: his demand, as he expressed it, that revolutionary men should be Romans.

'There is something tragic', Marx and Engels wrote

> in Saint-Just's illusion. On the day of his execution he saw hanging in the Hall of the Conciergerie the great tables of the Rights of Man, and with pride and self-esteem declared: 'After all, it was I who did that.' But those tables proclaimed the *rights* of a *man* who could no more be the man of ancient society, than his national–economic and industrial relationships could be those of antiquity.

My aim is to start out from Saint-Just's illusion, and by asking what made it an illusion, raise a question about the interpretation of ethical and political ideas, such as freedom, in different times and circumstances. This will lead us to consider a more extreme situation in which we have to interpret the life of other groups of human beings without sharing a history with them. That will lead us, finally, to some thoughts about moral philosophy and what it can do.

The idea which Marx and Engels put in that way, in terms of Saint-Just's illusion, had been expressed before, most notably by Benjamin Constant in his famous lecture twenty-five years earlier on ancient and modern liberty.[2] Constant had claimed that the ancient conception of liberty revered by the Jacobins, a conception centred on notions of public dedication, had been systematically and catastrophically unsuited to a large modern and commercial society. What Marx and Engels called an 'illusion', Constant called a 'mistake'. It was a mistake, very importantly, in several dimensions at once: in historical interpretation, in politics, and in ethical understanding as well.

First, in historical interpretation. We need not agree with Marx and Engels' specific diagnosis of it to accept, as we surely should, the general idea, common to them and to Constant, that the preconditions of political freedom vary with different social formations. Moreover, the extent to which a specifically *political* freedom can satisfy the need for freedom is itself something that varies with historical conditions. What is necessary for freedom and what is sufficient for it may reasonably and honourably be understood in different terms in different historical circumstances.

It is natural to put the thought like this. But how can we speak in this way of what is necessary or sufficient at different times for this one thing, *freedom*? What is this item that is differently understood at different times? If, as Constant said, the liberty of the ancients and the liberty of the moderns are not the same conception, what is the relation between those conceptions? It is clearly not just a matter of words: the Jacobins and their victims were not trapped by an unfortunate mistranslation from Greek or Latin. Nor is it a change of subject, like that which thirty years ago helped some to believe that if a colonized people became free from the colonizers, that process in itself would make each of its citizens free.

One obvious suggestion is that in order to understand the relations between ancient and modern liberty, we should look to a tradition, an historical narrative, in terms of which the earlier ideal was transmuted into the later. On such an account, it will be this transmutation that Saint-Just overlooked, and indeed he did so, since he overlooked the world that must have contained it: as he amazingly said in his condemnation of Danton, 'the world has been empty since the Romans'.

An historical account is necessary, and in principle it could be enough. Yet it is hard to believe that these conceptions do not have some more intimate connection with each other than is revealed simply by giving an historical derivation. Indeed, how could the supposed revival of the ancient conception have been announced to modern people, above all by Rousseau, with such electrifying effect, if it did not speak to something that in their actual circumstances they wanted under the name of freedom? At the root of both ancient and modern liberty there is one basic or primitive conception of freedom: this is freedom as power, action unimpeded, in particular, by other people. Some thinkers – such as Hobbes, and, some of the time, John Stuart Mill – think that this is *the* conception of freedom, and that it contains all that one knows or needs to know about its value. But this is to identify the seed and the plant, or the rhythm and the dance; it does not get us very far in answering questions such as that raised by Saint-Just's illusion or mistake, about freedom as a political value. As Ronald Dworkin has said, primitive freedom is not in itself a political value at all, perhaps not even a social one. A social value implies a social space in which that value can be intelligibly claimed, and to claim freedom must always involve more than simply claiming power. It is no news to anyone ever that people want the means to do what they want to do. If I make a claim in the name of freedom, then I must do more than say that I want power. I must provide some reason why specifically I should be able to do some certain thing to you, or you should not be able to do some certain thing to me.

The same point may be put in a perhaps less edifying way. There are only two ways of acquiring power, to claim it or to get it by using power you already have. Those two may indeed in many cases come to the same thing; but if they do not come to the same thing, and you need, distinctively, to claim it, then you need something to claim it with other than the power you have, and that must be something that others can understand as an assertion of value or right.

What is true, I believe, is that every conception of freedom as a social or political value is an elaboration in political or social terms of that primitive idea of freedom as power; it involves, for instance, an interpretation at the level of social experience and argument of the frustrations and resentments involved in the obstruction of power. The question of what is involved in what I have too easily called 'an elaboration' is of course enormous, and much philosophical and historical work is concerned with that question: work, for instance, on the varying conceptions of oneself as a public or a private person.

But it is not any further detail about this particular case, freedom, that concerns me here. For the present purpose, I want to retain from it three ideas. A value, in this case freedom, can demand different social and political expressions at different times, and it is not simply a misunderstanding that refers these to the same value. Historical understanding is necessary to see how this can be so, but there is also an underlying primitive idea of which these social expressions are, as I put it, 'elaborations'; though I suggested that, in this case at least, the primitive idea was not itself a social value. Last, we have the point that the social requirements in terms of which an expression is viable in one set of historical conditions may make it a disaster in another: that was the nature of Saint-Just's illusion.

There is at least one other case, justice, in which social values that make a claim on people in different forms at different times can be seen as cultural elaborations of a primitive idea or universal set of conditions: the quarrels, aggressions and demands for settlement of which (we may presume) Heracleitus spoke when he said 'If it were not for these things, they would not have known the name of justice'.[3] In this case, however, unlike the case of freedom, the way in which the basic or primitive situation is specified already introduces something that is nearer to being a social value. The primitive core of the desire for freedom, I suggested, lies in the frustration of our aims by other people; the primitive core of justice lies in such things as a loss that demands recompense, or a good that needs to be shared, and these ideas already introduce the schema of a social value. At this level, it is as yet a highly indeterminate value, and it has of course received a vast range of cultural elaborations. Some of the elaborations have been connected with one another by historical traditions, as in the case of freedom, but it is also true that every society – however exotic it may be from our point of view, and unconnected until modern times with Western history – displays some elaboration of justice, some social structures that must be understood in terms of those primitive demands.

When Constant said that Saint-Just made a mistake, he meant, as I mentioned earlier, not merely an historical but a political mistake; and Constant's description of the mistake itself offered a political and an ethical argument. The argument is clear enough: the Jacobin policies aimed to make French society into something that no modern society could be, and so they inevitably led to human disaster. There is certainly no conflict between the historical diagnosis, on the one hand, and the political argument, on the other; indeed the argument gets its materials from the historical interpretation. However, the fact that this is so does mean that the political argument is of a rather special kind. The way in which it is special is well brought out by Marx and Engels in their suggestion that Saint-Just's mistake was not merely a mistake, but an illusion.

In much of our everyday political discourse we argue *with* other conceptions of liberty, justice, equality, or whatever the value may be. When different political movements argue for programmes that variously claim the justice of letting the rich keep their gains or the justice of redistributing those gains to the poor, their arguments can get some grip because each starts from some conception of justice that we can culturally recognize, and they try to relate to those conceptions of justice policies that they claim to be viable for our world. The various conceptions of justice and of other values on which such arguments draw are the materials of politics and also, less institutionally or formally, of people's ideas of what their life ethically means. But Saint-Just's conception of freedom did not fit into such a pattern, and that is just the point of the historical diagnosis: the antique conception of freedom was in a sense alien, and belonged to a different world. When Constant and the others dismiss Saint-Just's conception and condemn him for trying to apply it to the modern world, they are of course engaged, as I have said, in a political argument against that conception; but there is an important difference in this from the more usual case in which we argue against a conception which does belong to the modern world and which proposes a way of governing our affairs in it.

Of course someone may want in some radical and indeterminate way to change the modern world – to change it back, for instance, so as to make it more receptive to an historically alien conception. That is the aspiration of Utopianism, a familiar enough strain in European politics. As a self-consciously revolutionary leader, Saint-Just had a vision which might be called Utopian, and to that extent he did not even want to engage with the political conceptions of the modern world as he found them. Unlike most Utopians, however, he was, for a while, among those in charge, and just in virtue of that he had to engage with a world that was obstinately there. To have a hope or a vision, even an illusory one, is not necessarily to suffer from an illusion; that begins when you cannot tell the difference between the vision and the world around you.

Saint-Just's illusion marks the meeting place of two spaces that we naturally treat differently. One is the space of our actual social and political life, within which we encounter various political and ethical demands and ideals, argue with them, adapt ourselves to them, try to form a conception of an acceptable life within them. The other space, of which we may be conscious only in a very shadowy way, is of other conceptions and ideals and world pictures that human beings have had, and may perhaps still have elsewhere, which are not part of our social and political space, are not even starters for a life we might now lead, and are – strictly in that sense – alien to us. I emphasize as strongly as I can that it is only in that sense that they are alien. They are not, for instance, the conceptions of aliens: they are human conceptions, ideas held by other human beings.

Nothing that is within our social space, and is something that we must actually address, is in this sense alien. Here it is extremely important that a claim to the effect that a particular conception lies within our actual social space is basically a social claim, not a conceptual one. What I mean by this is that there is no necessary expectation that the world of ideas and practices in which we find ourselves should conceptually hang together, or form one homogeneous ethical whole. Neo-Hegelian and other nostalgic writers typically exaggerate the extent to which any society has ever had a homogeneous outlook, and one may perhaps doubt whether contemporary societies are really more pluralistic in their composition than many societies of the past. But they are certainly more pluralistic in their outlook, and consciously accept that attitudes which are substantively different from one another in spirit and in history actually coexist. People realise, too, that this fact itself makes demands on ethical and political understanding and invention. Meeting those demands provides one dimension of ethical thought that is now particularly important.

Saint-Just's conception was alien to late eighteenth-century French society, just because it was drawn from a world in which the social structures, economic forms, and people's needs were very different. Yet although it was alien to that society, it was connected to it by an historical story. People had a picture of a past from which it was drawn – an idealised picture, for sure, but of a past that could be represented as modern Europe's own past.

A set of values might be more alien than this. It has been a concern of philosophy to ask how alien they might be and yet still be recognizably human values. Consider a society that, at least when we encounter it, has no relation to our history: an isolated, small, traditional society on the other side of the world. The people of this society seem to have beliefs, practices and values very different from ours, which are certainly in no way candidates for adoption in the world we live in. The ideas and values of such a society may seem to be alien in some more radical sense than anything we have yet considered. But how radical can that sense be?

It is a familiar idea that we are not merely *given* the beliefs, values and so forth of such a society: faced with their activities and utterances, enjoying (or otherwise) their company, we have to interpret these things. We are also familiar with the idea, developed powerfully in philosophy by Donald Davidson, that we could not come to understand these people without building into our interpretation at a structural level some assumptions about the ways in which the experience and thoughts of these people resemble ours. If we are to interpret what they are up to, we must rationalise it in terms that make sense of it to us.

What does this process involve if we are to make sense of these people's values: by which I mean primarily, what they think important, laudable, hateful, to be condemned or despised, and so forth, in the actions and reactions of human beings? We should not necessarily expect it to come out simply as a serial process in which we first ascribe to them simpler attitudes and then get on to understanding their values. Certainly we must understand some at least of their beliefs and desires in order to interpret their values, but it can be argued – as it has been by Susan Hurley[4] – that we must, equally, ascribe some values to them even in the course of crediting them with desires or preferences, because it is only by reference to some sense of their values, of what they think

140

worthwhile, that we can ascribe to them a rational structure of preferences. By the same token, those values must make sense to us as values
that human beings might have: and to *some* degree, at least, that must
mean values that we share. In the case of beliefs, we cannot rationalize
these people's activities and their sayings without ascribing to them a
substantial range of beliefs that we ourselves take to be correct. Similarly,
there has to be a bridgehead of shared human concerns, the argument
goes, for us to be able to recognise anything these people hold as values,
even as alien values.

Some philosophers[5] want to take the argument a step further, and
suggest that while the values of an exotic society may perhaps be alien in
the sense that I have introduced – in the sense, namely, that those values
and those people's way of life are not candidates for our serious consideration in our historical circumstances – yet at a deeper level, there are no
really alien values. On this account, we bring to that other society, as
interpreters, a structure of basic values such as a conception of what
human qualities are valuable and admirable, and we find in the others'
life and experience, as we come to understand it, a similar structure. The
others will doubtless not place the emphasis as we do; they will esteem
some qualities more than we do and esteem others less; their distinctions
between virtues and vices, good and bad kinds of actions, may not divide
up the field in quite the same way that ours do. But – the argument goes
on – these variations can be explained rationally in terms of their and our
different circumstances. We should not be surprised, for instance, if
special emphasis is put on certain kinds of courage and certain kinds of
solidarity where people have to hunt their food. This is not relativism but
quite the reverse: it is the appropriate adaptation to circumstance of
shared ethical concerns. Under the local variations, the argument goes,
there is a common human ethical sensibility of a fairly structured kind.
Moreover – and this follows from its being an argument from interpretation – this *must* be so, because it represents a condition of understanding
these people's life as a human life at all.

I am sure that in interpreting other people we have to take it that they
and we have a good deal in common; it may well be, further, that some of
what they and we have in common must be, if in a schematic form, some
values. But we cannot be compelled to think, it seems to me, that the
requirements extend as far as this argument claims, or that all human
beings must share, in some more or less determinate form, the same
materials of an ethical life. It is not so much that I do not believe it to be
true. It is rather that I cannot believe that it *has* to be true, that reflection
on the demands of interpretation should be able to lead us to so substantive a conclusion. If it could, then philosophy would now have succeeded

in doing what social anthropology and its intellectual ancestors over several centuries have failed to do.

European thought has passed this way before, more than once. In earlier centuries, for instance in the time of what were called, from the European perspective, the voyages of discovery, and again when Europeans encountered peoples of the South Pacific, there was intense speculation and discussion on the subject of a common human nature, and on questions of how the diversity of practices and ways of life that had come to light was to be read. Some of this discussion had, needless to say, powerful ideological motives, and was interwoven with such questions as the possibility of salvation for these creatures, and the legitimacy of enslaving them.[6] But once it was given that these were indisputably people, other human beings, and that they therefore had a good deal in common with the Europeans, the issues became central, of how determinate the basic similarities were, and at what level they were to be found: as needs, or values, or a shared moral reason, or – as it came to be put in a more recent time when anthropology had gained an identity – a capacity to live within symbolic systems.

Many of those earlier formulations have of course gone, and with them (at least in their more shameless forms) the ideological fantasies that sometimes went with them, of ignorant or noble savages. But the fact that those elements have departed, and that we are anxious to relegate them to the history of colonialism and slavery, may conceal the fact that the central questions – the questions, as we may summarily put it, of a common human nature – remain unanswered, and continue to recur in different forms, in such fields as cultural anthropology, cognitive psychology, and comparative linguistics. For the purpose of ethical understanding, we should distinguish two levels of question about a common human nature. One is the general level, at which we ask what are the basic psychological and social concepts that are needed to interpret both our own and other human activities. A second and more specific question, the question raised by the argument I am considering, is to what extent those concepts are both specific and ethical: how far, for instance, it is true that we shall be able to understand another culture's ethical practices only if we interpret them in terms of a range of virtues and vices that are familiar to us.

We need to assume a certain amount in common between us and the others; and we are trying to understand what might, very broadly indeed, be called their ethical life. But it does not follow from those two truths that what we must assume as in common with them is an ethical life, or to any determinate level, the materials of it. It may be, as I have said, that there are some, perhaps very schematic, values that we must see ourselves as sharing with them. I mentioned earlier in the case of justice, the primitive core, as I put it, that underlies the elaborations of this value that we might expect to find in any society. That core was to be found, I suggested, in certain situations of conflict and certain needs for settlement. That is, of course, so vague as barely to be a suggestion, let alone an interesting one. It may be that if we examined more interesting and more specific suggestions, and reached a better understanding of the basic forms of the need for justice, we shall come to see that we do need to ascribe to human beings in every society[7] a particular sentiment or disposition, something like a sense of fairness. Perhaps. But that questions, and many others of the same kind, are precisely the questions that have descended into the various social sciences, as well as into philosophy, from the old speculations about a common human nature, in particular a common ethical nature. The fact that these questions remain, and in such recalcitrant and dispersed forms, should discourage us, as it seems to me, from thinking that they are suddenly going to be answered by unaided philosophy.

The idea that they might be answered by philosophy, and in a way favouring very strong assumptions about the underlying similarities, has perhaps been encouraged by an idea that is implicit in some theories of language, particularly of a Wittgensteinian kind, to the effect that understanding someone else's language, and hence their form of life, essentially involves *identifying* with them. On this account, the essence of understanding someone else's concepts is to put yourself in the way of using them. But if you can do this, for instance with ethical concepts, then those concepts must in some sense respond to something that is already yours. (Indeed, the very phrase 'form of life' has helped to encourage the conclusion: it suggests at once an anthropological category and the limits of intelligibility, and so manages to imply that if we can understand others at all, then they cannot be culturally so distant from us.) But anthropologists, who actually have to do it, know that this image of interpretation through identification is inadequate. As Clifford Geertz has put it,[8] 'to see others as sharing a nature with ourselves is the merest decency', but it does not constitute a method. The whole problem is to deploy our concepts, some of which are nearer to theirs and some further away, 'so as to produce an interpretation of the way a people lives which is neither imprisoned within their mental horizons, an ethnography of witchcraft as written by a witch, nor systematically deaf to the distinctive tonalities of their existence, an ethnography of witchcraft as written by a geometer'. One must bring with one beliefs, models, patterns of explanation: it is they that will determine, in the end, how much identity there will turn out to be, and at what levels.

The fact that the questions about a common human ethical nature have not been solved may encourage a more radical thought: that, at the ethical level at least, these questions are based on a misunderstanding, and are never going to be solved by anything. It may be that in some form this suspicion may be correct, but it is not at all easy to express it coherently. To say, for instance, as is said quite often, that there is no such thing as human nature and that everything is interpretation, merely rides over the present question, of what it is we have to take for granted if we are to give any interpretations. To reject such formulations is so easy, in fact, that we may stop asking whether there might not be something in them after all. Perhaps it is not only our interpretation of ethical situations that inescapably involves elements local to our perspective, but our interpretation of other people's interpretations of ethical situations.

Even leaving aside more radical doubts about the question, it is clear at any rate that we do not have an answer to it. When we ask what underlies the variety of human ethical practice, the truth is that we do not know and have no very clear idea of what an answer would look like. We do know one thing, or at least have very good reason to believe it: that if there is anything that could be an answer, it will come from actual interpretations of actual people, and will involve the kinds of psychological and social study that I mentioned earlier. It could not emerge simply from a priori reflections on the requirements of interpretation. There is a very short argument, surely, to show that it could not. If it were true that to understand other people's ethical life we had to interpret them in a way that led us to recognize a high and determinate level of ethical resemblance between them and ourselves, then it would already have been recognized: it would have shone forth from all those devoted attempts to interpret. But it has not, which is why we are all still having this discussion. In this respect, the situation is exactly the same as with the age-old attempts to overcome moral disagreement by discovering a universal morality on the basis of nature. Nature seems, unhelpfully, to underdetermine human morality to just the extent that leaves open all the disagreements that the morality of nature was supposed to resolve.

What does it mean for moral philosophy that, as I have argued, no a priori considerations will answer the question about a shared ethical nature? At first glance, it looks like the sort of conclusion that philosophy has learned to live with over many centuries, that something it thought to be entirely its business turns out to be other people's business as well. Except for its perpetually discouraging implication that there are many things one needs to know if one is going to make any sense of the world, this conclusion need not in itself be too upsetting.

However, I think that the present conclusion reaches rather further than this way of putting it would suggest. There are some questions that philosophy is disposed to think are, if anything is, its own business. In moral philosophy, such a question is usually taken to be the objectivity or otherwise of ethics. But the questions we reached in talking about interpretation and the extent to which it assumes or reveals a determinate degree of ethical resemblance between human beings – those same questions about which I have just claimed that if they are answerable at all they must be answered with other help – these seem to be all that is now left to this issue that has often been supposed to be central to moral philosophy and special to it, the issue of the objectivity of moral judgement. Or rather: they are all that is to left to that issue if it is understood as a *theoretical* issue. (I shall come back shortly to what I mean by that qualification.)

Many different things have been discussed as the question of objectivity, but they all tend either to come to nothing, or to come back to one issue: the proper understanding of ethical disagreement. Some philosophers have been very exercised, for instance, with the question whether moral judgements can be true or false. But work has to be done to find what, and how much, that question means. Indisputably, remarks about the morally good and bad, right and wrong, are called 'true' or 'false': the question is how much follows on that use.[9] The concepts of truth and falsehood carry with them the ambitions of aiming at the truth and avoiding, so far as we can, error; the question must be, how those ambitions could be carried out with regard to ethical thought. I see no way of pursuing that question, which does not lead back to questions such as these: if an ethical disagreement arises, must one party think the other in error? What is the content of that thought? What sorts of discussions or explorations might, given the particular subject matter, lead one or both of them out of error? It is only in the context of such questions, as it seems to me, that issues of objectivity in ethics acquire any content and escape from the primitively reductivist charge that 'objective', 'true', 'really wrong', and so forth are merely devices we use to keep up our confidence. But those questions, in turn, can only lead us back to this one: how do we picture the underlying ethical material in other people and in ourselves? It is only in the light of our best understanding of this that we could understand how far disagreement might intelligibly reach, and how, at the limit, it might be intelligibly resolved. And that question is of course the one that we have already identified, the question about a common ethical nature: the question that philosophy by itself cannot answer.

The question was: how, *at the limit*, disagreement might be resolved. The philosophical question about objectivity is an extreme or limiting question, and it is because of this that it coincides with a question about the limits of interpretation. It is just the extremity of the question, of course, that might make us say that it was a typically philosophical question. It is just the same feature of it that, under the only line of enquiry that could make sense of it, reveals it as having no answer that philosophy by itself is going to discover.

Of course, most disharmonies between ethical outlooks are not as extreme as this. They are more like what we normally call disagreements: conflicts of outlook in some social space that the parties, to some degree at least, actually share, as opposed to the singular situation of the anthropological investigator, 'set down', in Malinowski's phrase,[10] among a strange people. In these more familiar cases we need not go to the limits of human similarity and dissimilarity: we will have, typically, more shared cultural materials to work with, more ways, at least if we are lucky, of resolving or accommodating our differences. Here we come back to the division in the road that was marked by the ambivalent case of Saint-Just's illusion. These are the cases in which we may see the alternative conception of an ethical life as a real possibility for us and for our world: it is now something to be argued with, not only something to be understood.

Moral philosophers, unlike in this respect political philosophers, have typically found these more realistic cases less interesting. Partly, this is just their professional interest in the extreme and limiting case, the interest that is often called (in a question-begging phrase) the interest in principle. However, there might be an argument to suggest that the problems of the extreme case were inescapable. It could be argued that if the more realistic cases were of any interest at all from the ethical point of view – if they did not turn, for instance, on some unproblematical disagreement of fact – then they must after all involve the issues that are up for interpretation in the extreme and limiting cases. One cannot understand one's disagreement with someone unless one understands how exactly his outlook contrasts with one's own, and this, it may be said, involves knowing just the relations between the structure of his moral consciousness and one's own that were at issue in the extreme and limiting case. How can I know where we differ, unless I know how to fit our difference into the common structure of human ethical perception, whatever that may turn out to be?

Of course I have to understand the person with whom, in limited and local terms, I am disagreeing, and this requires interpretation. But it is wrong to think that in order to interpret one another in these less extreme situations we must reach the ultimate basis of ethical understanding, if indeed there could be such a thing. We do not have to explore the outside limits of the possibilities for agreement and disagreement. To think that we do is to accept uncritically a kind of foundationalism. Part of what we are given, in being given to some degree a shared social space, is some shared understanding of the psychological bases of moral agreement and disagreement themselves: a sense of the virtues, perhaps, or of expected conduct, or of public principle, and with these we work, in seeking to articulate and perhaps resolve disagreements.

In a very self-conscious culture formed by an elaborate history, such as our own, there are exceptional opportunities for varying, re-emphasizing and recalling these materials. At the present time, for instance, some philosophers call for a revival of the ethics of the virtues, as contrasted with those familiar materials of modernity, principle and utility. It is reasonable for them to call on these ideas, which are to be found in our cultural reserves, but they err if they think that such concepts are the universal and ultimate basis of all ethical experience, and they err still more – err in the same way as Saint-Just – if they think that the virtues as described by Aristotle or St Thomas are the necessary and sufficient materials of ethical self-understanding at the end of the twentieth century.

There is another way in which the demands of ethical disagreement as we more ordinarily meet it may seem to call on the theory of the ultimate case. Can we possibly conduct any ethical argument in good faith or with conviction, it may be asked, unless we believe that some answer will be objectively correct? If not, then we implicitly deploy the idea of objectivity, and all its ultimate problems, as soon as we take an ethical disagreement seriously. The answer to this point, however, is basically the same as to the last. We do not need the idea of an ultimately objective answer – the answer, for instance, that would imply, if it were expanded enough, an account in terms of a universal moral psychology of where exactly at least one of the disputants had been in error. We need only something more restricted, the idea of the acceptable answer to this disagreement, an answer that might be reached in actual historical circumstances: an answer, or the refusal of an answer, to which the parties could honourably agree. Of course, any such agreement could be criticized from outside the disputants' perspective; this raises no new problem, and simply introduces the shared materials, whatever they might turn out to be, of another disagreement. What is indeed a problem, and needs much to be said about it, is the question of what might be counted as an honourable agreement. That question belongs to what might be called a theory of persuasion, and the essential point about it is that it would be itself an ethical discussion: a discussion of the proper role of rhetoric, and loyalty, and disinterestedness, and the value of truth – plain truth, the truth of historical and social truthfulness, rather than the phantasm of ultimate ethical truth.

To see things in this way represents a reversal of a familiar Platonic structure. For the Platonic spirit (Plato himself, needless to say, had more complex views) the aim is ultimate truth or rationality, and the powers that could lead us to it merely need to be protected from interference by persuasion. The present picture is rather of a world in which everything is, if you like, persuasion, and the aim is to encourage some forms of it rather than others. This is not a technical task, like clearing a radio channel of static. It is a practical and ethical task, like deciding who can speak, how and when. It is also not, as is often suggested by those of a Platonic disposition, a picture that is a product of despair, a mere second-best for a world in which the criteria of true objectivity and ethical truth-seeking have proved hard to find. To recognise how we are placed in this respect is, if anything, an affirmation of strength. To suppose that the values of truthfulness, reasonableness, and other such things that we prize or suppose ourselves to prize, are simply revealed to us or given to us by our nature, is not only a philosophical superstition, but a kind of weakness. If that is the best we can say for them, we probably do not deserve them anyway.

I said earlier that philosophy might find itself without the exclusive possession of the topic of ethical objectivity, so far as that was a theoretical issue. The contrast I had in mind there was the dimension we have now touched on, of the theory of persuasion, the ethical question of how in dealing with ethical disagreement we should best conduct ourselves. There is no reason to say that this is not a philosophical subject; the reason someone might have for saying so would probably be the false view that philosophy was cut off from substantive ethical issues. But it should remind us of how deeply impure philosophy is. The fate, as I have described it, of the theoretical issue of objectivity reminds us in one way of the impurity of philosophy; if it is to have anything to say about that question, it will have to address a lot more than philosophy. The ethical issues of objectivity, the questions of what truthfulness and an appropriate impartiality mean to us in our circumstances, remind us of that impurity in another way: to think about those questions is also to think about a lot more than philosophy. It is to try to think seriously about a decent life in the modern world, and it is a platitude to say that it needs more than philosophy to do that.

It is equally a platitude to say that philosophy should at any rate help one to do that. Moreover, it is true. But then, with professional ease and some self-congratulation, philosophers may draw from this another conclusion, that teaching philosophy to people must also help them to do that. Perhaps that is true, too. But before we take comfort from it, we should get clear that a good deal of what is called teaching philosophy is nothing of the sort. The word 'philosophy' occurs in the title of the activity only, so to speak, adverbially; what is being taught are the capacities to analyse issues, sort out one's terms, write clearly, and expound efficiently in a short time something one does not understand very well. Philosophy is a suitable vehicle through which to teach these useful skills, since it is intellectually complex, encourages analytical talent, and when suitably presented is not very threatening. I am not of a Wittgensteinian temper to find these activities an affront to philosophy. Moreover, it may be that acquiring these skills itself helps one to think about what is a decent life in the modern world. But it is not in the least obvious that acquiring these skills, and the exercises that impart them, help people to think about that question in the ways that philosophy, properly and impurely practised, would encourage people to think about it. Not for the first time in its history, the best hopes for philosophy, and what goes on in the name of teaching it, are in some conflict with one another.

Notes

1 Karl Marx and Friedrich Engels, *Die Heilige Familie* (1845), in *Die Heilige Familie und andere philosophische frühschriften* (Berlin, 1953).

2 Benjamin Constant, 'De la liberté des anciens comparée à celle des modernes', lecture given at the Athenée Royale, 1819; translated in *Constant: political writings*, edited by Biancamaria Fontana (Cambridge: Cambridge University Press, 1988). The observation that the 'illusion' referred to by Marx and Engels was a 'mistake' for Constant, I owe to François Hartog. The contrast was abolished, from a point of view opposite to Saint-Just's, by Fustel de Coulanges in *La cité antique* (1864): in the words of Albert O. Hirschman (*The Rhetoric of Reaction: perversity, futility, jeopardy* (Cambridge, MA: Harvard University Press, 1991), p. 104), 'Unlike Benjamin Constant, Fustel no longer allows that the Ancients had evolved and practised any important variety of liberty whatsoever.'

3 Heracleitus, fragment 23; Charles H. Kahn (ed.), *The Art and Thought of Heracleitus* (Cambridge: Cambridge University Press, 1981), LXIX. The fragment is cited in a similar connection by Martha Nussbaum, 'Non-relative virtues', *Midwest Studies in Philosophy* 13 (1988).

4 Susan Hurley, *Natural Reasons: personality and polity* (Oxford: Oxford University Press, 1989), chapter 6.

5 Hurley, *Natural Reasons*, does not explicitly claim this position, so far as I can see, but what she says does strongly suggest that she holds it. Variations between the practical judgements arrived at by different human groups are regularly ascribed to different weightings given to the same kinds of consider-

ation. She does allow for (p. 236) 'exotic conceptually possible counterevalua-
tive worlds', but 'our' 'familiar' values seem to be equated (p. 275) with 'sane
human values' and contrasted only with 'mad human values, Martian values,
Alpha Centaurian values, and so forth'. Barry Stroud argues to the conclusion
that we could not ascribe values to others without holding some ourselves
('The study of human nature' in *Tanner Lectures on Human Values* 10 (Salt Lake
City, 1988)), but rejects the stronger thesis (pp. 253–4). Nussbaum, 'Non-
relative virtues', argues towards a similar position, though not from a distinctively interpretational standpoint; but, admitting various sensible qualifications, perhaps stops short of it. Donald Davidson has written ('Expressing
evaluations', The Lindley Lecture, University of Kansas, 1982, p. 19): 'Just as in
coming to the best understanding I can of your beliefs, I must find you
coherent and correct, so I must also match up your values with mine; not of
course, in all matters, but in enough to give point to our differences.' I do not
disagree with this, but I go on to argue, in effect, that what is meant by 'giving
point to our differences' is significantly affected by the question whether those
differences lie within one social space or not.

6 On this topic, see in particular Anthony Pagden, *The Fall of Natural Man*
(Cambridge: Cambridge University Press, 1986.)
7 Not to every human being. The point is a cultural one about societies; it of
course has psychological implications, but it does not apply directly to each
person's psychology.
8 Clifford Geertz, *Local Knowledge: further essays in interpretive anthropology* (New
York: Basic Books, 1985), pp. 16, 57.
9 A related line of thought is developed by David Wiggins, 'Truth as predicated
of moral judgements', in his *Needs, Values and Truth*. See now Crispin Wright,
Truth and Objectivity (Cambridge, MA: Harvard University Press, 1992).
10 B. Malinowski, *Argonauts of the Western Pacific* (1922) (New York, Routledge
and Kegan Paul, 1961), p. 4.

III

Ethics

13

The point of view of the universe:
Sidgwick and the ambitions of ethics

Sidgwick's book *The Methods of Ethics* was first published in 1874, and he took it, with substantial alterations, through five editions, and partly through a sixth. It has been recently described as 'a systematic treatise on moral philosophy, examining in detail a far wider range of topics than any previous book on the subject, and setting new standards of precision in wording, clarity in exposition, and care in argument'.[1] It is not merely an historical monument. After a period of fairly resolute neglect, it is now beginning once again to be admired and, it may even be, to some extent read. It bears a very real intellectual relation to modern Utilitarianism and to certain of its problems. There are difficulties not only about Utilitarianism, but about the very project of a systematic ethical theory, which emerge with special clarity from the pages of Sidgwick's book, particularly because Sidgwick was in various ways both more and less conscious of them than modern writers have been. It is the relevance of Sidgwick's book to a large and still very pressing question, the possibility of ethical theory, that I shall discuss.

Of course Sidgwick was not only famous for this book, or for his other work in philosophy. Born in 1838, he had an interest from his undergraduate days in enquiries into supernatural phenomena, and he played an important part in the early history of the Society for Psychical Research, founded to pursue on a supposedly scientific basis what Sidgwick sometimes called his 'ghostological' interests. He felt in a way that was perhaps peculiar to his time, and indeed rather specially peculiar to Cambridge, that séances in darkened and stuffy sitting-rooms, with heavily unconscious ladies who might be hoped at least to hear voices from the departed and, with exceptional good luck, to extrude some ectoplasmic embodiment of them – that these undertakings could have some relevance to the truth of the Gospels (cf. Schneewind, p. 31). This might seem to many people now an error of judgement, as indeed it seemed at the time to Christians of other persuasions, but certainly Sidgwick's part in the revealing history of that strange subject was substantial.

Another substantial and certainly more beneficent claim to fame was the very large part that he played in the foundation of Newnham College. In addition to his own large expenditure of effort, time, and money on this project, his wife, Eleanor Mildred Balfour, the sister of the Prime Minister, was the College's second Principal. In his ethical theory, as we shall see, there is a rather notable tension between, on the one hand, Utilitarian principles that could lead to radical change, and, on the other hand, an application of those principles serving in good part to justify the status quo. That tension emerges particularly in passages of considerable unease about sex and the character and motives of women in contrast to men. It is notable, too, that in *The Methods of Ethics* the issue of women's rights gets no mention at all, though it was of course a salient feature of the political and social thought of his Utilitarian forebear, John Stuart Mill. But in practice Sidgwick was energetic to admirable ends in this respect. We must be grateful that he had no disposition to share, nor even to regard as utilitarianly valuable, a kind of conventional outlook which was expressed – I am afraid one has to admit, rather splendidly expressed – in a letter from W. B. Yeats to Katherine Tynan in 1889:

> [If women go through] 'the great mill called examinations', they come out with no repose, no peacefulness, their minds no longer full of secluded paths and umbrage-circled nooks, but loud as chaffering market places. Mrs Todhunter is a great trouble mostly. She has been through the mill and has got the noisiest mind I know. She is always denying something.[2]

There was quite a strong tendency, at least in liberal circles, to regard Sidgwick as rather saintly. This was a response in particular to his intellectual honesty, to be found both in the marked scrupulousness of the argument of *The Methods of Ethics*, and also in his resignation of his Fellowship because he could not subscribe sincerely to the Thirty-Nine Articles. That impression of saintliness, however, had about it an unremovable Victorian quality, which laid it open to question by those of the next generation. Maynard Keynes wrote to his friend Swithinbank about Sidgwick's Memoir in 1906, six years after Sidgwick's death:

> Have you read Sidgwick's Life? It seems to be the subject of conversation now. Very interesting and depressing and, the first part particularly, very important as an historical document dealing with the mind of the period. Really – but you must read it yourself. He never did anything but wonder whether Christianity was true and prove that it wasn't and hope that it was.

He even learnt Arabic in order to read Genesis in the original, not trusting the authorised translators, which does seem a little sceptical. And he went to Germany to see what Ewald had to say and fell in love with a professor's daughter, and wrote to his dearest friends about the American Civil War.

I wonder what he would have thought of us; and I wonder what we think of him. And then his conscience – incredible. There is no doubt about his moral goodness. And yet it is all so dreadfully depressing – no intimacy, no clear-cut crisp boldness. Oh, I suppose he was intimate but he didn't seem to have anything to be intimate about except his religious doubts. And he really ought to have got over that a little sooner; because he knew that the thing wasn't true perfectly well from the beginning. The last part is all about ghosts and Mr Balfour. I have never found so dull a book so absorbing.[3]

Yet Keynes and his friends, of course, had another saint of their own, and one equally involved in moral philosophy. Keynes had written to Lytton Strachey just a month before:

I am studying Ethics for my Civil Service.

It is *impossible* to exaggerate the wonder and *originality* of Moore; people are already beginning to talk as if he were only a kind of logic-chopping eclectic. Oh why can't they see!

How amazing to think that we and only we know the rudiments of a true theory of ethic; for nothing can be more certain than that the broad outline is true. What is the world doing? It does damned well bring it home to read books written before P. E. I even begin to agree with Moore about Sidgwick – that he was a wicked edifactious person.[4]

Insofar as this is not just about Moore's personality, it is about 'P. E.', the famous book that he had produced in 1903, *Principia Ethica*, a book still a great deal more read than *The Methods of Ethics* – or at least parts of it are, the wrong parts in fact. There are some merits, certainly, that it has of a kind inconceivable in Sidgwick's work, and which chiefly compelled Keynes's admiration: an intense conversational tone, at certain points, an immediate persuasive presence. Sidgwick never sounds like that.

But in other respects, especially in argument, *Principia Ethica* is not as admirable a book as *The Methods of Ethics*. In fact, despite some fundamental differences in their conclusions, a good deal of it actually comes from Sidgwick, with Moore simply ignoring a number of difficulties which Sidgwick, usually rightly, thought that he had identified. Certainly it was not any theoretical merit of *Principia Ethica* in comparison to *The Methods of Ethics* that should have persuaded Keynes that it was the more valuable work. Nor, really, should it have been that Moore's work was the more spiritually radical. It certainly seemed so: both in the values that it espoused, and in the way it went on about them, it was a good deal less dauntingly earnest than Sidgwick – but that was due in good part to a change in time and temper. As Keynes's remarks themselves show, there was no more *doubt* in the world of *Principia Ethica* than in that of *The Methods of Ethics* – and perhaps in certain ways less doubt – about the solid foundations of the whole enterprise.

It is a standard criticism of *The Methods of Ethics* that it is extremely boring. Roy Harrod wrote (p. 76): 'I remember Alfred Whitehead telling me that he had read *The Methods of Ethics* as a young man and found it so stodgy that he had been deterred from ever reading any books on ethics since.' Defenders of Sidgwick these days have a tendency to reply to this charge in the general style of the libel lawyer, to the effect that first, it isn't true, and second, if it is true it is justified by his unflashy concern to get things right in detail. The truth is, first, that a lot of it is boring; second, not all of it is. There are distinct moments of tension which grow out of passages of that very boredom. One might say indeed that the over-whelming Englishness of this book extends even to a similarity to a cricket match, which has the very sophisticated feature that one can appreciate the significant detail of the monotony that lies before one at a given time only because one understands remote and hypothetical moments of excitement that might grow from it. Third, the fact that a lot of *The Methods of Ethics* is boring is not the most important fact about it. It is not even the most important negative fact about it, because what is most deeply wrong with it emerges in the most interesting bits. Yet, nevertheless, it is still true that there is something revealing about the boringness, and that it has a certain quality which constitutes a quiet sustained comment on what is wrong with the work.

Here we have to recall one or two points about how the book is shaped. The 'methods of ethics' to which the title refers are egoism, intuitionism and utilitarianism. As Sidgwick admits, to call egoism a method of *ethics* at all may seem rather misleading, since pure egoism is easily contrasted with the very idea of an ethical outlook. But Sidgwick makes it entirely clear what he is talking about, and it is in fact one of the best features of his undertaking. Like Plato and Aristotle, of whom he said that 'through a large part of the present work' their influence had been 'greater than that of any modern writer',[5] he regarded the fundamental question of ethics as 'in what way is it reasonable or rational to live?' – a question to which egoism might conceivably turn out to provide the answer. If some moral or distinctively ethical (in the narrower sense) answer to that question is to be adopted, then it has to work its passage against egoism as much as against alternative answers of the moral, non-egoistic, sort.

The task of adjudicating by reason alone between the claims of egoism and those of morality was one which Sidgwick was not to claim that he had achieved.[6] He was left with the suspicion that it could be achieved only by appealing to religious principles, and those were principles which he neither thought it appropriate to introduce into a science of ethics – which he conceived, distinctively and rather originally, in a secular light – nor was himself prepared to put sufficient faith in.

What he did feel had been achieved by *The Methods of Ethics* was a demonstration that at any rate the moral option should take the form of the Utilitarian theory. In arriving at this conclusion he engaged in an extensive survey of commonsense morality, in which he set out a good deal of everyday moral thought, or at any rate those conclusions and arguments that might find favour with what he variously calls educated, cultivated, intelligent or morally sensitive persons. The main emphasis of this is to point out the doubtfulness, unclarity, and uncertainty of much of this thought, and the difficulty of deriving its conclusions from any clear and limited set of principles.

It is the aim of deriving these conclusions from such principles that gives the point to the label that Sidgwick attaches to the section of the book in which he surveys commonsense morality. It is the section that is supposed to display the method of 'intuitionistic ethics'. It is important in trying to follow Sidgwick's thought to see what this label does and does not imply. Some writers on ethics, including some later than Sidgwick and indeed Moore himself, made rather a lot of the notion of intuition, as being a particular kind of mental capacity for discerning fundamental ethical truths; and arguments about the existence or possibility of a power of that kind have taken up quite a lot of room in the literature of moral philosophy. They have been concerned with the theory of moral knowledge. However, Sidgwick is actually not very interested in this aspect of the question, which he regards as part of the 'psychology' of ethics – and in not being very interested in it he is importantly followed by some contemporary writers such as, notably, Rawls.

In talking about 'intuitionism' Sidgwick is concerned chiefly with a method – the method, roughly, that takes the reflective or even the relatively unreflective convictions of everyday moral thought and uses them to arrive at basic and supposedly certain moral truths or, again, to reach conclusions about unfamiliar cases. However, there are some important ambiguities in how ambitiously such a method is to be taken. At its least ambitious, it looks much like going on as people generally go on – using some cases to think about others, and not being immensely surprised if, as Aristotle always held and the results of Sidgwick's reflections illustrate, there are no very definite, clear and exceptionless moral principles to be found in everyday thought.

Sidgwick, however, finds this a reproach to commonsense morality;

157

though, as we shall see later, it may be that he finds it a reproach to that morality only if commonsense morality is seen in a certain light, as self-sufficient. He quite certainly finds it a reproach to any *theory* which tries to derive from that morality a set of clear, definite and certain moral principles which will be specific enough to decide uncertain cases. The outlook that claims to do this he calls *dogmatic intuitionism.*[7] He is less clear than he might be about what its success would consist in, but he is clear that it fails.

However, there is another, higher, level of intuitionism of which Sidgwick takes a different view. This, he says, 'springs from the demand to find some deeper explanation of why conduct commonly judged to be right is so: while accepting the morality of common sense as in the main sound, it still attempts to find for it a philosophical basis which it does not itself offer'. He equates with this the aim of getting one or more principles 'more absolutely and undeniably true and evident, from which the current rules might be deduced, either just as they are commonly received or with slight modifications and rectifications' (p. 102).

The conclusion that Sidgwick eventually arrives at is that this task can in fact be carried out – the task, that is to say, of starting from received moral opinion, justifying and explaining a good deal of it in terms of some more general principles, and applying those same general principles as a way of criticizing some other parts of received opinion which do not coherently hang together with the rest. This he thinks can be done, but he thinks it can be done only through the principles of Utilitarianism. Indeed, in the end he thinks that the contrast between intuitionism and Utilitarianism is wrongly drawn, since the only way of correctly carrying out the intuitionist objective is by reference to Utilitarianism, and the only justification of Utilitarianism itself is, as we shall see, dependent upon certain general principles which are intuitive. One difficulty of the book is that it is formed by a distinction between the intuitionistic method and the Utilitarian method, which at an ultimate level Sidgwick eventually rejects.

I think that it is this structural feature of the book, the fact that its design is not actually very well adjusted to its conclusions, that helps to make some of it so boring, in particular this survey of commonsense opinion. There are other reasons as well. It is a general feature of the book that the account of commonsense morality is very linear, lacking any sense of the possibility of alternative moral traditions or the idea that certain moral outlooks of cultivated contemporary opinion might represent interests less broad than those of society or mankind as a whole. His discussion, for instance, of the ethics of making a financial profit out of persons who are in a disadvantaged situation is one example where the notion of *common sense* itself demands to be examined in ways in which Sidgwick never examines it. The discussions of sexual morality, again, though they do get mildly more adventurous as we move from intuitionism to Utilitarianism, continue to make fairly uncritical use of a notion of purity which is no doubt part of what Bloomsbury found oppressive and stuffy.

The lack of any non-moral perspective on the morality of his time is a feature of the work in general. The structural failing that I mentioned before comes out rather in this, that the only example of a theoretical structuring of everyday morality that we are in the end given in the book is the Utilitarian example itself. When Sidgwick is discussing, in the intuitionist section of the book, an intuitionist method which is, at that point, supposedly *distinct* from Utilitarianism, there is no fixed set of expectations against which commonsense opinions are being tested for coherence, definiteness and completeness. We are constantly reminded that there are various kinds of cases to which common sense seems not to provide an absolutely clear and unambiguous answer. But we need some account of what kind of intuitionist theory is, as an ideal, in question; and in the absence of that we have no guiding sense of how far we should be disappointed by the absence of these clear and unambiguous answers. Without the guiding notion – and also without, as I have said, any sense of the possibility that social or economic causes might have played some part in all this – the trail of inconclusive commonsense considerations and unresolved commonsense questions is bound to leave a dispiriting impression.

While Sidgwick criticized those who wanted to draw up a rational morality distinct from Utilitarianism, it is very important that he nevertheless shared their aspiration to a rational morality. The aim of throwing 'the morality of common sense into a scientific form' (p. 338) was his aim too, and he shared with those intuitionists the desire to be able to answer moral questions of judgement with a 'clear and accepted principle' (pp. 249ff.) It is very revealing of his own outlook that he asks, just before starting on his treatment of Utilitarianism (p. 406), 'If we are not to systematize human activities by taking universal happiness as their common end, on what other principles are we to systematize them?'

In 1864, ten years before the publication of *The Methods of Ethics*, he had written (Schneewind, p. 44): 'I will hope for any amount of religious and moral development, but I will not stir a finger to compress the world into a system, and it does not at present seem as if it was going to harmonise itself without compression'. Yet in *The Methods of Ethics*, he certainly came to think that a system was needed that would ideally possess properties of clarity, reflectiveness and consistency, and would be such as to command the general agreement of unprejudiced people. The notion that this is what moral philosophy should produce, and that this is what gives it power to combat the irrational, the merely personal and the merely habitual, is one that is still very influentially with us.

No such system can be derived, Sidgwick concludes, by the intuitionistic method, so long as that method is regarded as operating at a fairly low level of generality, merely considering everyday principles of action or everyday models of virtuous conduct. The consequences of that, we have been shown by the long survey of commonsense opinion, are too often conflicting, unclear and inconclusive. However, if we move to a higher level of generality, there are some principles which when he reflects on them Sidgwick finds to possess geometrical certainty, and which he believes can command universal assent. This is the level of 'philosophical intuitionism', where intuition is required to deliver to us only propositions of a very abstract and general kind, which will need interpretation in order to give us definite resolutions of our moral difficulties. He offers us three such fundamental principles. They appear in fact in a variety of formulations, and a great deal of effort could be spent on discussing how those various formulations relate to one another. That, however, does not matter for our present purpose.

The first principle is closely related to that familiar item, the Golden Rule 'Do to others as you would have them do to you': one of Sidgwick's formulations is 'If a kind of conduct that is right (or wrong) for me is not right (or wrong) for someone else, it must be on the ground of some difference between the two cases, other than the facts that I and he are different persons'.

The second of Sidgwick's basic principles is a substantive principle of prudence: what it says is that it is rational to pursue 'one's good on the whole' where 'on the whole' implies that we should have an 'impartial concern for all parts of our conscious life', and 'Hereafter *as such* is to be regarded neither less nor more than Now'. Sidgwick explains (p. 381):

> It is not of course meant that the good of the present may not reasonably be preferred to that of the future on account of its greater certainty: or again, that a week ten years hence may not be more important to us than a week now through an increase in our means or capacities of happiness. All that the principle affirms is that the mere difference of priority and posteriority in time is not a reasonable ground for having more regard for the consciousness of one moment than for that of another.

One consequence of this principle is that 'a smaller present good is not to be preferred to a greater future good (allowing for difference of certainty)'.

This principle of impartiality over all the times of one's life is an interesting example of what Sidgwick wants from an intuitive principle, since it is certainly not tautological, but many people find it completely self-evident. Indeed, it is fair to say that almost everybody who agrees with it finds it completely self-evident. However, the trouble is that the world also contains a group of people, distinguished perhaps from the first on grounds of temperament, who find it to an equal degree self-evidently false. I personally am convinced that whatever merits such a principle of impartial prudence may have, it is certainly not a mere derivation from the notion of practical rationality, and does require the introduction of a special attitude towards one's own life and one's own future. Whether this is so, is a large and interesting question, which I cannot take any further here. The one remark I would make about it is that Sidgwick's own discussion of it, and indeed almost all the extensive discussions of it in the recent literature, have taken for granted a large falsehood, namely that the length of time over which this prudence is to be exercised – the extent of one's conscious life – is something that is given independently of one's own prudential or other practical reasoning: it is not a matter for one's own control. This is consistent for Sidgwick, who, at least in *The Methods of Ethics*, unquestionably accepts, without any comment at all, a prohibition on suicide. Others who do not subscribe to that restriction should for this reason, as well as for a number of others, take another look at that assumption.

The third of Sidgwick's basic principles that supposedly attract assent from all reflective persons lands us unambiguously in the territory of morality. He writes (p. 382):

> So far we have only been considering the 'Good on the Whole' of a single individual, but just as this notion is constructed by comparison and integration of the different 'goods' that succeed one another in the series of our conscious states, so we have formed the notion of Universal Good by comparison and integration of the goods of all individual human – or sentient – existences. And here again, just as in the former case, by considering the relation of the integrant parts to the whole and to each other, I obtain the self-evident principle that the good of any one individual is of no more importance, from the point of view (if I may say so) of the Universe,[8] than the good of any other ... and it is evident to me that as a rational being I am bound to aim at good generally – so far as it is attainable by my efforts – not merely at a particular part of it.

This, then, yields a principle of universal benevolence that 'each one is morally bound to regard the good of any other individual as much as his own, except in so far as he judges it to be less when impartially viewed, or less certainly knowable or attainable by him'.

'Accordingly', Sidgwick writes, 'I find that I arrive, in my search for

161

really clear and certainly ethical intuitions, at the fundamental principle of Utilitarianism' (p. 387). Sidgwick does in fact think that there remains one further task to be performed, in order to demonstrate that this set of principles uniquely determines Utilitarianism as the ethical theory capable of systematizing our moral intuitions – this is the identification of Universal Good with universal happiness. This is, for a rather technical reason, more of a problem for Sidgwick than it is for a modern theorist at a comparable point in the argument. Though Sidgwick's views on the subject of happiness are quite complex, he fundamentally believes, in the tradition of Bentham and Mill, that happiness is to be interpreted in terms of pleasure – and pleasure is a subject on which he has some complex views. A modern Utilitarian is more likely to interpret the ultimate end to which the tradition gives the name 'happiness' in terms of satisfaction of desires or some such notion as rational preference. When it is seen in these terms, Sidgwick's three premises do seem to deliver Utilitarianism virtually immediately. When, motivated by universal benevolence, we are concerned with the good of each person, we are required to be concerned with the very same thing that each of those persons has to be concerned with prudentially in his own case, so it will precisely be something like each person's objectives or rationally organized set of preferences that will become the raw material of the additive sum of universal good. Indeed, the fact that what we are concerned with is already assumed to be an additive sum, and that universal good is understood already as something that can be globally assessed in some such way, shows how far Sidgwick's three axioms already determine that the system that is going to satisfy these conditions will be a kind of Utilitarianism. It should also make us wonder once more how far the axioms do have to be accepted as rationally inescapable.

I shall come back to saying something about the merit of the axioms – in particular the last one, which is the one that both distinctively delivers morality, and also delivers this distinctive morality. However, there is one more thing to be said first about the way in which Sidgwick proceeds to apply the Utilitarian system at which he has now arrived. It is extremely distinctive of his system; it is what enables him, more than anything else, to reconcile his system with large areas of commonsense morality; and it is what very particularly brings out, in my view, a basic fault not only in his results but also in his approach. This is Sidgwick's insistence, perfectly correct in itself, that a moral system should not imply that actions must always be taken as the result of conscious rational calculation, whether it be of prudence or of universal good. It had been an old objection to Utilitarianism that it could lead to a denial of all natural affections and the stifling of impulse and spontaneity in the interests of a calculative spirit directed to universal good. As Scheewind has shown, this objection was in fact aroused much more by Godwin than it was by Bentham; Godwin's ferociously rational determination to respect almost any consideration other than those that an ordinary human being would find compelling did considerable damage to the image of Utilitarianism, as well as being something that Godwin, even when he adopted more moderate views in his later years, could never live down. This problem Sidgwick both saw and took resolute steps to avoid. He saw that from the point of view of Utilitarianism it must simply be an empirical question what motivations actually lead to the greatest good; and, in particular, whether the motivation of thinking about the greatest good is likely to lead to the greatest good. The Utilitarian consciousness, then, is itself made a problematical item about which it is necessary to think, and it is at least perfectly possible – and Sidgwick clearly regards it as true – that the Utilitarian consciousness should not, at least in many departments of life, be over-encouraged. Indeed, this is not just a point about the Utilitarian consciousness, although it very strongly applies to that: it is a point about the rationality of deliberation altogether. As Sidgwick puts it (p. 345) the dictates of reason ought always to be obeyed, but it does not follow that the dictation of reason is always a good.

From these considerations Sidgwick can offer a Utilitarian account of various things, particularly of certain dispositions of character which are often thought of as having an intrinsic or non-Utilitarian value. They include such things as the disposition to tell the truth, to be loyal to one's friends and to feel a particular affection and concern for one's own children. Such an account plays quite a large role in carrying out the task that Sidgwick assigns to Utilitarian theory, of explaining and also in some sense justifying various parts of commonsense morality which might at first glance not seem to be of Utilitarian inspiration, and which indeed had not seemed to the intuitionists to be of that inspiration, since they constantly cited them as counter-examples to the Utilitarian outlook. The values of justice, of truth-telling, of spontaneous affection, and so forth, were all items which it seemed the thoroughgoing Utilitarian would not endorse. But if it is not only permissible but indeed (according to Sidgwick) very important to consider the Utilitarian value of a state of affairs in which people have those dispositions, then the Utilitarian justification could extend much further than had at first been thought.

The business of giving these explanations or justifications is conducted by Sidgwick in a slightly desultory way and, in a manner which is shared by large numbers of later Utilitarian writers, he makes pretty cavalier use of what are supposed to be evident matters of fact, which in some cases may invite much the same doubt as the dispositions or rules that they are being invoked to justify. His account of the double standard in sexual morality, for example, not surprisingly makes use of some fairly ideological material about the differences between the sexes, as well as appealing to such notions as 'the contagion of unchastity' (p. 452). In pursuing his project of uncovering what he calls the 'unconscious Utilitarianism' (p. 454) of commonsense morality – a phrase that itself raises some extremely pressing issues in the philosophy of social explanation – he is also sometimes guilty of a mistake that, again, turns up in later writers; this is to infer that, because considerations of utility or the greater happiness are quite often used in order to resolve a conflict between two other values, it then follows that those values must all the time be directly or indirectly expressions of the end of utility or the greatest happiness. This simply does not follow.

But the most interesting problems that arise from Sidgwick's treatment lie not so much in these standard features of the Utilitarian enterprise, but rather in the view which his theory requires us to take of these various dispositions themselves. Unsurprisingly, Sidgwick has to treat these dispositions, when he is talking about them theoretically, in a very instrumental way, and the arguments that he produces about them are very linear. The dispositions are regarded just as devices for generating certain actions, and those actions, in the end, as the means by which practical reason produces certain states of affairs, those that minister most to universal good. That is what those dispositions look like when seen from the outside, from the point of view of the teleological Utilitarian consciousness. But it is not what they necessarily or usually seem like from the inside; and indeed what the Utilitarian argument may very well yield is the conclusion that they should *not* seem like that from the inside. Certainly it is empirically possible, and on the lines of Sidgwick's argument it must be true, that the dispositions will do the job which the Utilitarian theory has assigned to them only if the agents who possess those dispositions do not see their own character purely instrumentally, but rather see the world from the point of view of that character. Moreover, those dispositions require them to see other things in a non-instrumental light. Though Utilitarianism usually neglects the fact, they are dispositions not simply of action, but of belief and judgement; and they are expressed precisely in ascribing intrinsic and not instrumental value to various activities and relations such as truth-telling, loyalty and so on. Indeed, if Sidgwick is right in saying that the Utilitarian theory explains and justifies larger areas of everyday morality than had been supposed by the intuitionists, and that he has succeeded in his project of reconciling Utilitarianism and intuitionism by explaining in Utilitarian terms some of the phenomena on which the intuitionists were most insistent – if that is so, then is *must* be that in the actual world the dispositions do present themselves to their possessors, and also present other features of the world, in this non-instrumental light. It was these possessors who, just because they had these dispositions, were so strongly disposed to reject Utilitarianism and insist on the intrinsic value of these actions and of ends other than universal good.

It follows that there is a deeply uneasy gap or dislocation in this type of theory between the spirit that is supposedly justified and the spirit of the theory that supposedly justifies it. The gap is not very clearly perceived, if at all, by Sidgwick, nor, in my view, is its significance fully or at all adequately understood by later theorists who have adopted very much Sidgwick's position. In both Sidgwick's case and theirs, there is a distinction which has the effect of disguising from them this very deep area of difficulty: a distinction between theory and practice. That distinction, though regularly used, remains remarkably unexamined in this tradition of philosophy; and in fact I believe that if it is examined, it will be found to have, in these connections, virtually no saving power at all.

There is, first, the question of the practice of the theorist himself. The theorist may be presumed – at least as a first presumption – to possess the dispositions of which at a theoretical level he also possesses the Utilitarian justification. So in his mind at least the consciousness that goes with these dispositions, that they are directed to objects of intrinsic value, has to coexist with the consciousness of their justification, that both they and the objects to which they are directed have no intrinsic but only instrumental value. The conditions of this supposed coexistence are by no means easy, and they are hardly ever in Utilitarian writers made clear.

Sidgwick's failure to confront them is illustrated by the rather famous passage in which he discusses something that from a Utilitarian point of view he is certainly right to discuss, namely whether the Utilitarian theory is itself something that should be made known. He has been discussing exceptions to the general rules:

> the Utilitarian may have no doubt that in a community consisting generally of enlightened Utilitarians, these grounds for exceptional ethical treatment would be regarded as valid; still he may, as I have said, doubt whether the more refined and complicated rule which recognises such exceptions is adapted for the community in which he is actually living; and whether the attempt to introduce it is not likely to do more harm by weakening current morality than good by improving its quality. Supposing such a doubt to arise, ... it becomes necessary that the Utilitarian should consider carefully the extent to which his advice or example are likely to influence persons to whom they would be dangerous: and it is evident that the result of this consideration may depend largely on the degree of publicity which he

165

gives to either advice or example. Thus, on Utilitarian principles, it may be right to do and privately recommend, under certain circumstances, what it would not be right to advocate openly; it may be right to teach openly to one set of persons what it would be wrong to teach to others; it may be conceivably right to do, if it can be done with comparative secrecy, what it would be wrong to do in the face of the world; ... These conclusions are all of a paradoxical character: there is no doubt that the moral consciousness of a plain man broadly repudiates the general notion of an esoteric morality, differing from that popularly taught; and it would be commonly agreed that an action which would be bad if done openly is not rendered good by secrecy. We may observe, however, that there are strong utilitarian reasons for maintaining generally this latter common opinion; ... Thus the Utilitarian conclusion, carefully stated, would seem to be this; that the opinion that secrecy may render an action right which would not otherwise be so should itself be kept comparatively secret; and similarly it seems expedient that the doctrine that esoteric morality is expedient should itself be kept esoteric. Or if this concealment be difficult to maintain, it may be desirable that Common Sense should repudiate the doctrines which it is expedient to confine to an enlightened few. And thus a Utilitarian may reasonably desire, on Utilitarian principles, that some of his conclusions should be rejected by mankind generally; or even that the vulgar should keep aloof from his system as a whole, in so far as the inevitable indefiniteness and complexity of its calculations render it likely to lead to bad results in their hands. (pp. 489–90)

On this kind of account, Utilitarianism emerges as the morality of an elite, and the distinction between theory and practice determines a class of theorists distinct from other persons, theorists in whose hands the truth of the Utilitarian justification of non-Utilitarian dispositions will be responsibly deployed. This outlook accords well enough with the important colonial origins of Utilitarianism. This version may be called 'Government House Utilitarianism'. It only partly deals with the problem, since it is not generally true, and it was not indeed true of Sidgwick, that Utilitarians of this type, even though they are theorists, are prepared themselves to do without the useful dispositions altogether. So they still have some problem of reconciling the two consciousnesses in their own persons – even though the vulgar are relieved of that problem, since they are not burdened with the full consciousness of the Utilitarian justification.

Government House Utilitarianism is unlikely, at least in any very overt form, to commend itself today. A version more popular now is to identify the required distinction between theory and practice as a distinction between the *time* of theorizing and the *time* of practice, and to use the notion, deployed in moral philosophy by Butler, of the 'cool hour' in which the philosophically disposed moralist reflects on his own principles and practice. There are problems, no less severe, with that model – problems which in fact become deeper and deeper the more that, in some appropriate cool hour, one thinks about them. There is the relatively straightforward artificiality of supposing that the thorough commitment that is required to the values of friendship, truth or whatever it may be, can merely alternate, on a timetable prescribed by calm or activity, with an alien set of reflections. At a rather more interesting level, the model implies an extremely naive conception of what is going on in the cool hour itself. It is assumed that it is the cool activity of theorizing that will display to oneself the true value of one's own dispositions and reactions, where I mean by their 'true' value, the value that they really have for one. Should that be different from the value that one really believes that they have, when one is not reflecting on the value that one believes they have? The idea that cool and articulated reflection must be authoritatively revealing about one's structure of values is not itself a very sophisticated belief. Moreover, it can be seen as performing a function.

Utilitarians standardly present everyday, unschooled, moral reactions as at least presenting a problem of justification, and as running a serious risk of turning out, when unmasked, to be mere prejudices which should be dismissed in the light of Utilitarian reason. But it is at least as plausible, and the history of the subject very strongly suggests that it is true, that the theoretical reasonings of the cool hour are themselves only sustained and directed by some sense of the moral shape of the world as provided by the everyday dispositions. The belief that one can look at all one's dispositions from the outside, from the point of view of the universe, and that so doing is embodied in a cool hour of personal reflection, is a misrepresentation of that cool hour. What that hour does for one may be not to allow one to assume the point of view of the universe, but rather to disguise the fact that the affections and perceptions that mean most to one may well be not only contingent but also essentially incapable of being made totally transparent to oneself.

A suspicion related to that emerges, too, if one turns away now from the state of consciousness of the Sidgwickian theorist, to the result of his theorizing. Here we must remember what the objections to unreconstructed intuitionism were, and how it was to be a demand on ethical theory that conflicts, inconsistencies and unclarities in everyday thought should be resolved and some clear principle provided for answering these questions. We left aside at that point the question of why these intellectual improvements were required. The question might indeed scarcely seem worth asking: its answer would generally be supposed to lie, at least to an important extent, in the improvement of practice. If our practice can be related to a more complete and coherent ethical theory, then the questions which in practice (or at very least in the more reflective parts of practice) demand and do not receive an answer – how, for instance, to extend some recognized principle to a new kind of case – can receive some rational resolution. Yet on Sidgwick's account of the matter it is just very unclear, at the end of the enterprise, how far we have actually advanced towards these objectives.

There is more than one reason for this. First of all, our general unclarities and conflicts and our sense of divergent claims are quite certainly related to the dispositions of action and judgement that we actually possess. Indeed, in his treatment of dogmatic intuitionism, Sidgwick makes it repeatedly clear how that is so – it is just these various virtues, and various moral ideals related to them, that fail to yield determinate results in various places where he hopes for such results. Yet in the end we learn that it does actually serve the ends of universal good that we should have these dispositions, and that they should be expressed in the field of practice. But if so, then it is for universal good that we should live in a world which presents itself in at least quite a lot of these ways as raising conflict and divergence of sentiment.

To put it another way, these dispositions turn out to be a very valuable element in the world of practice. But that means that divergences of sentiment and various kinds of conflict that flow from those dispositions are themselves part of the world of practice, and the answers that they demand have to come from impulses that are part of the situation as it is actually experienced in the world of practice. It follows that a theory which stands to practice as Sidgwick's theory does cannot actually serve to eliminate and resolve all conflicts and unclarities in the world of practice, though *they* are the conflicts that were complained of when the method of intuitionism was unfavourably reviewed.

It is some consciousness, perhaps, of this point that encourages another feature of Sidgwick's treatment – again a feature which is displayed in the work of later Utilitarians: namely, that it seems not to matter very much if the immense calculation of additive satisfaction cannot actually be carried out. 'We have to observe', Sidgwick writes (p. 439) 'that the difficulties which we found in the way of determining by the intuitional method the limits and relative importance of these duties are reduced in the Utilitarian system to difficulties of hedonistic comparison.' In fact, we are not given many examples, and it is hard to see how we could be, of how those hedonistic comparisons do actually resolve those conflicts. It seems rather that it is this fact itself, the very idea that those conflicts and obscurities have been reduced to hedonistic comparison, that provides the intellectual comfort. It seems that the theorist has certain expectations of how

practice should relate to theory, and then finds that they are better satisfied by a certain kind of theory about that relation itself than they are by
the experience of putting any of it into practice.

Some of the problems presented by Sidgwick's Utilitarianism, and its
need for a dissociation between theory and practice, are peculiar to such
a Utilitarianism. Other schemas for ethical theory might at least satisfy
one test which, as we have seen, Sidgwick's notably and confessedly
failed (though he seems not to have regarded it as a failing), the test of
being *open*; the requirement, that is to say, that if the theory in question
governs the practice of a given group, then it must be possible for everyone in that group to know that it does. Rawls's theory, for instance,
reasonably introduces, and itself passes, this test. Yet there are warnings
and, I believe, finally negative lessons to be learnt from Sidgwick's theory
by ethical theories in general, even those less extravagently evasive than
his.

Here we have to go back to Sidgwick's third axiom, the principle of
impartiality which stated that from the point of view of the universe the
good of any individual is equally valuable. Of course, Sidgwick himself,
as we have already explained, immediately sets about to reverse this
emphasis, as soon as we get to practice:

> each one is morally bound to regard the good of any other individual as
> much as his own, except in so far as he judges it to be less when impartially
> viewed, or less certainly knowable or attainable by him. I before observed
> that the duty of Benevolence as recognised by common-sense seems to fall
> somewhat short of this. But I think it may be fairly urged in explanation of
> this that *practically* each man even with a view to Universal Good, ought
> chiefly to concern himself with promoting the good of a limited number of
> human beings, and that generally in proportion to the closeness of their
> connection with him. (p. 382)

The model is that I, as theorist, can occupy, if only temporarily and
imperfectly, the point of view of the universe, and see everything from
the outside, including myself and whatever moral or other dispositions,
affections or projects, I may have; and from that outside view, I can
assign to them a value. The difficulty is, however, as we have already
seen, that the moral dispositions, and indeed other loyalties and commitments, have a certain depth or thickness: they cannot simply be
regarded, least of all by their possessor, just as devices for generating
actions or states of affairs. Such dispositions and commitments will characteristically be what gives one's life some meaning, and gives one some
reason for living it; they can be said, to varying degrees and variously
over time, to contribute to one's practical or moral identity. There is
simply no conceivable exercise that consists in stepping completely

outside myself and from that point of view evaluating *in toto* the dispositions, projects, and affections that constitute the substance of my own life.

It is significant that this is not just the point, analogous to an important
truth in the philosophy of science, that the Cartesian stance or Archi-
medean fulcrum is impossible, and that one can evaluate beliefs only on
the basis of others. That is indeed true, and its analogue in moral thought,
that some values are needed to evaluate other values, is also true. But *that*
point has already been allowed for in Sidgwick's theory. There is one
evaluative disposition that one takes to the point of view of the universe –
or, perhaps one could say, finds waiting there, since it is the same for
everyone. This is, simply, the disposition of impartial benevolence – or
perhaps, in other versions of ethical theory, some other very general
principle of impartiality. But that does not meet the real point, which lies
rather in a *disanalogy* with the philosophy of science. Even though one
cannot reconstruct a scientific body of belief starting totally from outside
it, nevertheless it is an aim, in reconstructing it, to free one's view of the
world to the maximum degree from perspectives peculiar to one's historical or local situation – to correct for observer's bias, and indeed to try
to see the universe from the point of view of the universe, that is to say
from no distinctive point of view at all. Some contemporary philosophers
of science will say, of course, that this objective is actually impossible, but
certainly it has been a basic aim of science, and if it is impossible, even as a
limiting ideal, then of course so much the worse for any supposed
analogy to it in ethical theory. But, whether it is possible or not, the
analogy to it presents an insoluble problem to ethical theory. For, I agree
with Sidgwick, such a theory must aim to be a theory for practice, and to
be closely related to reasons for action. It cannot be a reasonable aim, with
regard to that purpose, that I or any other particular person should take
as the ideal view of the world – even if one then returns from it to one's
self – a view from no point of view at all. My scientific theory, if I have
one, is, as a scientific theory (as opposed to a personal achievement, or a
possible means to entry to the Royal Society), only incidentally *mine*: if it
is true, then anyone else's true theory will to that extent be the same
thing. But my life, my action, is quite irreducibly mine, and to require that
it is at best a *derivative* conclusion that it should be lived from the
perspective that happens to be mine is an extraordinary misunderstanding. Yet it is that idea that is implicitly contained in the model of the point
of view of the universe.

Sidgwick rightly emphasized, as I have said, the conception of ethics as
part of the theory of rational conduct. He also held that ethical theory
should yield objective truths about what is ultimately valuable. That is not
an aspect of his thought which I have emphasized. But I hope that I have

at any rate not begged the question against it – I have, if you like, implicitly allowed it to Sidgwick. Yet on that very showing, deep holes reveal themselves in Sidgwick's account, and an extensive indeterminacy appears in the relations that are supposed to hold between theory and practice.

The thoroughness and care of Sidgwick's work must support the belief that this is neither a superficial feature of his outlook, nor one due only to its peculiarities. My own view is that no ethical theory can render a coherent account of its own relation to practice: it will always run into some version of the fundamental difficulty that the practice of life, and hence also an adequate theory of that practice, will require the recognition of what I have called deep dispositions; but at the same time the abstract and impersonal view that is required if the theory is to be genuinely a *theory* cannot be satisfactorily understood in relation to the depth and necessity of those dispositions. Thus the theory will remain, in one way or another, in an incoherent relation to practice. But if ethical theory is anything, then it must stand in close and explicable relation to practice, because that is the kind of theory it would have to be. It thus follows that there is no coherent ethical theory.

The fact that Sidgwick's theory so clearly and significantly fails in these respects follows, I believe, simply from the fact that it is so clear and significant an example of an attempt at an ethical theory.

Notes

This is substantially the text of the Henry Sidgwick Memorial Lecture 1982, delivered on 18 February. I am grateful to the Principal and Fellows of Newnham College for their invitation to give the lecture. I believe that it may have been the first Sidgwick lecture to be concerned with Henry Sidgwick himself.

1 J. B. Schneewind, *Sidgwick's Ethics and Victorian Moral Philosophy* (Oxford: Clarendon Press, 1977), p. 1.

2 Quoted in Frank Kermode, *Romantic Image* (London: Fontana, 1971), p. 64.

3 R. F. Harrod, *The Life of John Maynard Keynes* (London: Macmillan, 1951), pp. 116–17.

4 *Ibid.*, p. 114.

5 Henry Sidgwick, *The Methods of Ethics*, 7th edn (London: Macmillan, 1907; reissued 1962), pp. 375–6.

6 Chiefly because the task must be impossible. However, the difficulties that Sidgwick encounters are certainly heightened by confusions in the distinctively hedonistic part of the theory. See in particular the footnote on pp. 499–500.

.7 Schneewind has usefully discussed the problems that arise because Sidgwick actually approaches the discussion of dogmatic intuitionism through some considerations about perfectionism. Sidgwick's discussion certainly involves his own 'thin' view of moral dispositions, criticised below.

8 The phrase recurs at p. 420 without the apology.

14

Ethics and the fabric of the world

John Mackie held[1] that values, in particular ethical values, were not objective, a denial which he took to mean that they were not 'part of the fabric of the world' (p. 15). He stressed that this was to be taken as an ontological thesis, as opposed to a 'linguistic or conceptual' thesis, and to arrive at it was, for him, a matter of 'factual rather than conceptual analysis' (p. 19). In this respect, he found a parallel between value properties and secondary qualities, as he did more generally, being prepared to say of both that they were 'projected' on to the world. The idea of 'factual analysis', and the exact contrast that he intended with conceptual analysis, are not entirely clear, and I suspect that he put it in this way because he closely associated the conceptual and the linguistic, and he wanted to stress – rightly – that the truth of what he claimed was not going to be determined by an enquiry into the use of ethical words. In any sense broader than that, it seems reasonable to hold, as McGinn has argued,[2] that the question of the subjectivity of secondary qualities is a conceptual question; and if that is, so will the same question with respect to ethical qualities (as I shall, for the moment, vaguely call them).

Mackie's own arguments for his conclusion make it unclear how this could be a factual issue. One, the so-called 'argument from queerness', says in effect that the idea of ontologically objective values explains nothing and offends against parsimony: and the grounds of this criticism seem to be entirely a priori. The other, the 'argument from relativity', cites facts about the variation of ethical belief between cultures, and the plausible explanations of it that might be given by the social sciences. The facts about cultural variation can be accepted to be factual facts, even though, as is well known, their interpretation leaves a lot of room for disagreement. But that does not make the conclusion which Mackie draws from them into a factual rather than (in the broader sense) a

172

conceptual conclusion. Even if humankind displayed more unanimity in its ethical reactions than it does, that would not seem to make the reactions more objective, on Mackie's view, but simply more like perceptions of secondary qualities. We shall see later that cultural variation does play a part in the argument, but it is at a different level.

Mackie was prepared to call his position 'moral scepticism', though he made it clear that this was not meant to imply any first order indifferentism, or the rejection of moral considerations as bearing on practical reason. He described his account as an 'error theory' of moral judgements. (The error in question seems, very roughly, to be that of taking moral values to be objective.) Mackie himself said that the name 'moral scepticism' was appropriate (p. 35) just because it was an error theory: presumably because the theory exposes as false something that common sense is disposed to believe. At the same time, however, he did not suppose that when this error was exposed, everyday moral convictions would properly be weakened or opened to doubt. I shall come back to the question of how these claims hang together. However, it is worth asking at this point why one should be more disposed, on the strength of the first of these claims (the error theory), to apply the name 'moral scepticism' to Mackie's view, than one is to withhold that name in virtue of the second claim – that everyday conviction is properly unshaken. That is not an obvious preference, and the fact that Mackie did choose to use 'moral scepticism' in this way reveals some assumptions. I take them to be, first, that scepticism is essentially concerned with knowledge or the lack of it, and, second, that in view of the error theory, there is no moral knowledge.

Particularly granted Mackie's own views, I do not think that this is the most helpful way to use this phrase. Scepticism is basically concerned with doubt, and not necessarily with (the denial of) knowledge. Where it is knowledge that is appropriately pursued in order to put an end to doubt, a denial that knowledge is possible will lead to a sceptical position; but in areas where, on a true view, there is no question of knowledge, and the search for it is inappropriate, this is not so. Scepticism will rather be whatever attacks conviction in those areas. On Mackie's view, which (as I take it) sees the moral as no candidate for knowledge at all, moral scepticism should rather be a position that upsets moral conviction, for instance by claiming that moral considerations have no place in practical reasoning. If the claim that ordinary moral experiences involved an error did properly shake everyday convictions, then there would be reason to say that the error theory was a form of moral scepticism.

Mackie applied the error theory in ethics very widely. It is not simply a matter of those ethical perceptions that are nearest to certain aesthetic reactions, such as that certain people or actions are horrible. Many might agree that the perception of those characteristics can reasonably be assimilated in some degree to the perception of secondary qualities. Nor is it simply a matter of goodness. He says (p. 15) that in claiming moral values not to be objective, he intends to include, besides moral goodness,

> other things that could be more loosely called moral values or disvalues – rightness and wrongness, duty, obligation ... and so on.

In the same spirit, he connects (p. 29) the denial of objective values with the rejection of a categorical imperative:

> So far as ethics is concerned, my thesis that there are no objective values is specifically the denial that any such categorically imperative element is objectively valid. The objective values which I am denying would be action-directing absolutely, not contingently ... upon the agent's desires and inclinations.

This claim raises very sharply the question of what the objectivity is that Mackie is denying. It is not immediately clear what it could mean to say that a requirement or demand was 'part of the fabric of the world'. It might possibly mean that some agency, which made the demand or imposed the requirements, was part of the fabric, but, even if it were, that fact in itself would not be enough to make its demand categorical in the relevant sense. In purely logical or syntactic terms, of course, the demands of such an agent might be categorical, but so might the demands of any agent whatsoever. The person who peremptorily says 'get out of the way' speaks categorically. What he is telling you to do is to get out of the way, not to get out of the way unless you don't mind getting hurt: if you don't mind getting hurt, and stay in his way, you still prevent the state of affairs that he means to bring about. In this, his imperative is (logically) categorical, while the imperatives in the washing-machine instructions are logically hypothetical, even though their antecedent, which is very obvious, is usually suppressed. But this, the question whether an imperative is *intended* categorically, is not the point. The question is rather about the status of some logically categorical imperative, whether an agent in some sense goes wrong who does not recognize it as a demand on him. Whatever that may turn out to mean, it cannot be the same as the question whether there is an agent 'in the fabric of the world' who makes that demand. If there is an exceptional agent in, or perhaps outside, the world whose demands do have that character, that will be because of his nature, not simply because he is 'out there'.

Consider another picture of what it would be for a demand to be 'objectively valid'. It is Kant's own picture.[3] According to this, a demand will be inescapable in the required sense if it is one that a rational agent must accept if he is to be a rational agent. It is, to use one of Kant's favourite metaphors, *self-addressed* by any rational agent. Kant was wrong, in my view, in supposing that the fundamental demands of morality were objective in this sense, but that is not the immediate point, which is that the conception deploys an intelligible and adequate sense of objectivity. It seems to have little to do with those demands being part of the fabric of the world; or, at any rate, they will be no more or less so than the demands of logic – which was, of course, part of Kant's point.

Kant's theory offers an *objective grounding* of morality that is not (as one might say) realist. Moral claims are objectively correct or incorrect, but when one gives a general explanation of what makes them so, that explanation does not run through the relation between those statements and the world, but rather through the relation between *accepting* those statements, and practical reason. There are other candidates for a theory that is objective but not realist, such as a theory which suggests that one must have the desires appropriate to the ethical life if one is going to be in good shape as a human being, where the idea of 'being in good shape' is one that can be explained at least partly (it need not be wholly) prior to the ethical life. This again would be objectivity, and there would be ethical correctness, but it would be basically a correctness of desire and arriving at it would be a feat of practical reasoning; or if of theoretical reasoning, then, to a significant degree, of a non-ethical kind (establishing, for instance, the appropriate psychological truths).

Even if no theory of these kinds is sound, the possibility of them is important for the present discussion. This is not because it shows Mackie to have been looking for objectivity in the wrong place. The significant point is that under these possibilities we are *still* presented with the phenomenon that attracted Mackie's diagnosis, and they help one to understand what needs diagnosing. Suppose that the ethical life could be objectively grounded in one of these ways. One could come to know that it was so grounded, by developing or learning philosophical arguments which showed that ethical life satisfied the appropriate condition, of being related in the right way to practical reason or to wellbeing. But ethical life itself would continue to involve various experiences and judgements of the kind that present themselves as 'objective' – and what they present is not the objectivity that, on these theories, they would genuinely possess. They are not experienced as satisfying any such condition. This is notably clear in the Kantian case, and Kant saw the point himself. In acknowledging the categorical demand of obligation or recognising a moral requirement (the kind of thing expressed in saying, for moral reasons, 'I must'), one does not experience it as an application of

175

the demands of practical reason, but as something more immediate than that, something presented to one by the situation. That is one reason why Kant identified an empirical psychological surrogate of one's rational relations to morality, in the emotional phenomenon of the sense of reverence for the Law. That feeling does, on Kant's theory, represent objectivity, but it also misrepresents it, by making it seem something different from what it is.

It is reasonable to think that no experience could adequately represent an objectivity that lay in the Kantian kind of argument. Kant claims that the requirements of practical reason will be met only by leading a life in which moral considerations play a constitutive, in particular a motivational, role. Moreover, that life is understood to be one in which moral considerations can, in contrast to other motivations, present themselves as objective demands. It follows that what it is for a consideration to present itself as an objective demand could never consist merely in its presenting itself as so related to that very argument. So, in the Kantian version at least, there is no alternative to the experience being a misrepresentation of genuine objectivity. The really important question that is raised here is whether the central experience of ethical life has to be the experience of being confronted by an objective demand.

There would be a certain misrepresentation, then, in that experience of objectivity even if there were genuine objectivity in the form of an objective grounding. What if there were acknowledged to be no such grounding? This covers two distinct possibilities. One is that the idea of such a grounding is intelligible, but there is no convincing argument of this kind. (This is my own view.) This possibility raises much the same range of questions about the experience of objectivity as would be raised if the grounding argument were valid. If that argument is not valid, then we are to that extent the more deceived if we think that there is objectivity, but we are not any the more deceived *by the experience*; and whether the argument is valid or not, the same questions will arise about the necessity of that kind of experience to the ethical life.

The second possibility is to be found in the outlook of someone who agrees that there is no objective grounding, but nevertheless thinks that there is objectivity. Such a person (Prichard was one) will believe that they are mistaken to look for any argument of these kinds to yield objectivity; objectivity is, rather, something to be grasped through these experiences themselves. He thinks that objectivism gets its content just from the sense that these experiences embody, of confrontation with something independent. He construes objectivism as a kind of realism. This possibility is simply misconceived, and in relation to this idea Mackie was right to detect error, since it takes the fact that an experience is demanding as sufficient evidence, indeed the only evidence, that it is the experience of a demand. It takes resonance to be reference, and that is certainly a mistake. The mistake, however, is not inherent simply in having that experience. It is not even inherent in having that experience and connecting it with objectivity. It lies in a theory which takes that experience to reveal all that one knows or needs to know about objectivity.

We can now go back to other kinds of what I earlier called 'ethical qualities', those that lie in the area of the good, the admirable and so forth, and also the more affective characteristics – the outrageous, the contemptible, and the rest. In these last cases, at least, it is obvious to reflection that there is a relativity involved. It is tempting to see in this, as Mackie saw, some analogy to secondary qualities. However, there is a significant difference between the two cases; it lies in the conception that it is appropriate to have of 'the world' of which these various qualities are said not to be part. The fabric of the world from which the secondary qualities are absent (in their presented form) is the world of primary qualities, and (to take for granted the answers to several large and contentious questions) the claim that the secondary qualities, as presented, are not part of that world comes to much the same as the claim that they do not figure in an 'absolute conception' of the world on which scientific investigators, abstracting as much as possible from their various perceptual peculiarities, might converge.[4] There is nothing unnerving or subversive in the idea that ethical qualities are not part of the fabric of the world in this sense. They do not need to do better than secondary qualities.[5]

The subjective conception of secondary qualities rests on the notion that in principle the perception of (say) colours can be explained in terms of perceptual psychology, on the one hand, and the world as characterised in terms of primary qualities, on the other.[6] In the case of ethical qualities, however, if subjectivism holds that they are added to or 'projected' on to the world, 'the world' has to be already construed in a psychologically and socially richer sense than 'the world' on to which secondary qualities are projected. Any conceivable explanations of variations in ethical reactions will have to include psychological and social elements in the cause. This would be so even if human beings as such converged in ethical reaction more than they do. However, the explanation of these variations can in fact be plausibly traced in many cases to cultural factors, and this is where we rejoin the 'argument from relativity', which earlier seemed not very relevant. It is not relevant, if (as I think Mackie had in mind) 'the world' is to be regarded in the same way for the two cases of secondary qualities and of ethics. But if this is not to be so, cultural variation and its explanations are relevant, because they help to make clear what kinds of convergence might appropriately be looked for in ethical thought, and how we might explain them.

The importance of those explanations comes out in the ways in which we might assess future processes of convergence in ethical thought. The mere fact that convergence occurred would not in itself be evidence of any kind of objectivity. What would matter would be the explanation of the convergence. Human beings might come to agree more on these matters than they do now just because of assimilation and a higher degree of interdependence, and that would tell us nothing about the status of ethical belief. It would be different if some argument for an objective grounding appeared to have gained increasing rational assent. Of course what we think about the chances of finding an objective grounding will themselves affect and be affected by the ways in which we understand existing ethical variation: the relations, as one would expect, run in both directions.

None of these understandings, however, could make more plausible what I earlier called the *realist* version of objectivism. So, to summarize, the position seems to be the following. Realist objectivism, in that sense, is not an option and Mackie was right in rejecting it, though he was wrong in thinking that cultural variation was relevant to it. Cultural variation is relevant, but not at this point. It is so in virtue of the explanations that it requires us to give of ethical reactions, explanations that both affect our conception of 'the world' that elicits those reactions, and also are related to the prospects for objectivism in a different sense, that of an objective grounding of ethical beliefs and attitudes. The question of whether there could be such a grounding is not answered by Mackie's kind of critique, in terms of the fabric of the world; but that critique does nevertheless attack a feature of ethical experience, which, even if there were an objective grounding, would tend to misrepresent it – most starkly, as we have seen, in the Kantian case.

I come back now to what I called earlier the 'two claims': that our ethical experiences involve an error, and that ethical conviction need not be upset by recognizing that fact. It will be helpful to take the second claim first. In the case of secondary qualities, the discovery that they are subjective has very little, if any, effect on everyday practice, and it is obvious why that should be so. The psychological capacities that underlie our perceiving the world in terms of certain secondary qualities have evolved so that the physical world can present itself to us in reliable and useful ways (it is an interesting question, discussed by McGinn, whether Kant was right in thinking that any world we could experience would have to present itself in terms of some secondary qualities). Coming to know that these secondary qualities constitute our form of perceptual engagement with the world, and how this mode of presentation works, will not unsettle the system. Indeed, in this case unreflective practice is so harmoniously related to theoretical understanding, that a good case can be made for rejecting Mackie's view that there is an *error* involved at all in everyday belief, though no doubt there is in naive philosophical theory about it.[7]

If we ask similar questions about ethical qualities and our experience of them, it seems that it is the second claim that is harder to accept. If the general direction of Mackie's critique is right, then ethical qualities, which are felt to be in some sense independent of us and our motivations, turn out in fact to be dependent on us and our motivations. Moreover, and more damagingly, this can be plausibly explained by supposing that ethical constraints and objectives have to be internalized in such a way that they can serve to control and redirect potentially destructive and unco-operative desires, and that they can do this, or do it most effectively, only if they do not present themselves as one motivation or desire among others, nor as offering one option among others. They thus present themselves as something given to the agent, but at the same time something from which he cannot feel himself entirely detached, as he could from some external, questionable, authority.

Similar experiences are involved when one's values come into conflict with other people's values. While one is involved in expressing one's own as against some other values, one cannot at the same time simply see those others as alternative ways of ordering society or of producing some very general kind of human good. One cannot, equally, think that, while as a matter of fact one sees the world from the perspective of one set of values, it might be more convenient if one could bring it about that one saw it from another; just as one cannot think it an acceptable way of dealing with some morally disagreeable phenomenon that one should stop being affected by it. It is for this kind of reason, indeed, that McGinn says that our moral consciousness is *not* like our experience of secondary qualities, since we accept that one could change the colours of the world if one could make a general enough psychological alteration. He may underestimate in this the momentum of our current conceptions of what colour things are: but, in any case, the consideration will not show that moral distinctions are not relative to our psychological and social constitution. It will only show how deeply entrenched they are.

If all this is so, then it is not easy to combine the two claims, and the consciousness of what the system is will not happily coexist with the system's working. In this respect, it is not like the example of secondary qualities. The fundamental difficulty is to combine the efficacy of a social system with consciousness of what it involves. Moreover, if one believes, as I think John Mackie did, that it is a desirable feature of a society that its practices could in principle become as far as possible transparent to it (though not all of them could do so at once), then one must ask whether, on anything like Mackie's view of it, ethical experience could itself pass that test.

Despite his second claim, Mackie did not think that things would go on exactly the same if subjectivism in his sense became known. He recognized that if subjectivism is true, then acquiring values is not the process it is supposed to be under objectivism (p. 22), and it must surely follow that if subjectivism were not just true but known to be true, those processes would be consciously conducted in some different way. Sometimes (e.g. p. 106) Mackie was disposed to conclude that if his views were right, 'morality is not to be discovered but made: we have to decide what moral views to adopt. ...' But, as so often when a conclusion of that kind is drawn from an ethical theory, it is unclear who 'we' are, and to what extent the process of decision is supposed to be individual or social or, indeed, concrete at all. It certainly cannot follow from Mackie's view that when we have come to realize what moral experience really is, we shall start to acquire our moral attitudes by self-consciously deciding on them, either individually or collectively. It is not clear that there could be such a process, and if there were, there is no reason at all to think, in the light of Mackie's theory itself, that it would be effective.

Mackie's theory, and any like it, leaves a real problem of what should happen when we know it to be true. I cannot try to take that problem further here. I shall offer just one speculation, that the first victim of this knowledge is likely to be the Kantian sense of presented duty. We have seen that it is the starkest example of objectification, and since there is virtually nothing to it except the sense of being given, it stands to suffer most if that sense is questioned. There are other ethical desires and perceptions that are better adapted to being seen for what they are. It is an important task for moral philosophy to consider what they may be, and into what coherent pictures of ethical life, philosophical, psychological and social, they will fit.

Notes

1 John Mackie, *Ethics: Inventing Right and Wrong* (Harmondsworth: Penguin Books, 1977); and first in 'A refutation of morals', *Australian Journal of Psychology and Philosophy* 24 (1946): the page references that I give in parentheses are to *Ethics*. I regret that John Mackie and I never had an opportunity to discuss the kind of question raised here, though we did talk about other issues in ethics, particularly utilitarianism. He would have certainly brought to the discussion of

our disagreements the clarity, honesty and shrewd perception that he so notably showed on all occasions, and he would also have recognized that on these questions, the disagreements are rooted in a deeper agreement.

2 Colin McGinn, *The Subjective View: secondary qualities and indexical thoughts* (Oxford: Oxford University Press, 1983), to which I am indebted at several points.

3 Some of the immense confusion that surrounds this subject comes from the fact that Kant, who started it off, expressed himself in terms of a logical distinction between categorical and hypothetical. Readers of the *First Critique* should not be surprised to find him using what seems to be logical distinction to make a different level of point.

4 See my *Descartes: the project of pure enquiry* (Harmondsworth: Penguin Books, 1978), especially chapters 1, 8 and 10; McGinn, *The Subjective View*, who well brings out how the absolute conception is not a perceptual one. For various formulations of the idea and assessments of its prospects, see N. Jardine, 'The possibility of absolutism', in D. H. Mellor (ed.), *Science, Belief and Behaviour: essays in honour of R. B. Braithwaite* (Cambridge: Cambridge University Press, 1980), pp. 23–42; and *The Fortunes of Inquiry* (Oxford: Oxford University Press, 1986).

5 The point is well brought out in David Wiggins, 'Truth, invention, and the meaning of life', in *Needs, Values and Truth*. McGinn (pp. 145ff.) does think that ethical qualities, or our actual understanding of them, need to do better than secondary qualities: I shall come back to this point later.

6 This is not to deny that variations in perceived colour may have psychological causes, as they do by juxtaposition and in many other cases. This is one area in which we invoke the difference between real and apparent colours: it is generally thought that a difference in the observer's expectations, for instance, cannot affect the colour a thing is. It is not the same with smells; and certainly not with affective qualities. Whether a substance is perceived as food can affect whether it *is* disgusting: the contrast with something's *seeming* disgusting is drawn at a different level.

7 McGinn, *The Subjective View*, chapter 7. The issue involves the question of how the relativity of secondary-quality predicates shows up in their semantics. It is not wholly clear what McGinn's view is on this: cf. pp. 119–20 with pp. 9–10. See also Wiggins, 'Truth, invention, and the meaning of life', and Williams, *Descartes*, pp. 242–4.

15

What does intuitionism imply?

Intuitionism in ethics is nowadays usually treated as a methodological doctrine. In the sense that John Rawls gives to the term in *A Theory of Justice*, an ethical view is intuitionist if it admits a plurality of first principles that may conflict, and, moreover, it has no explicit method or priority rules for resolving such conflicts.[1]

The use of the term to stand for this kind of view represents a change from the practice of the 1950s and 1960s, when it was taken for granted that intuitionism in ethics was an epistemological doctrine, a view about the way in which ethical propositions are grasped or known – the kind of view held, for instance, by W. D. Ross and H. A. Prichard. As such, intuitionism was much criticized at that time, to considerable effect.[2]

It seems to be mainly the influence of Rawls that has brought about this change in the understanding of the term. Interestingly, the change restored an earlier state of affairs. J. O. Urmson[3] tells us that when he was an undergraduate and attended Prichard's classes, it was assumed that intuitionism was to be understood as a methodological position: it was opposed, necessarily, to utilitarianism, and Moore (for instance) was not regarded as an intuitionist.

Rawls seems to regard the epistemological doctrine as an addition to the methodological, and sees intuitionists as a methodological genus of which the notorious epistemological intuitionists are a species. I shall be concerned with the relations between methodological intuitionism (MI), on the one hand, and, on the other, two different epistemological doctrines that may be called 'intuitionist' (EI). However, I do not want to follow Rawls's practice and treat EI only as a species of MI. The reason for this is well illustrated by the case of Henry Sidgwick, who insistently rejected MI, but claimed that the supreme principles of his utilitarianism were grasped by intuition. In saying this, he precisely wanted to indicate an area of agreement between himself and the traditional anti-utilitarian intuitionists. Again, someone could accept a *rationalized pluralism*, with explicit priority rules, and so not accept MI, but yet take an E-intuitionist view on the question of how the rules were grasped. The classes of positions associated with MI and with EI merely intersect.

This does not mean that the questions raised by the two sorts of position are entirely distinct. In particular, those who accept MI, such as Urmson and myself, should consider whether it has any particular epistemological consequences. In his brief article 'A defence of intuitionism', Urmson confines himself in effect to the claim that MI correctly describes our experience. That seems to me importantly true, but it is not enough for a defence; apart from the question of what that tells us about our experience, there is the issue, raised by many opponents of MI, whether our experience should be left in that state. Their challenge can be fully met only by considering what antecedent warrant there is for the demand that we should rationalize our ethical beliefs, and what conceptions of rationality are being deployed in that demand. This is particularly significant because a charge of unreflective conservatism is often applied to MI. But it is a mistake to think that in order to take a critical view of our ethical beliefs, we have to systematize them in a theoretical style. Indeed, the theoretical stance may not even encourage a critical view. Some systematizations are themselves very conservative, and the rhetoric of radical rationality conceals how conservative they are. The picture of rationality for ethics expressed in terms of theory and system is inadequate. Moreover, we do not have to think that what is principally wrong with our ethical life and our understanding of it is that they are insufficiently rational: they may be, for instance, insufficiently honest. The valid objections to uncritical conservatism can be represented within MI itself.

Here I am concerned more narrowly with the relations between MI and EI. I shall consider EI in two different versions. One version, the view to which the title 'intuitionism' was traditionally most often applied, rested on the idea that there was some instructive analogy between ethical propositions and truths of mathematics, particularly truths of mathematics that were supposedly self-evident. The criticisms of this are well known, and surely sound. It is hard to find ethical propositions with any content for which the required self-evidence can be invoked in the first place (Sidgwick's own fundamental intuition illustrates this.) Even if such propositions were available, it is not clear how far we should have got, since it is not clear how much is done by the notion of intuition even for mathematical truths. C. D. Parsons has made the interesting suggestion that it does some work only if 'intuition that' is linked to 'intuition of', and this is not going to be available in any helpful way for the ethical case, however it may be with mathematics.[4]

Why should anyone want to associate MI with an EI that is conceived in the mathematical style? On the face of it, it is an improbable connection. If the epistemology of ethics is to be mathematical, so (one might expect) should be its development and presentation. One would look for an ethical theory that would be axiomatized or organized in a deductive form. That aspiration, which few since Locke[5] have entertained, stands at the opposite pole to MI. So why should the mathematical analogy encourage any association with MI?

The answer presumably lies in the fact that the mathematical analogy did not go beyond considering ethical convictions individually. It was enough that they seemed to display immediate non-empirical certainty, which encouraged an analogy with the grasp of very simple mathematical relations, but offered no parallel to mathematical discovery. All that the analogy could do in the heuristic direction was to exclude any process of empirical inquiry; it provided no picture of the discovery of ethical truths except the intuition of them one by one. If the propositions that were supposedly intuited were very general and few in number (as in Sidgwick's case), empirical facts could be applied and subsumptive arguments used, and the way would be open to systematization. But if the intuitions were numerous (at the limit, particular in content and indefinitely many, as in Prichard's case), the absence of any model of how they might be associated naturally led to MI. In this case, all one has is an insistence that the ethical convictions are certain, with virtually no account of how such convictions might be corrected or rejected. This indeed offers a target to the utilitarian objection that intuitionism is conservative.

The supposed analogy between ethical and mathematical propositions was encouraged by the fact that the ethical concepts appearing in these propositions were very abstract and general. E-intuitionists in the mathematical style have been, to use Susan Hurley's term, 'centralists',[6] believing that very general ethical concepts were logically prior to more specific ones; and the truths that were supposedly intuited used very general concepts such as *good* and *right*.

If we look away from these very general notions to more specific or 'thick'[7] ethical concepts, such as *treachery* or *cowardice* or *promise*, we may be encouraged to accept a different style of EI, one in terms of an analogy to sense perception. Such a view has been advanced by John McDowell.[8] The point of calling this an (E-)intuitionist theory (though I do not know that McDowell calls it that himself) is that it presents a range of particular ethical convictions that are immediate and claim to represent something objective. McDowell regards their claim as justified, once an important distinction has been made between two senses of objectivity. In one sense, a quality is objective only if it can be characterized without any reference to experience at all. In another sense, it is objective if 'it is there to be experienced, as opposed to being a mere figment of the subjective state that purports to be an experience of it'.[9] In the first sense, values (as the objects of these intuitions may be called) are not objective, but neither are secondary qualities; in the second sense, they have as good a claim to objectivity as secondary qualities have.

McDowell considers the objection that value qualities play no real role in the explanation of value experience, whereas secondary qualities do play a role in the explanation of (say) visual experience. His answer to this is as follows. The right test with regard to explanation 'is not whether something pulls its own weight in the favoured explanation (it may fail to do so without thereby being explained away), but whether the explainer can consistently deny its reality'.[10] It is this test that admits secondary qualities. By this same test, values can figure in explanations, and this is all the more clear because the explanations are different from those appropriate to secondary qualities. McDowell illustrates this point by reference to something that is not itself a value: 'We make sense of fear by seeing it as a response to objects that *merit* such a response. ... For an object to merit fear just is for it to be fearful. So explanations of fear that manifest our capacity to understand ourselves in this region of our lives will simply not cohere with the claim that reality contains nothing in the way of fearfulness.'[11]

Before considering the relation of this kind of EI to MI (a question on which McDowell has something to say), I shall make some remarks about the epistemological view itself; they are not intended as a fully argued criticism of it. The crucial word in the passage I have just quoted (as so often in discussions of objectivity) is 'our'. Consider a people who are filled with terror, perhaps of a rather special, numinous kind, by certain features of their environment. They have a word to pick out things to which they react in this way. It is not a blankly causal, still less a merely individual, reaction, and children are instructed in what does and what does not merit it. We – the ethnographers – come to understand these reactions, and the word that picks things in terms of that reaction. We do not share the reaction, except to the extent that we imaginatively enter into their view of things: for instance, we do not share beliefs and attitudes that make this reaction intelligible. Is the quality for which they have this term 'there to be perceived'? It is part of their world; it is not part of our world. Is it part of *the* world? Or – we may put it another way – is it part of our world, when 'our' relates to a *we* for which there are no others?[12]

We can distinguish at least three different levels in the understanding of situations like this. There is, first, a *shared practice*, in particular a linguistic one: people in this society have a word that they can apply to new situations, teach to their children and so on. That raises a *psychological* question: there must be some explanation of how they can go on from one situation to another in using this term, and why one thing rather than another elicits from them the related reaction. Then there is the question of *objectivity*, whether 'there is something there to be perceived'; the answer to this is of course connected with the nature of the explanation that answers the psychological question.

In the case of secondary qualities, if we give a positive answer to the last question, this hangs together coherently with what we want to say about the shared practice and its psychological explanation. The reason for this is that if we find a group whose recognitional and classificatory practice differs from ours, we have an explanation of this that indeed refers to objective qualities; it is a matter of their and our capacities to perceive what is there. An important element in this is the fact that we can fit together what they can perceive with what we can perceive, in the sense that we can form a picture of one world, differently perceived, and that picture can contain these qualities. With the example of fear, and equally with what are clearly values, this is not so. We again have the phenomenon of a shared practice that requires psychological explanation. But here we can do nothing with the claim of objectivity, because here the explanation of why things are like that for them *and not so for us* does not bring in that quality. We could not, as in the case of secondary qualities, fit together into one world the qualities that they are supposedly perceiving and those that we are supposedly perceiving, let alone all the qualities demanded by the various value systems that there are or might be.

Nevertheless, the nature of the shared practice shows that it is world guided, and explanation will hope to show how that can be. What the explanation exactly may be, is to be seen: but we know now that a vital part of it will lie in the desires, attitudes, and needs that we and they have differently acquired from our different ways of being brought into a social world. The explanation will show how, in relation to those differences, the world can indeed guide our and their reactions. 'The world' in that explanation will assuredly not be characterized merely in terms of primary qualities; the account of it will need to mention, no doubt, both secondary qualities and straightforwardly psychological items. But it will not contain value qualities corresponding to their experience, or to ours. There is no room for all those qualities, and even if there were, there would be no coherent explanation of why we are able to perceive some of them, and they others. For what we already have good reason to believe about such explanations – that they must refer to different styles of socialization, for instance – would demand a model of a selective perceptual filter, culturally tuned, which is barely intelligible.

If we or they had an explanation of how the world guides the application of thick value concepts, it would not follow that we or they could take from the explanation some non-value concepts, combine them with a very general value term, and succeed in continuing the practice: that is to say, it would not reinstate centralism. Centralism is a doctrine about language and linguistic practice, and there is no reason at all to think that people could substitute for a linguistic practice the terms in which that practice was psychologically or sociologically explained.

These questions are directly relevant to ways in which McDowell's picture may bear on MI. McDowell thinks that if a 'projectivist' picture were correct, as opposed to the kind of picture he offers, 'having one's ethical or aesthetic reactions rationally suited to their objects would be a matter of having the relevant processing mechanism functioning acceptably.... The upshot is that the search for an evaluative attitude that one can endorse as rational becomes, virtually irresistibly, a search for ... a set of principles: a search for a *theory* of beauty of goodness.'[13] Such a theory would be opposed to MI, to which McDowell himself is attracted.

This seems to be a *non sequitur*. Even though there is no doubt more to 'projectivism' than there is to a minimal alternative to McDowell's objectivist picture, the point at issue is a quite general one. A theory of value is something that we are supposed to use in determining what is valuable, worth pursuing, and so on. Why should anything of that sort follow from or be contained in the correct explanation of how people share a practice and go from one case to another? McDowell's conclusion seems to be based on the idea that, if his picture is correct, then we have an account of rationality (based on objectivity) that is compatible with MI, since we can compare one case with another, appeal to a shared sense of resemblance, and so on; but if his picture is not correct, then the only rationality there can be will be that of theory.

Such an argument rests on two unsound assumptions. One is that case-by-case comparisons and appeals to a shared sense of resemblance are not available unless his picture is correct. That is not true. The possibility lies in the shared practice, not in McDowell's objectivist explanation of the shared practice, and when such a practice exists, such methods are available. To the extent that such practices do not exist – when, in particular, two groups use different thick concepts – the possibility of course does not exist; but then it does not, and McDowell's account is not going to bring it into being, particularly since that account contains no practicable theory of error or account of how each party fails to perceive things that other parties perceive.

A second assumption of the argument is that, without McDowell's picture, theory (as opposed to MI) provides the only rational way of discussing ethical convictions. (A form of this assumption is of course shared by the ethical theorists who oppose MI). This is also not true. To mention only one possibility, we can ask what understandings of human nature, society, and history are presupposed by a given shared practice, such as the use of some thick concepts rather than others, and those understandings may be open to criticism.

McDowell's objectivism is not necessary for a rational MI. Indeed, one may wonder why his picture should not lead in the opposite direction. Surely the world cannot simply contain a jumble of value qualities, perceptible to various differently trained observers? If there are such qualities, one would hope and expect that, as with secondary qualities, they had some discoverable theoretical structure. That McDowell's picture is not sufficient for MI (not that he claims it to be so) is suggested in an interesting way by the views of Hurley, some of which I have already mentioned. Her picture of the application of thick ethical concepts seems to be entirely compatible with McDowell's. However, she considers a further question, how a decision of what it is right to do can emerge when several such concepts apply in a situation and pull in different directions. Here she appeals to theory. Indeed, she adopts the very surprising claim that 'when we say that a particular alternative would be right, *it is part of what we mean* that there is some theory which is the best theory about the specific values that apply to the alternatives at hand and that this theory favours a particular alternative'.[14] It is not clear how much the term 'theory' is meant to imply (indeed it is hard to find a sense of the word weak enough to make this particular claim in the least plausible). But there is certainly nothing here to exclude, and much to encourage, the idea that on the basis of an intuitive application of thick concepts there needs to be erected a structure of ethical theory, of the kind that MI opposes.

The upshot of this discussion seems to be that EI and MI have no very close relations to one another. The closest association has been in the case of the EI in the mathematical style that accepted a large number of separate intuitions; and there the outcome itself gave some reason to distrust the epistemological model.

However, those E-intuitionists were not wrong in thinking that there is a large number of unobvious particular judgements to be made, and this fact is the starting point of MI. Few people suppose that all judgements of value, or judgements of right action involving value, are intuitively to be arrived at in isolation from one another. The question of MI's credentials is a question of how far we should expect all the values that we respect, and all the considerations that bear on decisions of right action, to be ordered in a systematic structure. That question arises at two levels, at least: we have to consider how far systematic connections and priorities can be set up between different values or principles at a general level, and also how straightforward the process is likely to be of applying them to particular cases.

There seem to me to be two very general kinds of consideration that should lead one to expect the kind of answer that MI gives to these questions. The first applies particularly to the general level, while the second applies to both the general and the particular levels. The first has some epistemological implications, or at least favours some tendencies over others in that area; the second should have some force whatever one's epistemological views.

The first consideration is to be found in a fact often neglected by ethical theorists, that our ethical ideas consist of a very complex historical deposit. When we consider this fact, and the relations that this deposit has to our public discourse and our private lives, there seems no reason at all to expect it to take, in any considerable measure, the shape of a theory. How compelling one finds this consideration certainly depends to some degree on one's epistemological assumptions. If one thinks that there is no other place to start ethical reflection than the life we actually have, it will seem compelling; the more independent leverage on that life one supposes possible, the less one will be impressed. But even those who believe in the independent leverage must find it hard to explain how, as ethical theorists seem often to assume, the theoretical structure is *already there* in our ethical thought and responses. How did it get there?

The second consideration, it seems to me, should have weight whatever one's epistemological assumptions. It rests on the fact that judgement is constantly required, and that judgement is overwhelmingly concerned with questions of what considerations, in a particular case or more generally, are more important than others. These need not necessarily be practical judgements, though practical judgements provide the central cases, and the weighing of ethical considerations in other connections is often closely relevant to possible practical judgements. Importance is of various types: something may be important to the agent, to others involved, to people in general, or, at the limit, it may be simply important.

The following points seem to me obviously true. Judgements of importance are ubiquitous, and are central to practical life and to reflection at a more general level about the considerations that go into practical decision. Moreover, judgements of importance indeed require judgement. There are certainly reasons why some considerations are more important than others, in any of the previous senses, but judgement is still needed to determine how far those reasons can take you. It may be obvious that in general one kind of consideration is more important than another (for instance, one kind of ethical consideration is more important than another), but it is a matter of judgement whether in a particular set of circumstances that priority is preserved: other factors alter the balance, or it may be a very weak example of the consideration that generally wins. Last, there is no reason to believe that there is one currency in terms of which all relations of comparative importance can be represented. On the contrary, any such currency (satisfaction of desires, for instance) consists of some consideration about which it will make sense to ask whether, on a given occasion or more generally, it is more important than something else.

Philosophy needs a better account of importance than it has at present, and such an account might display any of several epistemological inclinations. But whatever form it took, it would surely be a test of its adequacy that it preserved these banal truths; and any account that does preserve them is bound to leave a good deal of room for methodological intuitionism.

Notes

1 John Rawls, *A Theory of Justice* (Oxford: Oxford University Press, 1971), p. 34.
2 For instance, see Stephen Toulmin, *The Place of Reason in Ethics* (Cambridge: Cambridge University Press, 1950); R. M. Hare, *The Language of Morals* (Oxford: Oxford University Press, 1952); P. H. Nowell-Smith, *Ethics* (Harmondsworth: Penguin Books, 1954).
3 J. O. Urmson, 'A defence of intuitionism', *Proceedings of the Aristotelian Society* 75 (1974–75): 111–19.
4 C. D. Parsons, 'Mathematical intuition', *Proceedings of the Aristotelian Society* 80 (1979–80): 145–68.
5 John Locke, *Essay on Human Understanding*, IV, iii, 18.
6 Susan Hurley, 'Objectivity and disagreement', in Ted Honderich (ed.), *Morality and Objectivity: a tribute to J. L. Mackie*, pp. 54–97, in particular p. 56: 'I shall refer to accounts that take the general concepts in some category to be logically prior to and independent of the specific as *centralist*. Non-centralism about reasons for action rejects the view that the general concepts *right* and *ought* are logically prior to and independent of specific reason-giving concepts such as *just* and *unkind*.' I take it that in this formulation 'independent of' introduces a non-symmetrical relation. For comment on Hurley's own non-centralism, see below.

7 I have used this term for this purpose in *ELP*; see in particular chapter 8. If centralism is taken as a doctrine about the analysis or explication of such thick concepts as we have, I agree with Hurley – and, in this respect, with John McDowell – in rejecting it. However, I do not think, as they do, that the degree of autonomy enjoyed by non-specific terms such as 'right' is simply something to be determined by philosophical inquiry; the extent to which a society uses such terms as opposed to thick concepts is partly a historical question, and has important social implications. In this I agree with Alasdair MacIntyre; see *After Virtue* (London: Duckworth, 1982).

8 The statement to which the present discussion relates most closely is John McDowell, 'Values and secondary qualities', in Honderich (ed.), *Morality and Objectivity*, pp. 110–29.

9 McDowell, 'Values and secondary qualities', p. 114.

10 *Ibid.*, p. 117.

11 *Ibid.*, p. 119; McDowell's emphasis.

12 Cf. 'Wittgenstein and idealism', in my *Moral Luck*, pp. 144–63.

13 McDowell, 'Values and secondary qualities', p. 122; his emphasis.

14 Hurley, 'Objectivity and disagreement', p. 57; my emphasis.

16

Professional morality and
its dispositions

A leading example of a 'professional morality', the one that I shall have in mind for this discussion, is that of lawyers, particularly as that profession is practised in the United States,[1] but many of the considerations apply more widely.

What gives interest to the idea of a professional morality is the possibility that such a morality may diverge from 'ordinary' or 'everyday' morality. Indeed, it is this possibility that gives content to the idea of a professional *morality* at all, as opposed merely to a set of conventions or styles of etiquette associated with certain professions. Such divergences are a datum of the problem, but it is not entirely clear at a theoretical level how they are to be described. Divergences, first of all, do not necessarily generate conflict, though I shall argue later that they involve the possibility of conflict. They do not necessarily produce conflict in the professional agents themselves, since those agents may be totally at home in their professional morality and assuredly discriminate professional situations from others, and so on. Moreover, if others in the community equally accept the existence of the professional morality, there will be no conflict between those other people and the professionals.

First-person conflict within members of the profession and conflict between them and other people are of course both possible, and they are in principle independent of each other. Professionals who are complacent or convinced, or both, may be surrounded by a dubious public; on the other hand, it may be the professionals, or some of them, who are worried, and the public reassuringly traditionalist. (The clergy – in England, at least – provide a good example of the latter, to the extent that 'the public' is identified as their public, that is to say, the public of believers; but the fact that a special public needs to be identified in this way is itself part of their problem.) A complete separation from the public

192

is most naturally associated with a caste rather than simply with a profession. In an open society, the two types of conflict are likely to be associated; it is important, of course, as contrasted with the case of a caste, that people decide to enter or leave a profession, thus moving from one of these two groups to the other.

These possibilities help to make the important point that a professional morality is not just a *different* morality and professionals are not merely an out-group relative to the moral community. Two considerations are connected here, that the profession is (broadly) morally acceptable to the community and that the professionals see themselves as members of that community, members moreover who exercise their profession there.

We started from divergences between professional and general morality, but now it may be wondered how there can be divergences at all. For, it may be said, either there is a justification of this profession in terms acceptable to the community and its everyday standards, or there is not. If there is not, then it is not a professional morality but a different one. If there is, then there can be only superficial divergences – the everyday morality will contain the professional morality as an application of itself to special circumstances. So how can there be divergences?

It is natural to say, and it has been said in the literature, that divergences between professional and everyday moralities arise because the profession requires some acts that would be immoral if done in other than a professional context.[2] This is not very helpful. It leaves a very thin sense of 'divergence', if any at all – there are many sorts of acts that, relative to the general standards of everyday morality itself, would be immoral unless performed in special, specified circumstances. Moreover, this approach raises a problem about 'the same act' being done in a professional or a non-professional context. Many professional acts simply cannot be done in a non-professional context (e.g., harassing witnesses).

This is the familiar point that under some descriptions the action is the same, but that under some other, morally relevant descriptions, it is not the same. Moreover, it is rarely the case that the morally relevant difference between a professional (and permissible) action and a non-professional (and impermissible) action consists solely in the fact that the agent acts in a professional capacity in the one case and not in the other. What comes closest to that specification is the case in which the context is in all ways like the usual professional context, but the agent is only pretending to discharge a professional function, or wrongly believes himself or herself to be doing so, as with those who are impostors or have been disbarred, and so forth. Such a case gives us no help in understanding divergences between professional and everyday morality, which are called up, rather, by situations that typically display some larger difference between the professional act and the non-professional act that is being contrasted with it. We are then back with the absolutely familiar point that what is, under some description, the same act can be acceptable in some contexts and not in others. Yet, once again, there obviously are divergences: we are not discussing nothing.

A natural model to help us understand the problem is a two-tier structure of the kind that is familiar from the discussion of indirect utilitarianism.[3] The model will not help, however, unless we correctly specify in it what kind of item is being justified at the first level. It is often said that this is a set of *rules*. But what comes about or continues to exist if the second-order argument is accepted in practice is some social or psychological item, such as a rule's being followed in a group, people having a disposition to follow a rule, and so forth.[4] It is this concrete social or psychological item to which we should direct our attention, and if we are going to consider second-order justifications, it is usually most helpful to apply them to psychological dispositions and to such things as an educational system that encourages some dispositions rather than others. In the present connection, it is only in these terms that the problem can be understood at all. I shall correspondingly be concerned with the set of professional reactions, dispositions of deliberation, and so forth, that lawyers or other professionals acquire as a result of their training. (What they acquire as a result of their training is of course not to be understood merely in terms of what they get from their training and from nothing else, since the effects of their training will be very much a function of their general socialization.)

Let us call, then, the first-order item that is going to be discussed – the relevant psychological item that corresponds to this professional morality – 'the professional dispositions'. The second-order considerations that are to be applied to justify, or perhaps criticize, the professional dispositions will consist of some more general considerations. They need not be completely universalist, but they will have a wider application than the first-order system of professional dispositions. They do not have to be utilitarian. They must be able to take up in some way consequences of the first-order dispositions and of the institutions that go with them, but they do not have to treat those consequences merely in welfarist terms. Thus the relevant considerations about what follows from encouraging certain legal dispositions in society could well include reference to rights, such as the likelihood of one or another set of dispositions on the lawyers' part bringing it about that people will get their legal rights.

Those who have the professional dispositions must sometimes, in virtue of those dispositions, give answers to practical questions, or react to situations with which they are presented, in ways that differ from the decisions or reactions that would be appropriate merely on the basis of the wide system. If that were not so, there would be no point in the two-tier structure and the problems that it is supposed to help us to answer would not arise. This basic fact can give rise to serious problems for systems of this kind. The problems come out when one asks how the dispositions in question are supposed to coexist, psychologically or socially, with the consciousness of the general considerations that justify them. The difficulty is most acute when the justifying considerations are utilitarian. Disposition-utilitarianism typically tries to banish the problem by alienating the dispositions from the consciousness of their justification, but the outcome is never satisfactory.[5]

Let us make it a condition of applying the two-tier structure to our topic that the alienation problem should not arise. If there is to be a second-order justification of professional dispositions, then the consciousness appropriate to those dispositions should be able to coexist coherently with the consciousness of their justification, not just in one society, but in one head. To a limited extent, this follows from its being a professional morality that is in question. As has already been said, a profession is something that one can choose to leave or try to join, and the choices involved at those points must surely allow the two kinds of consciousness to come together. More important than this, however, is the substantive demand on a rational society that its institutions and the conceptions that legitimate them should be as far as possible transparent to it.[6]

We can now explain how it is that, despite the argument that there can be no divergence between professional and general morality, there really are such divergences. The two-level structure permits conflicts between its levels, and the fact that alienation has not been ruled out does not decrease that possibility, but if anything increases it, since alienation is itself a device for evading conflict. Conflict can arise because the justifying considerations are part of the general morality, wider than the professional system, and this has its own dispositions, not identical with the professional dispositions. It may simply be a fact that a natural expression of these is to feel repugnance at certain acts that are perfectly all right, or indeed required, as an expression of the professional dispositions.

In effect, divergence is being understood through the possibility of conflict, rather than the other way round. There is a distinction – of course there must be – between professional acts and 'similar' non-professional acts that are objectionable, but it is an expression of the general moral dispositions to see those two sorts of acts as relevantly similar. If one sticks merely to the perspective of rules, distinguishing conditions, and so on, where these are regarded purely as abstract propositional items – what we may call the perspective of casuistry – one will never see how there can be such a thing as a professional morality nor get any hold on the real problems that can arise from it. These will come out only within a psychological perspective that uses the idea of how people with certain dispositions naturally see things.

Suppose, then, that there is a spontaneous tendency for people to reject, in virtue of their general moral dispositions, acts that are expressions of certain professional dispositions. In what sorts of ways may the professionals or the general public adapt to the situation? There are several possibilities. One is that the spontaneous tendency will be modified by professional training, so that the trained professional ceases to react in this way. An analogy is the case of surgeons and the disposition of squeamishness. It is important, though, that this is only an analogy and not an example: this is because squeamishness – or at least this sort of squeamishness – is not a moral disposition. This possibility might be called *specific professional adaptation*.

A second possibility is that the general disposition is not specifically modified in this way, and at the same time the other general dispositions are not modified. This will have the result that the professionals get used to doing, from time to time, as an expression of their professional dispositions, acts that they find distasteful in virtue of their general dispositions. In that case, they have to sustain a certain level of conflict or uneasiness in their professional capacity. However, it may well be that the professionals do not want to sustain that degree of conflict. It may even be that in virtue of the general justification, we prefer, in some cases, professionals who are slightly different from the rest of us to professionals who are disposed to feel uneasy. This leads to a third possibility, that we should have professionals who lack to some degree the general dispositions. This is unlikely to go to the length of the professionals' having a different morality (we may remember here the different matter of a caste) but they could be seen by some others as up to a point rather horrible people. They can be consistently seen like this even by people who also think that there is a good justification of their profession and that the justification does require some of them to be like that.

This last possibility, of *non-specific professional adaptation*, is surely appropriate to some cases, or at least it is so in the society we have got and in any that we may reasonably foresee. Those of more utopian hopes or expectations may look to a society in which there is no need for such a possibility, one in which everybody is equally virtuous and nothing needs to be done that the virtuous cannot do. But that is not the society we have, and it would be a society in which not everything that we need and admire could be done. It is a real question for reflection, and for the political imagination, to what extent that would be so. It is important that, in considering these questions, we are asking what could be achieved, in what kind of society, by people who are independently, in virtue of the general dispositions, recognized as virtuous. That is why it is a substantive, and perhaps also a utopian, question. One can of course solve the problem much more easily, by simply regarding as virtuous the disposition to do what needs to be done, or what there is a good argument for doing. That idea short-circuits the appeal to dispositions and turns the language of virtue into the language of casuistry. The aim of the present discussion is not to do that, and in my view a decent polity should aim not to do that. I shall come back at the end to one or two more general questions about these strategies.

Even under the third possibility, the agents will probably lack only certain aspects of the general dispositions, because of course they do not lack discrimination between professional and non-professional acts, and they may display the general dispositions in non-professional contexts. But what distinguishes this possibility from the first, specific, adaptation, is that the agent's dispositions are not simply tailored to the shape of professional contexts and that there is some degree of generalization. The professional contexts may lack a very definite outline, and even in the case of the law, which is a favourable one in this respect, serious issues can arise about where the boundaries of the professional are. But apart from that, it may be psychologically hard or impossible for the professional dispositions to express themselves only professionally, and the profession, in hard cases, may retain, or only attract in the first place, a significant number of people whose dispositions would not be admired outside the profession. The military are often thought by liberal critics, probably wrongly, to provide conspicuous examples of this.

Most training in the respectable professions seeks, not surprisingly, the first possibility – a highly specific adaptation. Under this, the category of a professional context is paramount, and the person being trained is encouraged to use that notion in order to disconnect the less agreeable requirements of professional life from the effects of everyday dispositions. This approach has important limitations. One concerns relations with the rest of the community. We are assuming that the dispositions formed by the professional training differ in some degree from those of the rest of the community, and that some of the professional activity would spontaneously be poorly regarded by people outside the profession. There is then a tendency for the profession to become morally alienated from the community. This can be prevented in various ways, but none of them is entirely desirable. The community might be ignorant of what goes on, but this offends against transparency. Alternatively, it may be that the community knows what goes on, spontaneously regards it poorly, but swallows that reaction and puts it aside out of respect for the profession.

This can to some extent be rationalized in terms of the second-order arguments that justify (we are assuming) the profession's existence. It is often assumed that if the profession and its dispositions can be rationalized in this way, this is all that is needed for professional confidence and a good conscience all round. This relies on too abstract a conception of the problem. Knowing a justification of certain dispositions is not the same thing as having those dispositions themselves. What will be needed in concrete social terms will be a respect for the profession that takes the form of appropriate sentiments and is expressed in certain practices. If too much is asked of those sentiments, they will break down or will have to fall back on mystification.

Such processes involve risks for the professionals themselves. Since reliance on the dignity of the profession can become a mystification, and since, as I mentioned earlier, the boundaries of professional and non-professional activity are not always as clear or as indisputable as the mechanism of specific adaptation requires, the professionals may come to suppress their other reactions and take the third way, non-specific adaptation. They may become to some extent the sort of people that other people do not want to be. If this goes far enough, this can undo the respect for the profession on which the mechanism relied. The American taste for jokes against lawyers suggests that to some degree this has happened to the legal profession in the United States.

Granted all this, there is perhaps more to be said than is usually supposed for the second possibility, by which the professional consciousness is to some extent uneasy. There is indeed not much to be said for a system that makes the people who come out of it simply unhappy and ineffective; moreover, if it is too much like that, it will simply be rejected. Nevertheless, it is worth asking whether it may not be worthwhile encouraging some qualms rather than devoting all efforts to making the qualms go away. It will make a difference what form the uneasiness takes. A system of training will be no good if it merely punctuates an otherwise ruthlessly professional course with occasional encouragements to moral discomfort, like a weekly address at a military camp by a pacifist minister. What is needed is something different, a general structure or tone that makes it clear that the imperfections of the world in which the professionals operate include the fact that they cannot entirely reconcile what they need to do with what they would like only to have to do. Such a formation seems all the more appropriate to lawyers, whose profession, more than most, exists because of imperfection.

Concentrating now on lawyers, one can see quite a few reasons why some conflict, qualms, and moral unease might be usefully encouraged – or perhaps merely left – by a legal education. An education that properly allows for such things, and not just in the spirit of the padre's hour, will straightforwardly encourage lawyers to question the reality of what they are doing and to ask whether certain practices that cause suffering or (in at least an extra-legal sense) injustice are necessary. It will help them to ask how in detail the justifying arguments for the profession as a whole apply to this or that practice. It will provide some antibodies against absorbing a mystifying conception of the dignity of the profession. It will neutralize some of the mechanisms of self-deception, and so not only increase the human appeal of lawyers, but perform a social service, since lawyers are often powerful people with a strong interest in success, and it is a good idea that their self-image should leave them with inhibitions about how their armoury is being deployed. It is even a good idea for the legal profession itself, to help in heading off that alienation that I referred to earlier. It is desirable – certainly for lawyers themselves, and, perhaps, for society – that the legal profession should be as far as possible self-policed. This will not be acceptable to those outside if the dispositions of lawyers are too divergent from theirs.

These last suggestions, indeed the whole direction of this discussion, have been based on assuming that the dispositions encouraged by a professional training, and those that form a part of an everyday morality, are somewhat resistant to modification and are not simply malleable by casuistical argument. This follows from the claim that professional moralities and their relation to general morality are best discussed (as are many other subjects in ethics) in a way that pays attention to the psychological form in which ethical considerations have to be embodied. If ethical dispositions had no resistance or (to change the metaphor) momentum, not much would be gained by introducing them into the discussion. Another way of putting this is to point out that we can have, and we need, more than the one ethical disposition of asking the question 'what ought to be done?' and abiding by the answers to it. There is more to the ethical dispositions than their giving psychological effect to the results of casuistry.

This is not to deny that one important disposition of a professional person is to work by professional rules or codes, where these are acknowledged to be conventions that can be changed by agreement. The professionals would be very strange and mechanical creatures if all their professional practices were built into their dispositions. A disposition to follow the received or appropriate convention is a different thing from a direct disposition to do or to refrain from some related kind of act: sticking by rules of confidentiality, as David Luban has remarked, is not the same as having a secretive disposition. Much ethical discussion of professional conduct will concern such things as codes of conduct and what they should be. But that leaves room for us to recognize the importance of professional dispositions beyond a general disposition to follow the code. They will be expressed in discussions, from within the profession itself, of what the code should be. Moreover, the codes themselves can only be understood as rules to be applied in a certain spirit, from within a certain professional perspective, by people trained in certain professional dispositions.

Those dispositions can in their turn be discussed, as, very briefly, they have been discussed here, but the results of that discussion could not be reached merely by asking the question 'what should the lawyer (or other professional) do?' It involves the different question, 'how should the lawyer be?' The answer to that has to come in part from what we, the people who are discussing the question, are, and from what we understand that we are. That point is also important. Too often in this chapter it will have seemed that I have contrasted a professional morality with the general dispositions of the community and implied, moreover, that the professionals' dispositions are less admirable. It would be wrong to leave that emphasis uncorrected. The 'division of moral labour', in Virginia Held's phrase,[7] does not work like that. A professional morality is likely to emphasize some virtues, as well as laying less weight on others, compared with the rest of society, and society itself is more various than phrases such as 'the general moral dispositions' imply.

Even with regard to the more negative aspects of the professional outlook, a further qualification or reflection is needed. I have deliberately not said that concerned people outside a profession 'disapprove' of the professional dispositions or of what the professionals do. That would imply, it seems to me, a judgement that the profession should not exist or should not be as it is, and we are assuming that those outside do not make that judgement. They may well accept the second-order justification of the profession's existing and of the professionals' doing more or less what they do. Nevertheless, those outside, or some of them, may, as I have sometimes put it, regard the professionals poorly, and I have claimed that there is no incoherence in that. Certainly there is no logical incoherence in it. It is the product of our needing things done that cannot be done, or cannot be well done in present circumstances, without the help of activities which in virtue of some more general ethical dispositions we regard poorly. One is under no necessity to bring it about that one's ethical dispositions should be made exclusively responsive to approval and disapproval, in the sense of what one thinks ought or ought not to obtain. That, once more, would involve the reduction of disposition to casuistry.

It is very important that there is no logical or analytical necessity to deny the partial autonomy of ethical dispositions, their resistance to being schooled by judgements about what, as things are, ought to be the case. Their partial autonomy leaves room for types of ethical reflection that otherwise would be impossible. One type involves what I earlier called the political imagination. Recognizing what ought to be the case as things are – what *certainly* ought to be the case as things are – does not have to stop one thinking of ways in which things might be better. Political thought that is both liberal and rational (I do not regard those characteristics as equivalent, only as compatible) has to find some space between conservatism and utopianism, and the kinds of ethical experience that are in question here are necessary if that space is to exist. They help to stop the sores of realism forming the self-protective crust of cynicism.

There are personal as well as political thoughts that one needs to have at this point. While the two kinds of disposition that I have been discussing have to be kept distinct, and the question of what one feels about a certain kind of professional life from outside it is not settled just by the thought that one needs it to exist, one had better not forget that one needs it to exist. Academics (in particular) are sometimes tempted to feel superior to such professional labours. They should not do so. Those labours serve our needs, which are often the deepest we have – the need for a social order, among others. If those needs are essentially served by some activity or institution, such as a profession, then there is nowhere to go to be superior to that institution, except by climbing out of oneself. The only decent direction in which to move is into thoughts about how things might be otherwise, thoughts in which one is quite likely to be joined, indeed led, by members of the profession itself.

Notes

1 This chapter was a paper that was contributed to a Working Group on Legal Ethics organized by the Center for Philosophy and Public Policy of the University of Maryland. It benefited a lot from the group's discussions, which yielded the volume in which it first appeared. It has been somewhat revised for this reprinting.
2 Benjamin Freedman, 'What really makes professional morality different: response to Martin', *Ethics*, 91 (1981): Mike W. Martin (*ibid.*, pp. 619–25), to whom Freedman is replying, takes in effect a 'no divergence' view.

3 For the use of this term, rather than 'rule utilitarianism', which is both more restricted and also (as the present discussion itself suggests) misleading, see J. J. C. Smart and Bernard Williams, *Utilitarianism: for and against* (Cambridge: Cambridge University Press, 1973), pp. 118ff.

4 Cf. David Lyons's distinction between rule-adoption and rule-following in *The Forms and Limits of Utilitarianism* (Oxford: Oxford University Press, 1965), pp. 137ff.

5 I have argued this in 'The point of view of the universe', and in *ELP*, chapter 6.

6 'Rational' here is merely a place-holder, perhaps not the most appropriate one. It is an important question what virtue of a society is mainly in question here. For Rawls, it is of course justice, as involving what he calls 'publicity'. See: *A Theory of Justice*, section 23 and elsewhere.

7 Virginia Held, 'The division of moral labor and the role of the lawyer', in Luban (ed.), *The Good Lawyer*.

17

Who needs ethical knowledge?

An old question, still much discussed in moral philosophy, is whether there is any ethical knowledge. It is closely related, by simple etymology, to the question of cognitivism in ethics. Despite the fact that the terms 'cognitivism' and 'objectivism' seem sometimes to be used interchangeably, I take it that the question whether there can be ethical knowledge is not the same as the question whether ethical outlooks can be objective. A sufficient reason for this is that an ethical outlook might be taken to consist of rules or principles, which do not admit of truth or falsehood and so cannot be objects of knowledge, but which can be seen as having an objective basis.[1]

However that may be, it is usually thought that cognitivism is the form that objectivism should take if ethical claims can be true or false. Why should we think this? It may be said: if ethical claims can be true, then the most desirable state one can be in with regard to them is knowledge. By itself, that argument comes close to a simple assertion – it is, at least, very short. However, the argument may perhaps be given a rather richer content, on the following lines. A desirable state for one to be in with regard to one's ethical views is confidence. If one's state is not confidence, then it is doubt, and, at the limit, scepticism; and while it is certainly a good thing that people should be to some degree open to doubt about their ethical convictions, general doubt can hardly be desirable. But we do not want the confidence of bigotry – if there is to be confidence, it should be reasonable confidence. But reasonable confidence in what is indeed true is knowledge.

This is, at any rate, an argument, and that is already something with regard to an assumption which, so far as I can see, is usually unargued. However, the argument's conclusion can be challenged by a set of considerations suggesting that the concept of knowledge has only a limited usefulness in ethical matters (more limited than this argument would imply). It is these considerations that I want to examine. In doing so, I am going to sustain the assumption that ethical claims can be true or false. A serious problem in doing this is that it is unclear how large an assumption one is sustaining, and this itself bears on the question of ethical knowledge. If the concept of truth itself has epistemic implications, then the two matters cannot ultimately be kept apart.[2] However, I think that there is something to be learned from keeping the matters apart for as long as possible. For the purposes of this discussion, I shall leave the account of truth itself to one side and shall try to see, rather, what may be learned from considering ethical matters in the light of characteristics possessed by the concept of knowledge in general.

Philosophy's engagement with knowledge has taken at least two different forms. One, the Cartesian form, is not so much concerned with what knowledge is; rather, it makes some assumptions (usually rather demanding assumptions) about the conditions that knowledge has to satisfy, and asks whether we have any. The other approach, familiar in the recent literature, asks for the truth-conditions of 'A knows p'.[3]

In concentrating on the truth-conditions of that particular statement, the second approach implies what is in fact a peculiar stance to the person A. It is not merely that we are asking whether that person knows something that (it is implied) we already know ourselves. In addition to that, the question does not even have the force that it usually has when we ourselves have the knowledge in question, namely whether the truth has got to A, whether he even believes it. Rather, we are asking whether the true belief we know him to have has adequate warrant; our stance towards A is that of an examiner. The point of concentrating on the examiner's stance is, of course, precisely to isolate the question of warrant, but isolating the question in this way is not in fact the best way of answering it, because it does not help us to grasp the point of the demand for warrant. More generally, the method of starting from the examiner's stance conceals the point of our having a concept of knowledge at all. The point of the concept of knowledge comes out better if we start from questions such as 'who knows whether p?' – questions implying the more basic situation in which a questioner needs information that someone else perhaps has. Starting from this situation will not only give us a more realistic conception of knowledge, but will in particular shed light on the vexed question of warrant (the so-called 'third condition' on knowledge), by setting it against helpful ideas of what the point of imposing such a condition might be. To proceed in this way is to take up what E. J. Craig has called 'the practical explication' of knowledge, an undertaking which he summarizes as follows: 'We take some prima facie plausible hypothesis about what the concept of knowledge does for us, what its role in our life might be, and ask what a concept having that role would be like . . .'[4]

The third condition has its roots in the fact that 'we need some detectable property to lead us to informants with true information'. It is important, as Craig emphasizes, that we are being led to informants, not just to sources of information; we are dealing with other people, people who themselves know and do not merely record and display information. A useful informant on a given question must be reliable, and our ideas of what contributes to reliability are naturally shaped by various opportunities to acquire information at different places and times; in relation to these opportunities, we form the idea of a witness. Again, there are differential investments in inquiry, which produce various kinds of expert. (There is also the ideal of a good journalist, who is – though not in the forensic sense – an expert witness.)

If these are, in their most basic form, the kinds of consideration that provide the roots of the third condition, and hence of knowledge, then it may seem immediately clear that the notion of knowledge does not apply to the ethical, since there are, notoriously, no ethical experts, and, we may add, it is not in the least clear how there could be ethical witnesses. This familiar point has considerable weight, but it needs more careful handling than it sometimes gets. Many of the most convincing arguments on this subject show only that there are no *theoretical* experts in ethics or morality, that these are not sciences. This is indeed a plausible conclusion, and anyone who is tempted to take up the idea of there being a theoretical science of ethics should be discouraged by reflecting on what would be involved in taking seriously the idea that there were experts in it. It would imply, for instance, that a student who had not followed the professor's reasoning but had understood his moral conclusion might have some reason, on the strength of his professorial authority, to accept it; or that someone who did not entirely understand what was involved in some set of ethical sentences might (as with certain formulae of physics) know at least this much, that they expressed some ethical truths.

These Platonic implications are presumably not accepted by anyone, but something like the view that leads to them is implicit in one (it is only one) interpretation of 'applied ethics', in particular medical ethics. This interpretation takes expertise in ethical theory as a qualification for assisting in decisions about such matters as terminating supportive treatment of a comatose patient. It is clear why there is a social need for some kind of authority to help in legitimating ethically controversial policies in publicly answerable institutions, and clear also why this should, in a technical and secular context, be thought to take the form of an expertise. But the readily comprehensible reasons for introducing such a practice hardly lessen the paradox, that it invites us to appeal in matters of life and death to someone who has a PhD in ethical theory but whose judgement, quite possibly, we would not trust on any serious practical question.

All of this shows only that the model of a theoretical expert does not apply to the ethical case. But this is not the only model. Perhaps the idea of a reliable ethical informant should be construed rather in terms of practical experience and judgement. Indeed, Aristotle's famous description of such a person offers a hint of the other basic form of the division of epistemic labour, the idea of a witness. The valuable informant can be seen as one who, so to speak, has been down this road before:

> So we should attend to the undemonstrated sayings and opinions of people with experience, and older or sensible people, no less than to demonstrations; from their experience they have the eye, and so they see aright. (*EN* 1143 b11–14)

There are some emphases in this that belong to a traditional society (though it is worth saying that the reference to age is not unqualified, and also that Aristotle suggests only that one should attend to these people's sayings, not that one should always accept them). We can, in any case, lay aside the suggestion of a traditional authority figure, together with Aristotle's inevitable assumption that such a figure must be male. If we do this, who would such a person be? What is our relation to him or her? He or she is, paradigmatically, an advisor, someone who may see better than you do how things stand and will help you to see them aright. An advisor, above all, helps you to understand. This process can express and perhaps impart knowledge.

We should resist the temptation to think that this will be only non-ethical knowledge. It is true of some advisors, financial or legal for example, that they primarily offer straightforwardly empirical information, which they possess in terms of an expertise. An all-round advisor, however, who is prepared to help you to decide what is the best thing to do *period*, may well contribute some ethical insight to this, and that insight may take the form of certain kinds of knowledge under ethical concepts – that a certain course of action would be cowardly, for instance, or would count as a betrayal, or would not really be kind, and contributions of this kind can offer the person who is being advised a genuine discovery.

So here there is, in a sense, some ethical knowledge, it seems: knowledge of truths under 'thick ethical concepts'.[5] We have, then, advisors, who may be better than others in helping us to see how things stand under ethical concepts, can assist us in understanding the situation and in making, perhaps, a certain kind of discovery. We have also some 'marks of reliability'. However, these are not best characterized in terms of possessing information, but rather in terms of certain capacities, such as judgement, sensitivity, imagination and so forth. There is a question of how exactly such capacities are related to distinctively ethical knowledge. They can be applied to practical issues more broadly, and also can yield interpretations which, although they may deploy ethical concepts, shade into the psychological, as that a certain person cannot be trusted because of her vanity. Such a judgement can reasonably be called an ethical judgement, but is knowledge of it an example of ethical knowledge?

This matters less than the question of how much these structures, and these kinds of knowledge, do for the larger concerns of cognitivism. The question becomes very pressing when we consider that a good advisor of one person need not be a good advisor of another – and not merely in the sense that there are some people who cannot be advised by anyone. An advisor, and the person seeking advice, may not share the same presuppositions. Someone could be a capable and insightful advisor, to Catholics, for instance, who accepted the value of chastity, but be no use to someone who did not; in the opposite direction (so to speak) a seeker after advice might think that some well-regarded and shrewd advisor displayed a louche and opportunistic consequentialist outlook. In these ways, ethical knowledge, to the extent that it is identified through the advisor model, remains local. Moreover, the advisor model itself cannot be extended to identify a kind of knowledge that could itself overcome these difficulties. You cannot identify an advisor by marks that do not already include the degree of ethically shared outlook that would enable the person seeking advice to trust and understand the potential advisor. (This is concealed in Aristotle's account, because he speaks from a society which he pretends to be homogeneous and to concede authority to a certain kind of advisor.)

The point that the authority of a potential advisor must depend in part on the degree to which he or she shares the presuppositions of the person seeking advice should not be confused with a well-known argument against moral authority, which invokes the idea of autonomy: that nothing can be a moral belief of mine unless I have freely adopted it. This is no more true of moral beliefs than of any others. What is true is that I cannot reasonably, perhaps even intelligibly, come to accept an ethical belief just because I know that some reputably informed person holds it. We have already considered this in dismissing the idea that a model of theoretical expertise could apply to the ethical. But a similar point applies also to the model of the advisor. There are indeed situations in which one may reasonably take someone's word for it on an ethical matter although one lacks complete insight into the grounds of his judgement. But for that to be so, one has to trust his judgement, and not only in the sense that one can trust him, and regard him as an honourable person, although one disagrees with him on some important ethical matters. To take his word on an ethical question, one has to trust his ethical judgement as applied to oneself, and this requires that there should be enough ethically in common for one to be assured that when he uses the basic formula of advice, 'if I were you', it does not mean 'if you were me'.

Even if the advisor model provides a structure analogous to the practical explication of knowledge, and if the grasping of truths under thick ethical concepts provides some content for that structure, it still remains, as things are, to a considerable extent local. This means that the model does very little for the larger concerns of cognitivism. Cognitivism's question has often been expressed simply by asking whether there is any ethical knowledge or not, but in fact it has typically been concerned with the hopes of resolving the kinds of disagreement that separate from one another the local practices of advice under shared ethical presuppositions. The ideal of ethical knowledge was meant to offer the hope that such disagreement should be revealed as involving error.

Since local ethical knowledge fails to meet the larger demands of cognitivism, it might be wondered whether it is really knowledge at all. The question can be related to the argument which I considered at the beginning of this chapter (as at least *an* argument) for the view that if ethical claims can be true or false, then the desirable state of mind with respect to those claims would be knowledge. The argument distinguished between reasonable and unreasonable states of confidence, said that the former are what we need, and identified those states with knowledge. Does the advisory model, as developed in its local form (the only available one), meet the demands of this argument? The good advisor, master of the local thick concepts, indeed has a reasonable confidence in their application. That implies a confidence in using these rather than some other ethical concepts, but it is not clear that this confidence itself is reasonable in a sense that meets the demands of knowledge as expressed in this argument. The confidence is not necessarily *unreasonable*. But one thing that we have learned from the attempts to give conditions for knowledge is, surely, that if an alternative which rules out a given judgement has been *actually presented*, then if one is to know the first judgement one should have reason to rule out the alternative.[6] (The practical account of knowledge will, I believe, deliver this conclusion, and also explain why merely conceivable alternatives do not count.) In the modern world, at least, alternatives are presented to particular thick ethical concepts, and indeed thick concepts more generally are often replaced by the thinner resources typical of some modern ethical outlooks such as contractualism and Utilitarianism. Nothing in the advisory model, the only model we so far have for ethical knowledge, gives us grounds for applying the notion of knowledge to discriminations made at that level, between one set of thick ethical concepts and another, or between thick ethical concepts and their replacement by the thin. One can conceive of a reflective advisor and a reflective advisee arriving at some particular conclusions of that order: to the effect, say, that vanity is a failing, conceit is a vice, and humility is not a virtue. But more generally, there seems no reason to think of the local advisory model as capable in itself of offering us knowledge at such a level. I do not think that this conclusion should lead us to deny that the local practices can offer knowledge, but we shall have to accept the strongly anti-foundationalist consequence that ethical knowledge may rest simply on confidence, and not on a broader knowledge. (We should also consider how strong the original argument, from truth to the aim of knowledge, really is.)

Might we extend the practical explication of ethical knowledge so as to get beyond the local advisory model? The only way that I can see of doing so would lie in the Millian idea that the variety of human cultures, with their various thick concepts and ethical practices, should itself be understood in terms of an epistemic division of labour, as a kind of spontaneous and poorly co-ordinated research programme into the best way for human beings to live. (The unfortunate inhabitants of the previously Communist world, for instance, were no doubt taking part in an ethical experiment, among other things, though the description of it and of its results would certainly differ between different points of view on it.) As things are, our best candidates for ethical knowledge are local, and this fails to match up such ethical knowledge to the ambitions of cognitivism. The further proposal tries to overcome this limitation through interpreting the division between the various local ethical practices in terms appropriate to knowledge, as a version of the division of epistemic labour.

It may seem natural to test this suggested model by asking whether it fits the subject matter of ethical judgements, as understood in terms of metaphysics or the philosophy of language. There is certainly much more to be learned about the subject matter of ethical judgements, as an object of knowledge.[7] But I doubt in fact that the question of this model's ultimate appeal can be answered now, a priori, by the unaided resources of these areas of philosophy. What the extended model would need would be a plausible account of how the variety of different human cultural circumstances could be assimilated to the sorts of differences that intelligibly ground an epistemic division of labour: differences of location, for instance, or of subject matter, or of method, or of specialized observational skill. None of these in itself, it must be said, does offer a very convincing analogy. But in order to say that there could not be any adequate analogy, we would need a better understanding than we have of cultural variety, and of how it is related to what used to be called a theory of human nature. Some philosophers' theories imply that we understand more about this than we do. They suggest, for instance, that anything we can recognize as ethical value must be capable of being mapped on to a structure in which it will be intelligibly related in ethical terms to values we ourselves accept (as an application, extension, limitation, or so forth of them),[8] much as anything we could understand as a colour perception would have to be related to the dimensions of colour that we recognize. This demand is too strong, and certainly cannot be established a priori from, say, the theory of interpretation. We simply do not know how we may come to understand the relations between the various local practices that offer, as things are, the most convincing models of the practical explication of knowledge in ethical matters. We correspondingly do not know to what extent it may turn out that the differences between local practices can be assimilated to differences in fields of enquiry, so that the whole of human ethical experience might look more like an epistemic undertaking.

Whether or not it turned out to be so, there are two considerations that we are in a position to register now. One is that an interest in the ethical uniformity or otherwise of human nature has been a persistent concern for many centuries, and it would be a little naive to suppose that some new turn of the social sciences was going definitively to answer it. It is more likely that it will always remain a matter for scepticism, or else that the question itself will be swallowed up by global developments in human ethical life. Indeed, even if an answer seemed to emerge, the answer itself might well be a product of developments in human life. Human beings might arrive at a point where it seemed best to understand the process that led to that point in terms (for instance) of a convergent epistemic endeavour, but this impression itself might be a function of the social state that they had reached, an understanding caused by history rather than explanatory of it.

The second consideration is that if the hopes of a larger cognitivism are, in this way, at best in the hands of future historical interpretation – interpretation, moreover, the direction of which may well be indeterminately shaped by the same forces that it will be trying to interpret – the status of the claim that such a cognitivism is (so to speak) already true is unclear. It is even less clear that its truth could make any important ethical difference in the world we actually have now. As the practical explication of knowledge reminds us, we are interested in knowledge because we are interested in finding helpful knowers, and cognitivism's best hopes give us no way of doing that in ethical connections except the ways we are already familiar with. Perhaps a hopeful cognitivism, imaginatively construed, may encourage us to make the best sense we can of ethical variety. If so, well and good, but we have many reasons anyway for trying to do that; it is fair to say, too, that in the past outlooks calling themselves cognitivist have not always done much to encourage us to make good sense of ethical variety.

Notes

1 With some qualifications, this is Kant's position: for discussion, see 'Ethics and the fabric of the world', and *ELP*, chapter 4. I take it that it also represents Hare's later theory, though Hare himself has, reasonably, been sceptical about distinctions between the 'subjective' and the 'objective'. In a theory such as Hare's, moral principles and their particular consequences are taken to be prescriptions, and hence not possible objects of knowledge; their objectivity consists in their passing a certain test, which is itself said to be grounded in the nature of the moral point of view (in Hare's case, moral language). This raises, of course, a question of the relation between, on the one hand, a moral principle P, which cannot be an object of knowledge, and a claim of the form 'P passes the test', which presumably can be.

2 A focus for recent discussion of these questions has been provided by ideas of convergence: see notably 'Truth as predicated of moral judgements' in Wiggins, *Needs, Values, and Truth*. Wiggins's view is criticized by Crispin Wright (*Truth and objectivity* (1992), chapter 3), though it is unclear how far the notions of normativity that he uses avoid similar ideas. Contrary to some things that I have said earlier (particularly in 'Consistency and realism' in my *Problems of the Self: philosophical papers, 1956–1972* (Cambridge: Cambridge University Press, 1972)), I am now in sympathy with the aim of Wright's book, to give an account of truth itself that will have minimal substantive implications and will, so far as possible, leave epistemic and metaphysical issues to be discussed later. An adequate 'minimalism', as Wright argues, will need more than is offered by the 'redundancy theory'; for recent support of the latter, see Paul Horwich, *Truth* (Oxford: Blackwell, 1990).

3 Both approaches go back to Plato, the first to the *Republic* and the second to the *Theaetetus*. For the criticism of 'the examiner's stance', which follows, see my 'Knowledge and reasons' in *Problems in the Theory of Knowledge*, ed. G. H. von Wright (International Institute of Philosophy) (The Hague: Nijhoff, 1972).

4 Craig, *Knowledge and the State of Nature* (Oxford: Clarendon Press, 1990), chapter 2. I put forward a sketch in this style in *Descartes: the project of pure enquiry*, chapter 2, having got the idea from the Australian philosopher Dan Taylor, who may have been influenced in this direction by John Anderson. Craig's rich and illuminating development of the approach includes a

convincing demonstration that attempts to define the third condition so as to produce sufficient and necessary conditions of knowledge are bound to fail.

5 I have discussed such concepts, and, to some extent, their possible relations to knowledge, in *ELP*, chapter 8.

6 There seems to be a serious problem in this area for the idea which David Wiggins has advanced in several publications (e.g. Wiggins, 'Moral cognitivism, moral relativism and motivating beliefs', *Proceedings of the Aristotelian Society*, 91 (1990–91)), to the effect that with regard to some straightforward ethical judgements, as with some plain mathematical and factual judgements, 'there is nothing else to think but that p'. Nothing else to think about what? If the question about which we are to have something to think is whether setting fire to the cat was cruel or not cruel, then we must think that it was cruel. But people need not have this thought if they are asked 'is it all right to set fire to the cat?' or 'what did they do?' Wiggins's argument assumes that the concept of cruelty is always ethically to hand, but the problem is that it is not. With arithmetical examples and also, differently, plain factual examples, it is not like this.

7 As I implied in referring to the outstanding problems of truth (note 2) and of plain truth (note 6).

8 On this and related questions, see 'Saint-Just's illusion', in particular pp. 140–44 and note 4. The qualification 'in ethical terms' is important here. If there were a theory that understood cultural variety in terms of basic needs and physical circumstances, it would relate to that variety of human nature, but it would hardly advance the interests of a larger cognitivism, because the difference in circumstances would bear too remote an analogy to conditions of enquiry.

18

Which slopes are slippery?

In many ethical connections, including those in which the discussion concerns what the law should be, there is a well-known argument against allowing some practice, that it leads to a slippery slope. The argument is often applied to matters of medical practice. If X is allowed, the argument goes, then there will be a *natural progression* to Y; and since the argument is intended as an objection to X, Y is presumably agreed to be objectionable, while X is not (though of course it may be objectionable to the proponent of the argument – the slippery slope may be only one of his objections to it). The central question that needs to be asked about such arguments is what is meant by a 'natural progression'. Before coming to that, however, we need to make one or two preliminary points. First, it is worth distinguishing two types of slippery-slope argument. The first type – the *horrible result* argument – objects, roughly speaking, to what is at the bottom of the slope. The second type objects to the fact that it is a slope: this may be called the *arbitrary result* argument.

An example of a *horrible result* argument is that sometimes used against *in vitro* fertilization of human ova. IVF gives rise to extra fertilized ova, and experimentation is at least permitted, and perhaps required, on those ova. The period of time during which such experiments are allowed is limited, but (the argument goes) there is a natural progression to longer and longer such periods being permitted, until we arrive at the horrible result of experimentation on developed embryos.

All the arguments that I shall be considering use the idea that there is no point at which one can non-arbitrarily get off the slope once one has got on to it – that is what makes the slope slippery. Arguments that belong to the first type that I have distinguished involve, in addition, the further idea that there is a clearly objectionable practice to which the slope leads. The second type of argument, by contrast, relies merely on

213

the point that after one has got on to the slope, subsequent discriminations will be arbitrary. Suppose that some tax relief or similar benefit is allowed to couples only if they are legally married. It is proposed that the benefit be extended to some couples who are not married. Someone might not object to the very idea of the relief being given to unmarried couples, but nevertheless argue that the only non-arbitrary line that could be drawn was between the married couples and the unmarried, and that as soon as any unmarried couple was allowed the benefit, there would be too many arbitrary discriminations to be made.

Not all cases in which a slippery slope comes into the discussion are genuinely slippery-slope arguments. Sometimes the slope is invoked in order to express some other ground of objection. This is sometimes the case with Catholic objections to abortion. If it is said that early abortion is on a slippery slope that ends in infanticide, this may be a way of expressing another objection, itself regarded as basic, to the effect that early abortion is an example of killing an innocent human being. The slippery-slope considerations are intended to make one see that point, but the point itself goes beyond them. (I shall come to that sort of argument at the end of this chapter, and also to the point that some arguments fail to make clear the ways in which they depend on slippery-slope considerations.) By contrast, someone might base an objection to abortion directly on the slippery-slope argument itself, without agreeing that all abortion consisted of killing an innocent human being. He or she might think that early abortion did not involve doing that, but that there was a natural progression to cases that did.

There is another distinction to be made – a particularly important one. If it is said, in the course of one of these arguments, that two different cases or practices, A and B, cannot appropriately be distinguished, one thing that this may mean is that a distinction between them cannot *reasonably* be defended. It may be said, for instance, that any criterion or principle that admits A must admit B. Alternatively, it might be said that even though some distinction between A and B can reasonably be defended (there is a decent argument for distinguishing them), they cannot *effectively* be distinguished, and, as a matter of social or psychological fact, if A is admitted, B will be. Both these ideas, of a reasonable distinction and of an effective one, are relative to the nature of the practices and purposes in question. There must be some difference between A and B for the discussion even to get going, but that difference (between two foetuses, one of which is a day older than the other, for instance) may be said not to be reasonable in relation to what is being discussed (abortion), or not to be effective, or both.

A reasonable distinction need not be an effective one. Consider first-personal cases of temptation and discipline (to which indeed social cases of the slippery slope are often assimilated). If someone is trying to regulate smoking or eating, it may well be that in terms of the effects that are to be controlled – ill health, obesity, and so on – the distinction between no cigarettes or chocolate biscuits a day, and one, is not significant, and certainly less significant than that between one a day and thirty; but nevertheless the distinction between none and one is effective, while that between one and thirty is not, just because none does not lead to one, but one does lead to thirty.

When one is considering cases in which policies are to be adopted socially, and not solely for one person, there are further reasons why a distinction which was reasonable in terms of the original issues may turn out not to be effective. It may be clear, for instance, that the original case will be diffusely and inaccurately perceived in society. Again, not everyone in society may share the original judgements of what was reasonable. There may be a consensus on not allowing X, but as soon as X is allowed, there may be no consensus on what further distinctions can be drawn, and this may predictably lead to the undesired result Y. In such cases, we can have distinctions which are reasonable but not effective. They are distinctions that are intrinsically reasonable merely in terms of the subject matter, but if one tries to base a policy on those distinctions, there are social factors which mean that it will not stick. In similar terms, there can be distinctions which will be effective but are not (otherwise) reasonable.

There are some special questions about the distinction between the reasonable and the effective when one is concerned with *arbitrary result* cases, as I have called them. These questions arise particularly where issues of justice are involved, and the agent is publicly answerable for the equitable character of what is done. It may be argued, for instance, that no exception should be made to a certain rule, even though the particular exception being proposed is perfectly reasonable in terms of the purpose of the rule and the nature of the particular exception: the argument being that one will not be able to distinguish reasonably between the many possible exceptions that may then be claimed or, again, that the distinctions involved could not effectively be justified to the public.

This is of course the territory of the academics' friend, the Thin End of the Wedge, or what Keynes used to call the Principle of Equal Unfairness, that one should not do a good turn to one person, for fear that you might have to do one for someone else. There are, of course, cases in which this kind of argument is sound, but there are at least two ways in which it may fail. One is that the agents may be taking too narrow a view of what can count as a relevant distinction. Thus if somebody applies for a grant on grounds that are all right in themselves, it may not be much of an objection (though it is often heard) to say that if the grant is given, there will be no money for some other applicant with a similar claim: *being the first applicant* can itself be a relevant characteristic in such cases. Another way in which the argument can fail is that it may simply not be true that this exception or good turn will generate more demands for exceptions or good turns. The mere idea that there *could* be a row of claimants whose cases one could not distinguish cannot be enough to support this kind of slippery-slope argument.

But what does it mean to say that one cannot distinguish one case from another? A fundamental point here is that, in these applications of it as in others, *indistinguishable from* is not a transitive relation: from the fact that A is indistinguishable from B, and that B is indistinguishable from C, it does not follow that A is indistinguishable from C. This is familiar with regard to distinguishing colours by eye, but it applies equally to drawing reasonable distinctions among ways in which different cases are to be treated.

If indistinguishability in a given respect is made the basis of the application of a general term, a problem can notoriously arise, often discussed in terms of the paradox of the heap;[1] problems about slippery slopes are interestingly related to paradoxes of this sort. If a pile of n grains of sand constitutes a heap, it is plausible to say that so must a pile with one less grain; but equally obviously there is a number of grains too small to make a heap. In general, suppose we have a range of objects which we can place in order, on the basis of some varying characteristic, so that each object in the series will differ from its immediate neighbours, in terms of this characteristic, by only a tiny amount. (Piles of sand ordered by the number of grains they contain would be merely one example of this.) Let the objects be numbered $0[1]$, $0[2]$, and so on, according to their position in the series. Now suppose there is some property, call it the property of being F, which seemingly relates to this characteristic in such a way that:

(1) $0[1]$ is F.

(2) For any number n, if $0[n]$ is F, so is $0[n + 1]$.

(3) For some number m, $0[m]$ is not F.

(For simplicity's sake, I have put this in terms of an ascending series; to represent the sand example, F should be read as something like 'less than a heap'.) There is now a paradox, since the conjunction of (1), (2), and (3) is self-contradictory.

There are many ethical predicates that are vague in ways that invite the paradox. (Aristotle's doctrine of the Mean, indeed, taken strictly, implies

that all expressions standing for virtues or vices display such vagueness.[2])
In some cases, so long as the structure within which judgements are
being made is relatively informal, or contains a high degree of consensus,
and it is not under pressure, we may be able to proceed as we proceed
with many other vague predicates: we adopt the resource of what might
be called *restricted judgement*, and make judgements that involve the
predicate in question only in cases that either clearly display it, or clearly
fail to do so. How precisely that resource deals with the paradox is
another question; one way of understanding it might be that there is
nothing in our practice to commit us to the assertion of the induction step
(2), nor to its denial. However this may be, the practice at least keeps the
paradox at bay.

If we consider the special case, however, of normative predicates, such
as 'may reasonably be given a grant', 'may rightfully be aborted', and so
on – a class which is particularly relevant to slippery-slope arguments –
this resource is less likely to succeed. If a case presents itself at all, the
practical question of what one should do cannot be avoided. So virtually
the only circumstances in which the resource of restricted judgement
remains available are those in which the cases that actually present
themselves come from distinct parts of the range (as if, for example,
requests for abortions obligingly only ever came very early or very late in
pregnancy). One is not necessarily (as I pointed out earlier in connection
with certain *arbitrary result* cases) compelled to make a decision for cases
that never in practice arise.

There are, however, several factors that may upset that situation. One
may not be that lucky with the cases (we shall consider shortly circumstances that make it unlikely that one will be lucky.) Moreover, it may
well be that judgements *are* demanded about cases that have not actually
presented themselves. This is likely to be so if the structure in which these
decisions are being made is formal, public, and less consensual than those
that typically sustain the resource of restricted judgement. In particular, it
will be so if there is a requirement of publicity, and a declaration is
demanded of what principle is being employed: a demand that may be
made so that the practices can be understood and criticized, and so that
people can have determinate expectations of how they might be affected
by those practices. In these circumstances – and they are not confined to
the use of the law, though that is an obvious example – the resource of
restricted judgement will not do.

I mentioned that there were circumstances in which one was unlikely
to remain lucky with the selection of cases that present themselves. These
are the circumstances that most typically offer the conditions for a
slippery-slope argument. It is particularly so when there is a precedent

effect. Here, the fact that a given case has presented itself makes it likely that the next case will present itself, because there are people who have an interest in the next case being decided in the same way as the last, and it seems unreasonable that the next case, since it is indeed the next case in the spectrum, should not be decided in the same way as the last.

There is more than one reason why this process is likely to be repeated. It is not merely that, at any given stage, there seems no adequate reason to refuse the next step. In addition, it may well be that when a number of steps has been taken, the original objections to the process, or to this degree of it, now seem misplaced. The cumulative process has itself altered perceptions of that process. It is a mechanism very like that in terms of which Nelson Goodman explained the fact that increasingly incompetent forgeries by van Meegeren were accepted as genuine Vermeers.[3] Each new one was compared to a reference class that contained the earlier ones, and it was only when all the forgeries were bracketed, and the latest ones compared to a class of Vermeers free from van Meegerens, that it became obvious how awful they were. It is often this kind of process that critics have in mind when they claim that allowing some process will lead to a slippery slope. It is a process that they see in terms of corruption or habituation, just as reformers may see it as a process of enlightenment or of inhibitions being lost.

When may one rightly appeal to a process of this kind, and what are the correct conclusions to be drawn from it? The first requirement – to repeat a point that has already been made – is that it should be probable in actual social fact that such a process will occur. This requires that there should be some motive for people to move from one step to the next. Those who favour conservative policies sometimes simply assume this, perhaps because they have in mind a model of social addiction: once started in some given direction, society has, like the incipient alcoholic, an irresistible urge to go progressively further down the same path. In some cases, there certainly are reasons for thinking that the process is likely to occur. Besides the sort of examples suggested up to now, where interested parties have the same motive in relation to later cases as such parties had with earlier cases, there is also the competitive or many-party situation, supposedly exemplified by the arms race,[4] in which each party has a reason to take the next step because some other party took the last step. The conditions for a slide can be fulfilled in various different ways, but one must try as best one may to find out whether in a given situation they will be fulfilled or not. Possible cases are not enough, and the situation must have some other feature which means that those cases have to be confronted.

Suppose it is plausible that there will be a slide, and that there will be, at each stage, pressure to take the next step. What follows from that? The slippery-slope argument concludes that one should not start, and that the first case (whatever exactly that may be) should not be allowed, on the ground that after the first step there is nowhere to stop. In terms of the paradox, the argument wants us not to let premiss (1) above be true. But there is an obvious alternative. Granted that we are now considering cases in which a definite rule or practice is needed, which can be applied to any case and does not rely on what I called earlier 'restricted judgement', we have the alternative of sharpening the normative predicate in question, and drawing a sharp line between cases that are allowed and cases that are not. In terms of the paradox, the effect will be that premiss (2), the induction step, is falsified: for some n, we shall have decided that F applies to $0(n]$ but not to $0[n + 1]$. We lay down a maximum length of pregnancy for abortion, a number of days during which experiments on a fertilized ovum are permitted, a minimum age for admission to certain sorts of films, and so on.

Is drawing a line in this way reasonable? Can it be effective? The answer to both these questions seems to me evidently to be 'Yes, sometimes', and as that unexciting reply suggests, there is not a great deal to be brought to deciding them beyond good sense and relevant information. It may be said that a line of this kind cannot possibly be reasonable since it has to be drawn between two adjacent cases in the range – that is to say, between two cases that were not different enough to distinguish. The answer is that they are indeed not different enough to distinguish, if that means that their characteristics, unsupported by anything else, would have led one to draw a line there. But it is, all the same, reasonable to draw a line there. That follows from the conjunction of three things. First, it is reasonable to distinguish in some way unacceptable cases from acceptable cases; secondly, the only way of doing that in these circumstances is to draw a sharp line; thirdly, it cannot be an objection to drawing the line just here that it would have been no worse to draw it somewhere else – if that were an objection, one could conclude, by cumulation, that one had no reason to draw it anywhere, a path that leads to the grave of Buridan's ass (which allegedly starved through indecision, when placed between two equally attractive bales of hay). In practice, of course, the point at which the line is drawn is often chosen because it is salient in some way. Moreover, and significantly, it is rarely set directly in terms of the characteristic that the argument is about (development of a foetus, emotional maturity of a filmgoer), but is based rather on something else (a date, an age) which can be clearly established and is roughly correlated with the relevant characteristics. This makes it all the clearer that it is not the precise merits of one rather than another step in the range that is in question when the line is drawn. The Warnock Committee, in recommending a time limit of fourteen days for embryo experiment, made it very clear that this was indeed a regulatory line; though it bears a rough relation to a salient developmental feature, it was not intended to be an approximation to some characteristic which might be thought in itself relevant to the issue of experiment, such as sentience.[5]

A line such as the Warnock report proposed may be unreasonable on some other grounds, but it is not so merely because it is this kind of line. Whether such a line is effective is another question. If it is less effective than the alternative of allowing no cases at all, that will be because of special circumstances, such as those in which there is a consensus of allowing no cases, if that is all that can be achieved, but there is no consensus for anything else. Equally familiar, on the other hand, is a situation in which there is a consensus for allowing something rather than nothing, and a further consensus gradually emerges about what is to be allowed – a consensus, perhaps, formed as a result of recommending or legislating just such a line.

On this account, the slippery-slope argument should be properly understood as in good part an empirical, consequentialist, argument. It does of course assume certain evaluations; in the case of embryo experiment, all parties are assuming that experimentation on a neonate would be unacceptable. It also has to make various judgements about what would be reasonable or equitable discriminations to make. But at the end of the line the argument is about what sort of social practice will in fact follow from adopting what kind of rule, and this is in good part an empirical argument. Many of the consequences to be considered will no doubt be of the kind that utilitarians are particularly concerned with, consequences for utility or welfare. But the consequences can be evaluated in other ways as well, for instance with respect to rights. The considerations about rights, if they are brought into the argument at this point, will not themselves be consequentialist arguments; but the slippery-slope argument will itself be a consequentialist argument, to the general effect that if a certain rule is adopted or a certain practice allowed, then social consequences will follow in which (among other things) people's rights may be violated.

Seen in this light, it seems to me that the slippery-slope style of argument can carry weight, and is to be taken seriously; but that, equally, it need not necessarily carry the day, in the sense of proving that the first step should never be taken. We may, instead, take the path of drawing a line, and that is a perfectly reasonable reaction, in the right circumstances, to the challenge that is indeed posed by the slippery-slope considerations.

Some people, however, feel that this level of argument is too super-ficial to deal with the kind of ethical problem posed by abortion or embryo experimentation. They seek some 'absolute' consideration that will clearly settle the issue without invoking this sort of argument at all. Thus some people feel that they are on stronger ground if they say straightforwardly that the embryo is from the beginning a human being, and we should not kill or experiment on any human being (or, with regard to killing, at least on any innocent human being: there are various casuistical complications at this point which we can leave aside). This may be called the *definitional* approach. It looks different from the sort of thing that I have so far been discussing, and, as I have said, some people think that it is more solid and robust. But I think that this impression is an illusion, and in the last part of this chapter I shall try to show that inasmuch as this approach has any rationale, it is one that itself rests on the slippery-slope argument – indeed, on two separate applications of it.

An embryo which, if all goes well, will develop into a human being is certainly a human embryo, but that does not imply that it is itself a human being. Those who insist that it is, make a great deal of its potentiality for normal development into a human being, thus distin-guishing it from an ovum or a spermatozoon (which may be human but is not a human being). But in general this is not a natural way to describe or think of items which in the normal course of events have the potentiality of developing into a mature form that belongs to a given species. We do not naturally regard viable acorns as oak trees, or cater-pillars as butterflies, and, as Jonathan Glover said in a televised debate, his opponent would be put out if, having been invited to a chicken dinner, he were served with an omelette made of fertilized eggs. This rather brutal joke outraged his opponent, but it made an entirely valid point.

More immediate and obviously significant than these general points is the fact that women do not regard an early embryo in the same light as a neonate or a fully developed foetus. Their experience of miscarriage can take many different forms, and for some, no doubt, an early miscarriage can be almost as traumatic as stillbirth. But it does not have to be, and it would be a cruel impertinence for some metaphysician to insist that the loss involved in each of these things had to be equivalent.

It is thus not true to our experience, with regard to human birth, or more generally, that the embryo has to be seen as a human being, and there is much in our experience to make natural the description that many would give, that the embryo is something that develops into a human being. So what basis is there for insisting that, despite these appearances, it must be a human being? The insistence may, of course, be based merely on supposed supernatural revelation. But if not, I suspect that it comes from an argument something like the following:

(1) 'Human being' is an absolute term.

(2) Development is a gradual process.

(3) Development ends in a human being.

(4) If development starts with a non-human being, there must be a cut-off point.

(5) Any cut-off point is arbitrary.

(6) There cannot be an arbitrary cut-off point.

Therefore, development must start with a human being.

This is itself a slippery-slope argument, of what I called earlier the *arbitrary result* kind. The idea behind it is that since 'human being' is an absolute term – that is to say, nothing is more or less of a human being – it must be unacceptable to have a situation in which there is no definite starting point to something's being a human being, or only an arbitrary imposed starting point. But from a purely logical or semantic point of view, there is no reason to accept this. Very many terms, such as the names of many artifacts, are 'absolute' in this sense, but no-one would insist on imposing a definite moment for the start of their being the sort of thing that they come to be.

In this argument, we can certainly accept premisses (5) and (6), while premisses (1), (2), and (3) are indisputable. The implausible premiss is (4), and without this, of course, the *arbitrary result* slippery-slope argument will not work. Why should anyone accept (4)? It is certainly not imposed on us by purely logical or semantic argument. The reason, I suspect, actually lies in another slippery-slope argument, this time of the *horrible result* kind: namely, that unless some definite point is imposed, we shall have a slippery slope that ends up with the horrible practice of killing or experimentation on neonates.

The definitional approach, then, seems either to be quite arbitrary in its assumptions, or else to rely on the superimposition of one slippery slope on another: in the form of an *arbitrary result* argument, it presses the results of a linguistic practice which is itself only motivated by a *horrible result* argument.

The definitional approach has at least two disadvantages. One is that it fails to reveal what its real basis is: if slippery-slope arguments are to be used sensibly on these matters, then a first requirement is that they should be recognized for what they are. The second disadvantage is that if people insist that the early embryo is a human being, this may produce results quite different from those that they want. It is as likely, or indeed more likely, that the result will be, not to suppress all experiments on embryos, but to admit an exception to the rule that human beings should not be killed for medical purposes or experimented on without their consent. If exceptions are admitted to that rule, we shall certainly be confronted with a slippery slope – one more threatening than those already considered.

Notes

1 This is traditionally called the Sorites. An important discussion of some basic issues is Michael Dummett, 'Wang's paradox', *Synthèse* 30 (1975), reprinted in his *Truth and Other Enigmas* (London: Duckworth, 1978), pp. 248–68. (Wang's paradox is an inverted version of the Sorites.)
2 I am alluding here to the theory of virtue which Aristotle advances in his *Nicomachean Ethics*. Aristotle's doctrine is that every virtue of character lies between two vices or failings which represent extremes in opposite directions. Thus courage, for example, is viewed by Aristotle as a mean between the deficiency that is cowardice and the excess we call rashness.
3 Nelson Goodman, *Languages of Art – an approach to a theory of symbols* (Indianapolis: Hackett Publishing, 1976), pp. 110–11.
4 The conventional Prisoners' Dilemma picture of the arms race overlooks the respects in which it was a co-operative undertaking.
5 Mary Warnock: *A Question of Life* (Oxford: Blackwell, 1985).

19

Resenting one's own existence

We distinguish in general between the case in which two thoughts (statements, speakers) refer to one and the same object, and that in which they refer to two distinct but similar objects. We distinguish, that is to say, between identity and mere similarity.

The notion of identity relevant to the present discussion is not so much identity over time as *identity in relation to possibilities*. Given a particular object, we can consider various ways in which its properties might have differed from the properties it actually has; yet it can retain its identity through these speculations – we are all the time thinking about the same thing. 'If Robert had been born in France (as he might have been, if his mother, pregnant with him, had gone there), then ...' seems a speculation of this kind; one about an alternative possible life-history of the person Robert. In other cases, however, the thoughts start with a particular object, but do not succeed in preserving its identity through the speculations. The possibilities invoked in that case are not possibilities involving *that object*, but rather possibilities involving some other, perhaps similar, object that might have existed instead. 'If Robert had been the son of his mother's first fiancé, then ...' is not genuinely a thought about Robert, but about someone else, with a different father, who might have existed instead of Robert.[1]

The question whether a possibility preserves identity or not is not the same as the question of how similar the object in the imagined circumstances would be to the object in the actual circumstances. Let us suppose twins, of which one dies soon after birth; the survivor, Frank, is now aged ten. We think of the possibility that Frank might have died and the other twin survived; that child might well have been very like Frank as Frank is, but he would not have been Frank. On the other hand, suppose as we did that Robert had been born in France, instead of England, brought up

224

as a French speaker, perhaps been injured there, etc.: he would have been very different from Robert as Robert in fact is, but he would still have been Robert.

What is the principle underlying the distinction? An influential and plausible proposal[2] is that the identity of human beings, as of other sexually reproducing creatures, lies in the union of two given gametes: if either the sperm, or the ovum, or both had been different, a different human being would have been formed and born. A possibility in which a given human being, A, features is one that preserves the identity of the zygote from which A developed. Call this the Zygotic Principle (ZP).[3]

The Zygotic Principle is not motivated by any particular belief about the extent to which genetic information is important in causing the characteristics of a human being. (That this is not the point, emerges already from the consideration I just mentioned, that the difference between identity and non-identity does not turn on the question of how much the object that appears in the hypothetical speculation resembles the actual object.)

The motivation of ZP lies, rather, at a more general, metaphysical, level, in the importance of origins to our idea of a particular living thing (and of other kinds of thing as well). When we speculate about possibilities, we consider different possible life stories. We have to distinguish between *life story of a different individual* and *different life story of the same individual*. We understand the latter in terms of forward-branching alternatives in the life-history of the individual, with branches running from points at which what might have happened to him diverges from what actually happened. Since they provide alternative versions of one life story, they are branches from one stem; and they are forward-branching because the notion of a life-history is the notion of a causally structured sequence, a series in which later stages are explained by earlier stages. ZP provides the minimum basis for the stem of such a structure.

ZP affects the ways we should think about prenatal damage. Before we consider some consequences it does have, it is important to notice one consequence it does not have. If Mary is born handicapped because of damage to the foetus *in utero* (e.g. because of alcohol abuse by her mother), common sense will readily say three things: (a) Mary is handicapped, (b) Mary was damaged *in utero*, (c) Mary was damaged by what happened to her *in utero*. (a) is indisputable; in a sense ZP implies (b); it may well seem that it implies (c) as well. But since 'she', Mary, is a person, a human being, etc., it may seem to follow that ZP implies that the destruction of the foetus, however early, will be the killing of a human being, and conservative conclusions for abortion may be drawn.

In fact this does not follow, because either (c) does not follow, or, if it does, it does not imply that Mary was present at the time of the damage (cf. 'she was conceived on the night of August 4th'). ZP was formulated to say that a possibility in which Mary features is one that preserves the identity of the zygote from which Mary developed. This does not imply that the newly formed zygote is itself already Mary. It is a separate question whether that is so, or whether a human being is present only at some later time, e.g. at viability. If the second line is taken, then it will follow even on ZP that if the foetus is destroyed earlier than that time, then no human being came into existence from that event of fertilization. What does follow from ZP (and is consistent with the previous conclusion) is that if a person is born handicapped, then it is that person who would have been born without a handicap if that foetus had not been damaged, e.g. if her mother had not abused alcohol. The thought of that possibility might give Mary a grievance against her mother.

This leads to the main question of this chapter. Under ZP, some grievances apparently of that kind will not be grievances. Consider the case (discussed by Parfit[4]) of a couple who, if they have a child now will probably have a handicapped child, but if they have one later, will have a child who will probably not be handicapped. They have a child now, and she is handicapped. The child may have some grievance, but if ZP is correct, it cannot coherently be to the effect that if they had made a different choice *she* would not have been handicapped. If her complaint is not the impersonal objection to the effect that it would have been better for the world to contain a non-handicapped rather than a handicapped child, it can only be to the effect that it would have been better for her if she had not existed; and since that cannot mean that of the two states – existing and not existing – the latter would be nicer for her, it must mean that in some sense her life is not worth living.

This point obviously applies to screening for corrigible genetic damage; indeed, the case I just mentioned could easily be of that sort. Related considerations would apply to the case, at present merely theoretical, of genetic improvements. Suppose that there were a feasible and legal programme for polishing up people's DNA so that their offspring had enviable characteristics. Frank is annoyed that he is less clever, handsome, etc., than Hugh, whose parents took the trouble and had the resources to enter the programme, while Frank's did not. Frank cannot coherently think that if his parents had entered the programme, he would have been more clever and handsome: he would just have been a non-existent person with a smarter sibling. Moreover, in this case, he has no focus for the thought that his life is not worth living – unless he is so consumed by these thoughts, and by envy of Hugh, that it has become not worth living. He has no grievance at all.

Suppose that a certain condition is necessary for A not to have a certain disadvantage, but also sufficient for A not to exist (that is to say, anyone who lacked the disadvantage would not have been A). Not everything that can reasonably be called a genetic defect is a disadvantage of quite this kind, because of the complex interactions of genome and environment.[5] But for the present argument we may ignore these complexities and consider only what I shall call *a strongly genetic defect*, with which the character of the genome is unalterably expressed as the defect, if the foetus develops at all.

In general, if a person A has a certain disadvantage; if circumstances C would have prevented that disadvantage – i.e., they are circumstances in which A would have existed without that disadvantage; and C could have been brought about but was not – then A, so far as this goes, may have a grievance or resent the fact that C was not brought about. But if C is at once necessary for A not to have the disadvantage and sufficient for A not to exist, then A may indeed resent the fact that C was not brought about; however he can do so coherently only by resenting his own existence, and this implies that he would prefer not to have existed. This is *the All or Nothing principle of counter-identical grievance*.

I am going to suggest that this leads to a paradox. However, it is not that I think that the very idea of resenting one's own existence or having a grievance about it is paradoxical or incoherent. In legal cases of 'wrongful life', where the question concerns granting legal standing to a child's case against his parents or their doctors for letting him be born, some courts have held that the whole idea is incoherent because it involves the plaintiff's comparing two states of affairs from his own point of view, one in which the plaintiff exists and one in which he does not.[6] But this must be wrong; resenting one's existence does not involve this comparison, but can rather be constructed from inside the actual life. What it requires is that the person should prefer not to have existed, and I take it that this implies thinking that his or her life is not worth living. This is not in itself a paradox, but, in relation to strongly genetic defects, it does seemingly lead to one.

Resentment can vary with various things, such as the extent of the responsibility of the parties who are its objects; one way in which it conspicuously varies is with the severity of the disadvantage. The All or Nothing principle leads to the conclusion that one can resent a strongly genetic defect only if one thinks one's life is not worth living. But not all strongly genetic defects are very severe. They may be less severe than defects that are not strongly genetic; in particular, they may not be severe enough to make the person think that his or her life is not worth living. Suppose A resents having a defect which he believes would not have happened if his parents had taken certain action, but he does not actually think his life is not worth living. He then learns that the defect is strongly genetic. Does his resentment then disappear, as though it were a product of misunderstanding (as it might, for instance, if he learned that it was in no way his parents' fault)? Again, suppose that in similar circumstances A is in doubt whether his defect is strongly genetic or not; is he in doubt whether he has a grievance?

It does seem paradoxical that if a defect is strongly genetic you can resent it only if it is so severe that it makes your life not worth living, whereas this is not true of other defects. The consequences of the argument seem not at all to fit the ways in which someone would naturally think or feel about such situations. If it is a paradox, we must ask what we can most plausibly deny in order to avoid it. One way might be to deny ZP itself. But ZP, or something of the same general kind, is an otherwise intuitively acceptable and well-motivated account of a distinction that we certainly need; and one would in any case not know how much one would do for the paradox by rejecting ZP, unless one had some idea of what might take its place. So I shall not pursue this line.

I see no way of denying that one who resents his own existence prefers that he should not have existed; and no way of interpreting that preference except in terms of thinking that one's life is not worth living. Certainly the wish not to have been born, Job's wish, is not incoherent; equally, there is no way of understanding it except from inside the actual life, and from inside the life, it surely cannot involve less than the thought that life is not worth living.

The only obvious possibility left is that there is something wrong with the idea that if one resents one's defect, and there is no way in which one could have existed without that defect, then one must resent one's own existence. The underlying principle seems to be something like this: if one resents x, one prefers to x some alternative to x; any alternative to one's having the strongly genetic defect would involve one's not existing; so if one resents the defect, one prefers a situation in which one did not exist. This last preference is still in the mode of resentment, so to speak, so one's resents one's own existence.

This involves an argument of the following pattern:

(1) There is some alternative to x that A prefers to x.

(2) Every alternative to x implies P.

Therefore, assuming that A accepts (2),

(3) A prefers to x an alternative in which P.

Call this argument *the preference inference* (PI). It may seem that (PI) is obviously invalid. Consider a situation in which James dislikes working with his father, but his father has made it clear that if James goes and works elsewhere, he will not inherit the family fortune. We cannot argue:

(i) There are alternatives that James prefers to working with his father.

(ii) Any alternative to working with his father involves losing the family fortune.

Therefore:

(iii) James prefers to working with his father an alternative in which he loses the family fortune.

This is invalid. However, it should not lead us to give up (PI) altogether. What it shows, rather, is that we need care in interpreting statements about preferences and alternatives. 'Prefers' in (PI) is a very general term, standing in for a range of different attitudes, and the important point is that different attitudes may relate to different ranges of alternatives. The argument about James fails because one of the things that he would like is that the fortune should not be linked to his present job; but a state of affairs in which they are not linked is one that, as things are, he cannot attain. The sense in which (i) is true is that he *wishes* he had not to work with his father: correspondingly, the range of alternatives with respect to which it is true is that of *conceivable* alternatives. With respect to this large range of alternatives, (ii) is false. Conversely, if we fix the range of alternatives with respect to which (ii) is true, which is the range of practicable or available alternatives, with respect to that range (i) is false. (PI) is sound, but only if the relevant range of alternatives understood in the premisses is held constant throughout the argument.

What range of alternatives should be understood is given, broadly, by the attitude represented by 'prefers'. Wishing, which makes (i) true in James's case, is the attitude that puts the weakest constraints on the range of alternatives: one can *wish* even for the impossible. Correspondingly, if an example of (PI) offers a premiss (1) that represents a wish, there will be few values of P for which (2) will be true. Not every *conceivable* alternative to James's situation involves his losing the fortune; what he conceives of, and wishes for, is an alternative in which that would not be so.

In the matter of genetic defects, there would clearly be no problem or paradox if the only attitude involved were a wish. The person with the defect can, only too obviously, wish that he did not have his defect, without running into any implications for his own existence; he can wish both that he did not have the defect and that it was not strongly genetic. The attitude we are considering, however, is resentment, the attitude that goes with having a grievance. What in the way of alternatives does that import? If resentment is directed against people, rather than against God

229

or the universe, then (at least in the sense that concerns us here) it is directed against someone for an act or omission that one supposes it was possible for them to avoid. So if resentment is what is represented in premiss (1) of the argument (PI), the relevant range of alternatives must be alternatives accessible to the objects of the resentment (in cases of strongly genetic defect, typically the parents.) But with respect to that range of alternatives, premiss (2) – taking 'P' as 'A does not exist' – is indeed true.

It seems that we have no reason to deny that the argument (PI), with the premisses appropriate to the paradox, goes through. This approach to removing the paradox, seemingly the most promising, has left it where it was. The paradox applies to a certain sort of grievance, and if it is sound, it will apply to justiciable grievances of this sort. This means that a legal action with respect to a strongly genetic defect will be equivalent to a wrongful life action.

I see no way of removing the paradox: perhaps its conclusion should simply be accepted. I shall end with a consideration that may at any rate alleviate its effects. Even if resenting one's strongly genetic defect has the paradoxical implications, *disliking* the defect does not. Disliking one's defect naturally means that one dislikes suffering from the defect. This of course implies that one prefers some alternative to this suffering, but it is not true that all such alternatives involve one's not existing. If the sufferer receives compensation, help, and so forth, he may achieve some alternative that he prefers to his present suffering. With these improvements, his life may well be worth living, and if he recognizes this, then by the argument of the paradox itself, he must conclude that he cannot consistently resent his defect. The argument of the paradox, used contrapositively, leads to an encouraging conclusion, that compensation and help can logically banish resentment.

Postscript A: ZP and twinning

ZP raises a problem about twinning. ZP might at first sight be put like this: *a hypothetical story is about an individual A if it is about some individual who (in the story) developed from the same zygote as that from which A in fact developed.* If this means that *any* individual who developed from that zygote would count as A, then monozygotic twinning is fatal to it: any story about A would equally be a story about A's sibling, and conversely. So the principle has to be adapted to deal with splitting. The simplest way of doing this might be to say: *a story is about A if it is about an individual who uniquely developed from the earliest item from which A in fact uniquely developed*, where 'uniquely developed' refers to development in the course of which there is no splitting. Where there is no twinning, this is equivalent to the original principle – the 'earliest item' from which A uniquely developed is the zygote. Where there is twinning, the history of A goes back to the splitting, and no further.

This revised principle yields the results that where no twinning ever occurred, and A correspondingly in fact has no monozygotic sibling, it is not a thought genuinely about A that he or she might have had one; but if twinning did occur, and the other product of it did not survive to term, then of course it is a thought about A that he or she might have had a twin sibling, namely if that product had survived. Similarly, where A has in fact got a monozygotic twin, it is not a thought genuinely about A that A might never at any stage have been going to have one; but is a thought about A that the sibling might not have survived to term. The principle underlying these consequences is that where A and B are monozygotic twins, a situation in which the item from which B developed never existed would be a situation in which A never existed either.

One reaches the same result if one starts from possibilities about the zygote. It is (a) a possibility about a split zygote that it might not have split, and (b) a possibility about an unsplit zygote that it might have split. Possibility (a) does not give a sense to 'A, who has a twin, might not have had one': for which, of A and B, would the unsplit zygote have become? Similarly, if perhaps less obviously, possibility (b) does not give a sense to 'A, who has no twin, might have had one', for which of the twins would A have been?

Postscript B: the identity of the zygote

The argument of the chapter takes as unproblematic the identity of the zygote itself.[7] The identity of the zygote presumably depends on that of the gametes. It would be possible to rule that the genetic character of a gamete was necessary to its identity; in this case, it will be unqualifiedly true that in a case of strongly genetic defect there is no alternative that excludes it while preserving the existence of the person in question as defined by ZP. However, it seems counterintuitive to make this ruling. To take the clearer case – though the point applies to both gametes – a woman's ova are identifiable items which last through her life and might, moreover, be genetically damaged; a zygote formed from a given ovum with some given sperm would be the same zygote, even if the ovum sustained some changes. This intuition seems to fit better the motivation of ZP, which I remarked earlier was connected with the importance of origins, not with the importance of genetic information. But if this is accepted, and if the identity of the zygote depends on the identity of the gametes, it will be the same zygote, whether the ovum was damaged or not. This leaves room for the possibility that the same individual might have been born undamaged; and if the damage to the ovum were due to action on the mother's part, then there might be room for resentment against the mother, without the child necessarily thinking that his or her life was not worth living.

We could simply rule this out by saying that the identity of the zygote does not depend simply on the identity of the gametes, but on their genetic character when they form it; we can say that the zygote's own genetic character is necessary to its identity. This in fact seems a reasonable thing to say. But it is instructive that even if we do not say this, and we allow the possibility that the same individual might have been born undamaged if the gamete had not been damaged before fertilization, this still does not help with the paradox. To have any chance of helping with the paradox, it would have to be the case that there was a practicable alternative under which the subject would exist but without the defect. But that is not secured merely by that ovum's being undamaged, but by its being undamaged and fertilized by the same sperm, and there is no reason to think that this was a practicable alternative. What exactly we say about the identity of the zygote does not in fact make a great difference to the paradox.

Notes

1 I leave on one side theories in which no two possible worlds contain the same individuals. Such theories must in any case do something in their own terms to reinstate the idea of two different possibilities for the same person. Without this idea in some form, deliberation (for one thing) makes no sense.

2 Saul Kripke, *Naming and Necessity* (Cambridge, MA: Harvard University Press, 1980).

3 ZP does need some refinement. However, the problems involved are not important to the central argument of this chapter, and I have left discussion of them to two postscripts: see pp. 230–2.

4 *Reasons and Persons* (Oxford: Clarendon Press, 1984), chapter 16.

5 Phenylketonuria is a textbook example: there is a genetic abnormality which, granted a normal diet, is expressed as a severe mental deficiency, but if the condition is detected early enough and the child is given a special diet, development is normal.

6 I am indebted to David Heyd, 'Are "wrongful life" claims philosophically valid?', 21 *Israel Law Review* (1986), p. 579. See also his *Genethics* (Berkeley, CA: University of California Press, 1992), especially chapter 1.

7 I am indebted on this point to comments by Michael Devitt and Louise Antony.

20

Must a concern for the environment be centred on human beings?

What is the role of philosophy in questions about the environment? One helpful thing that philosophy can do, obviously, is to apply its analytical resources to clarifying the issues. This is excellent, but it is an aim not exclusively cultivated by philosophy; clear analytic thought is something offered by other disciplines as well. There are more distinctively philosophical lines of thought that bear on these issues, and it is some of these that I should like to pursue. They raise, for instance, questions about the nature of the values that are at issue in environmental discussion.

Questions of this kind are likely to be more distant from practical decision than many that come up for discussion in this area. They are, in particular, difficult to fit into the political process. They can indeed run the risk of seeming frivolous or indecently abstract when questions of practical urgency are at the front of political attention. Moreover, it is not simply a matter of urgent political decisions; some of the broader philosophical considerations are not immediately shaped to *any* practical decision, and it is a mistake to make it seem as though they were. They are, rather, reflective or explanatory considerations, which may help us to understand our feelings on these questions, rather than telling us how to answer them.

There is no special way in which philosophical considerations join the political discussion. They join it, rather, in various of the ways in which other forms of writing or talking may do: ways that include not only marshalling arguments, but also changing people's perceptions a little, or catching their imagination. Too often, philosophers' contributions to these questions seem designed only to reduce the number of thoughts that people can have, by suggesting that they have no right to some conceptions that they have or think that they have. But equally philosophy should be able to liberate, by suggesting to people that they really have a right to some conception, which has been condemned by a simple or restrictive notion of how we may reasonably think.

If we ask about the relations between environmental questions and human values, there is an important distinction to be made straight away. It is one thing to ask whose questions these are; it is another matter to ask whose interests will be referred to in the answers. In one sense – the sense corresponding to the first of these two – conservation and related matters are uncontestably human issues, because, on this planet at least, only human beings can discuss them and adopt policies that will affect them. That is to say, these are inescapably human questions in the sense that they are questions for humans. This implies something further and perhaps weightier, that the answers must be human answers: they must be based on human values, in the sense of values that human beings can make part of their lives and understand themselves as pursuing and respecting.

The second issue then comes up, of what the content of those values can be. In particular, we have to ask how our answers should be related to our life. Few who are concerned about conservation and the environment will suppose that the answers have to be exclusively human answers in the further sense that the policies they recommend should exclusively favour human beings. But there are serious questions of how human answers can represent to us the value of things that are valued for reasons that go beyond human interests. Our approach to these issues cannot and should not be narrowly anthropocentric. But what is it that we move to when we move from the narrowly anthropocentric, and by what ethical route do we get there?

Many cases that we have to consider of course do directly concern human interests, and we shall perhaps understand our route best if we start with them. There is, first, the familiar situation in which an activity conducted by one person, A, and which is profitable and beneficial to A and perhaps to others as well, imposes a cost on someone else, B. Here the basic question is to decide whether B should be compensated; how much; by whom; and on what principles. A further range of problems arises when various further conditions hold. Thus there may be no specific B: the people affected are identified just as those who are exposed to the activity and affected by it, whoever they may be. When this is so, we have *unallocated* effects (all effects on future generations are unallocated). A different range of questions is raised when we ask whether B is affected in a way that essentially involves B's states of perception or knowledge. Thus B may be affected by the disappearance of songbirds or the blighting of a landscape. These are *experiential* effects. It is important that an effect on B's experience may take the form of a deprivation of which, just because of that deprivation, B is never aware; living under constant atmospheric pollution, B may never know what it is to see the stars. Beyond this, and leaving aside the experiential effects on human beings, there are effects on animals other than human beings. These are *non-human* effects. Finally, what is affected may be neither human nor a member of any other animal species: it may, for instance, be a tree or a mountain. These are *non-animal* effects.

It is of course a major question in very many real cases whether an activity that has one of these other effects on the environment may not also harm human beings: the cutting down of rainforests is an obvious example. To the extent that human interests are still involved, the problems belong with the well-known, if difficult, theory of risk or hazard. This aspect of the problems is properly central to political discussion, and those arguing for conservation and environmental causes reasonably try to mobilize human self-interest as far as possible. But the human concern for other, non-human and non-animal, effects is misrepresented if one tries to reduce it simply to a kind of human self-concern. Since, moreover, the concern for those other effects is itself a human phenomenon, humanity will be itself misrepresented in the process.

Our attitudes to these further kinds of effect are not directed simply to human interests, and in that sense they are not anthropocentric. But they are still our attitudes, expressing our values. How much of a constraint is that? What is involved in the ineliminable human perspective itself? Where might we look for an understanding of this kind of human concern?

There is a point to be made first about the experiences of non-human animals. I have so far mentioned experiential effects only in the context of effects on human beings, but, of course, there are also effects on the experience of other animals to be taken into account. This is also important, but it is not at the heart of conservation and environmental concerns, which focus typically on the survival of species. An experiential concern is likely to be with individual animals rather than with the survival of species, and it is bound to be less interested in the less complex animals; in these respects it is unlike a conservation concern. It also, of course, has no direct interest in the non-living. In all these ways an environmental concern in the sense relevant to conservation is at least broader than a concern with the experiences of other animals. This particularly helps to bring out the point that an environmental concern is not just motivated by benevolence or altruism. (Inasmuch as vegetarianism is motivated by those feelings, it is not the same as a conservation interest.)

There is a well-known kind of theory which represents our attitudes as

still radically anthropocentric, even when they are not directed exclusively to human interests. On this account, our attitudes might be understood in terms of the following prescription: treat the non-animal effects,
and also the non-human effects that do not involve other animals'
experiences, simply as experiential effects on human beings, as types of
state that human beings would prefer not to be in, or, in the case of what
we call good effects, would prefer to be in. The badness of environmental
effects would then be measured in terms of the effect on human experience – basically, our dislike or distaste for what is happening. It might be
hoped that by exploiting existing economic theory, this way of thinking
could generate prices for pollution.

This way of looking at things involves some basic difficulties, which
bring out the fairly obvious fact that this interpretation has not moved far
enough from the very simply anthropocentric. It reduces the whole
problem to human consciousness of the effects, but people's preferences
against being conscious of some non-human or non-living effect are in
the first instance preferences against the effect itself. A guarantee that
no-one would further know about a given effect would not cheer anyone
up about its occurring; moreover it would not be an improvement if
people simply ceased to care. A preference of this kind involves a value. A
preference not to see a blighted landscape is based on the thought that it
is blighted, and one cannot assess the preference – in particular, one
cannot decide what kind of weight to give to it – unless one understands
that thought, and hence that value.

A different approach is to extend the class of things we may be
concerned about beyond ourselves and the sufferings of other animals by
supposing that non-animal things, though they have no experiences, do
have *interests*. This directly makes the attitudes in question less anthropocentric, but I myself do not think that it is a way in which we are likely
to make progress. To say that a thing has interests will help in these
connections only if its interests make a claim on us: we may have to allow
in some cases that the claim can be outweighed by other claims, but it will
have to be agreed that the interests of these things make some claim on
us, if the notion of 'interests' is to do the required work. But we cannot
plausibly suppose that all the interests which, on this approach, would
exist do make a claim on us. If a tree has any interests at all, then it must
have an interest in getting better if it is sick; but a sick tree, just as such,
makes no claim on us. Moreover, even if individual members of a species
had interests, and they made some claims on us, it would remain quite
unclear how a species could have interests: but the species is what is
standardly the concern of conservation. Yet again, even if it were agreed
that a species or kind of thing could have interests, those interests would

certainly often make no claim on us: the interests of the HIV virus make no claim on us, and we offend against nothing if our attitude to it is that we take no prisoners.

These objections seem to me enough to discourage this approach, even if we lay aside the difficulties – which are obvious enough – of making sense in the first place of the idea of a thing's having interests if it cannot have experiences. The idea of ascribing interests to species, natural phenomena and so on, as a way of making sense of our concern for these things, is part of a project of trying to extend into nature our concerns for each other, by moralizing our relations to nature. I suspect, however, that this is to look in exactly the wrong direction. If we are to understand these things, we need to look to our ideas of nature itself, and to ways in which it precisely lies outside the domestication of our relations to each other.

The idea of 'raw' nature, as opposed to culture and to human production and control, comes into these matters, and fundamentally so, but not in any simple way. If the notion of the 'natural' is not to distort discussion in a hopelessly fanciful way, as it has distorted many other discussions in the past, we have to keep firmly in mind a number of considerations. First, a self-conscious concern for preserving nature is not itself a piece of nature: it is an expression of culture, and indeed of a very local culture (though that of course does not mean that it is not important). Second, the disappearance of species is itself natural, if anything is. Third, and conversely, many of the things that we want to preserve under an environmental interest are cultural products, and some of them very obviously so, such as cultivated landscapes, and parks.

Last of these general considerations, it is presumably part of the idea of the natural that kinds of creatures have 'natures', and we cannot rule out at the beginning the idea that we might have one, and that if we have one, it might be of a predatory kind. It is one of the stranger paradoxes of many people's attitudes to this subject (and the same applies to some other matters, such as animal rights) that while they supposedly reject traditional pictures of human beings as discontinuous from nature in virtue of reason, and they remind us all the time that other species share the same world with us on (so to speak) equal terms, they unhesitatingly carry over into their picture of human beings a moral transcendence over the rest of nature, which makes us uniquely able, and therefore uniquely obliged, to detach ourselves from any natural determination of our behaviour. Such views in fact firmly preserve the traditional doctrine of our transcendence of nature, and with it our monarchy of the earth; they merely ask us to exercise it in a more benevolent manner.

Granted these various considerations, the concept of the 'natural' is unlikely to serve us very well as anything like a criterion to guide our activities. Nevertheless, our ideas of nature must play an important part in explaining our attitudes towards these matters. Nature may be seen as offering a boundary to our activities, defining certain interventions and certain uncontrolled effects as transgressive.

Many find it appropriate to speak of such a conception as religious. A sense that human beings should not see the world as simply theirs to control, is often thought to have a religious origin, and a 'secular' or 'humanist' attitude is thought to be in this, as in other respects, anthropocentric. In one way, at least, there must be something too simple in this association; while some traditional religious outlooks have embodied feelings of this kind, there are some religions (including many versions of Christianity) that firmly support images of human domination of the world. However this may be, an appeal to religious origins will in any case not be the end of the matter, for the question will remain of why religious outlooks should have this content, to the extent that they do. In particular, the religious sceptic, if he or she is moved by concerns of conservation, might be thought to be embarrassed by the supposed religious origin of these concerns. Other sceptics might hope to talk that sceptic out of his or her concerns by referring these attitudes back to religion. But they should reflect here, as elsewhere, on the force of *Feuerbach's Axiom*, as it may be called: if religion is false, it cannot ultimately explain anything, but itself needs to be explained. If religion is false, it comes entirely from humanity (and even if it is true, it comes in good part from humanity). If it tends to embody a sense of nature that should limit our exploitation of it, we may hope to find the source of that sense in humanity itself.

I end with a line of thought about that source; it is offered as no more than a speculation to encourage reflection on the question. Human beings have two basic kinds of emotional relations to nature: gratitude and a sense of peace, on the one hand, terror and stimulation on the other. It needs no elaborate sociobiological speculation to suggest why these relations should be very basic. The two kinds of feelings famously find their place in art, in the form of its concern with the beautiful and with the sublime. We should consider the fact that when the conscious formulation of this distinction became central to the theory of the arts, at the end of the eighteenth century, at the same time the sublimity and the awesomeness of nature themselves became a subject for the arts, to a much greater extent than had been the case before. Art which was sublime and terrifying of course existed before, above all in literature, but its theme was typically not nature in itself, but rather, insofar as it dealt with nature, nature's threat to culture: in Sophocles, for instance[1], or in

238

King Lear. It is tempting to think that earlier ages had no need for art to represent nature as terrifying: that was simply what, a lot of the time, it was. An artistic reaffirmation of the separateness and fearfulness of nature became appropriate at the point at which for the first time the prospect of an ever-increasing technical control of it became obvious.

If we think in these terms, our sense of restraint in the face of nature, a sense very basic to conservation concerns, will be grounded in a form of fear: a fear not just of the power of nature itself, but what might be called *Promethean fear*, a fear of taking too lightly or inconsiderately our relations to nature. On this showing, the grounds of our attitudes will be very different from that suggested by any appeal to the interests of natural things. It will not be an extension of benevolence or altruism; nor, directly, will it be a sense of community, though it may be a sense of intimate involvement. It will be based rather on a sense of an opposition between ourselves and nature, as an old, unbounded and potentially dangerous enemy, which requires respect. 'Respect' is the notion that perhaps more than any other needs examination here – and not first in the sense of respect for a sovereign, but that in which we have a healthy respect for mountainous terrain or treacherous seas.

Not all our environmental concerns will be grounded in Promethean fear. Some of them will be grounded in our need for the other powers of nature, those associated with the beautiful. But the thoughts which, if these speculations point in the right direction, are associated with the sublime and with Promethean fear will be very important, for they particularly affirm our distinction, and that of our culture, from nature, and conversely, the thought that nature is independent of us, something not made, and not adequately controlled.

We should not think that if the basis of our sentiments is of such a kind, then it is simply an archaic remnant which we can ignore. For, first, Promethean fear is a good general warning device, reminding us still appropriately of what we may properly fear. But apart from that, if it is something that many people deeply feel, then it is something that is likely to be pervasively connected to things that we value, to what gives life the kinds of significance that it has. We should not suppose that we know how this may be, or that we can be sure that we can do without those things.

As I said earlier, it is not these feelings in themselves that matter. Rather, they embody a value which we have good reason, in terms of our sense of what is worthwhile in human life, to preserve, and to follow, to the extent that we can, in our dealings with nature. But there are, undeniably, at least two large difficulties that present themselves when we try to think of how we may do that. First, as I also implied earlier,

239

there is no simple way to put such values into a political sum. Certainly these philosophical or cultural reflections do not help one to do so. It may well be that our ways of honouring such values cannot take an economic form. The patterns must be political; it can only be the mobilization, encouragement and expression of these attitudes, their manifest connection with things that people care about, that can give them an adequate place on the agenda.

The second difficulty concerns not the ways in which we might come to do anything about them, but what we might do. What many conservation interests want to preserve is a nature that is not controlled, shaped, or willed by us, a nature which, as against culture, can be thought of as just *there*. But a nature preserved by us is no longer a nature that is simply not controlled. A natural park is not nature, but a park; a wilderness that is preserved is a definite, delimited, wilderness. The paradox is that we have to use our power to preserve a sense of what is not in our power. Anything we leave untouched we have already touched. It will no doubt be best for us not to forget this, if we are to avoid self-deception and eventual despair. It is the final expression of the inescapable truth that our refusal of the anthropocentric must itself be a human refusal.

Note

1 As has been admirably shown by Charles Segal in *Tragedy and Civilization* (Cambridge, MA: Harvard University Press, 1981).

21

Moral luck: a postscript

When I introduced the expression *moral luck*, I expected it to suggest an oxymoron. There is something in our conception of morality, as Thomas Nagel agreed, that arouses opposition to the idea that moral responsibility, or moral merit, or moral blame, should be subject to luck. This is so, I still think, because the point of this conception of morality is, in part, to provide a shelter against luck, one realm of value (indeed, of supreme value) that is defended against contingency. However, there are some misunderstandings that I now think my formulations in *Moral Luck* may have encouraged.

One misunderstanding is fairly superficial. The conception of morality that has these associations is very well entrenched, with the result that if one says that there is a certain difficulty with (this conception of) morality, one may be taken to mean that the difficulty must arise with (any) morality; that is to say, with any scheme for regulating the relations between people that works through informal sanctions and internalized dispositions. One way of getting around this, which I have suggested more recently,[1] is to use the words *ethics* and *ethical* in the more general sense, reserving the term *morality* for the local system of ideas that particularly emphasizes a resistance to luck. (The emphasis that this system places on resisting luck is connected with other characteristics, such as its insistence that the conclusions of moral reasoning should take the form of obligations.) The suggestion that we might use these words in this way has hardly, as yet, swept all before it, and it no doubt has its own powers to mislead, but I will follow it here. In these terms, morality does try to resist luck, in ways that my and Nagel's articles bring out, but not every ethical outlook is equally devoted to doing so. I entirely agree that an Aristotelian emphasis in ethics, for instance, need not run into the same difficulties.

Morality, in the restricted sense in which I am now using the term, is to some extent, of course, a theoretical construct, and even those who agree that there is a special formation of this kind may reasonably disagree about what exactly is central to it. It is this kind of disagreement, I think, as well as the general distinction between morality and the ethical, that helps to sustain controversy on the question of how significant or interesting morality's resistance to luck may be. About that controversy, it seems to me that there is at any rate a fair dialectical point to be made: critics who claim that morality is not so concerned about luck as I suggested are at least matched in numbers and weight by those who manifestly are concerned about luck and are anxious to show that *moral* evaluations, properly understood, do not apply to those aspects of a situation that are matters of luck.

The distinction between morality and the ethical may help me to focus my view of the analogy that Nagel drew with epistemological scepticism. I entirely agree with him, and indeed it is central to my view, that the resistance to luck is not an ambition gratuitously tacked on to morality: it is built into it, and that is why morality is inevitably open to sceptical doubts about its capacity to fulfil this ambition. In this respect, there is an analogy to the idea (which I also accept) that there are intrinsic features of the concept of knowledge that invite scepticism. Indeed, I suggest in the article that this is more than an analogy: the concept of knowledge is itself committed to discounting luck.[2] However, there is also an important disanalogy. Everyone needs the concept of knowledge, but if morality is a local species of the ethical, and the resistance to luck is (at least in a strong form) one of its idiosyncrasies, then not everyone is stuck with these sceptical problems. Human beings have lived, do live, and doubtless will live, by conceptions of the ethical that do not invite these problems, or invite them in a much less drastic form. For these problems to be endemic not just in morality (in the narrow sense) but in our life, it would have to be the case that morality (in the narrow sense) was inevitably the form that ethical life took, and this is not so.

Nagel does suggest in his article, and has developed the idea in subsequent work,[3] that the general structure of these perplexities is inherent in the tension between a subjective and an objective view of action. Although I cannot argue it here, I do doubt whether it is simply the nature of action as a metaphysical problem that gives rise to these difficulties. It is reasonable to think that if we are to have the concept of an action, we must have the concept of a voluntary action; that is to say, very roughly speaking, the idea of an intended aspect of something done in a state of mind that is deliberatively normal. But we should recognize, and we can perfectly well recognize, that the idea of the voluntary is

242

essentially superficial.[4] Stronger demands on the idea of the voluntary come not from the mere need to recognize human actions, but from ethical sources. We feel the need to exempt agents from (some) blame for (some) things done involuntarily and also, perhaps, to deepen the idea of the involuntary, because we think it unjust not to do so.

It can be readily pointed out that this idea, though it certainly expresses morality's concerns, can hardly be deployed to back them up: the notion of injustice at work here is morality's own. That is correct, but it is not very helpful. If these are our feelings and our dispositions of judgement, then that is what they are, and a historical or philosophical distinction between morality and a more general conception of the ethical is not, in itself, going to make them go away. We need, not that general formula, but insight into what the distinctions of the voluntary and the involuntary, and the other conceptions related to the avoidance of luck, mean to us. Among the questions raised here are the following. Since, necessarily, we cannot ultimately avoid luck, what do we actually do about it? Why do we mind more about it in some connections than in others? Among our reactions to things that are done wrongly or badly, what does blame, in particular, do? Does it apply in the same way to others and to one's own self?

We also need to understand the demands we make on the justice of public processes, in particular the criminal law. In framing these demands, we may suppose that we are being guided by an ideal of perfect justice, embodied in a notion of moral responsibility, and that what we are trying to do, in a necessarily imperfect way, is to make our institutions reflect that ideal. There is a striking phrase in a paper by Judith Andre that expresses this[5]; she says that even an atheist who does not believe in an all-just, omniscient, judge 'can ask what such a judge would do'. My own view is that we have very little idea of what such a judge would or could do (the history of Christian belief, particularly of the doctrine of grace, perhaps bears me out on this) and that the very conception of somebody's knowing everything that bears on the judgement of a person's life or action, and giving indisputably the right weight to each element in it, is unintelligible. Atheists say that in forming ideas of divine judgement we have taken human notions of justice and projected them onto a mythical figure. But also, and worse, we have allowed the image of a mythical figure to shape our understanding of human justice.

Morality wants to understand everyday blame as a finite anticipation of a divine, perfect, judgement, but blame cannot be coherently understood in those terms. Granted this, we need to ask why blame should matter so much, who morality is disposed to make such a lot of it. This question has two sides to it, and they are equally important. On one side, we should ask why blame should be thought to be such a fearsome thing that, like weapons of destruction, it can be loosed only in circumstances that ultimately justify it. On the other side, we have to think of all those hostile and painful reactions, to oneself and others, that are not blame – or, at any rate, not blame as morality would wish it to be.

This second aspect raises a question that I still think needs to be pressed: what is the point of insisting that a certain reaction or attitude or judgement is or is not a *moral* one? What is it that this category is supposed to deliver? Writers on these subjects who agree that in some problematical context an agent may reasonably feel bad about something that he or she has done, and may perhaps reasonably attract negative reactions from others, are still often concerned to insist on the further question whether these various reactions belong to *morality*. I can only urge again the point I have tried to make in various other places, that invoking this category achieves absolutely nothing, unless one has some account of the singular importance of morality in this restricted sense. I still cannot see what comfort it is supposed to give to me, or what instruction it offers to other people, if I am shunned, hated, unloved and despised, not least by myself, but am told that these reactions do not belong to morality.

The most important source of misunderstanding in *Moral Luck* was that I raised, as I now think, three different issues at once. One was the question that I have just mentioned: how important is morality in the narrow sense as contrasted with a wide sense of the ethical? The second question concerns the importance, for a given agent and for our view of certain agents, of the ethical even in the wide sense. Any conception of the ethical will include in some form a concern for people directly affected by one's actions, especially those to whom one owes special care: suppose that my fictional Gauguin offended against such a conception. The question remains of where we place our gratitude that he did so.

The points have been made that my Gauguin is not the real Gauguin, and that he (that is to say, my Gauguin) owes something to romantic conceptions of artistic creation. Both points are true. The first is uninteresting. The second is more interesting, but in itself does not contribute to understanding the problem: for it to do so, we will need to understand what values are involved in, or ignored by, a 'romantic' conception of the artist. In any case, the question goes a long way beyond the example of Gauguin, however he is pictured. The question, as I would now express it, is directed to the placing of ethical concerns (even in the wide sense) among other values and, more broadly, among other human needs and projects. I discussed it in terms of an example that pictured, perhaps in 'romantic' or bohemian terms, an artist's life. I took the case of artistic activity because the products of that activity, not least in a 'romantic' or bohemian form, are things that people concerned about the ethical, or even about morality in the narrow sense, often take to be valuable; I took an individual life, even if a partly imaginary one, because I wanted to relate all these matters to personal decision, rationality, and regret. But this is just one application of two wider questions. What human activities have we reason to be grateful for? How can that gratitude be related to a concern with the ethical, or, more particularly, to a concern for morality in the narrow sense? Indeed, the question extends to a gratitude for morality itself. As Nietzsche constantly reminds us, morality owes a great deal, including its own existence, to the fact that it is not obeyed; it can seem to achieve closure on its own absolute kind of value only because the space in which it operates is created, historically, socially, and psychologically, by kinds of impulse that it rejects. *Moral Luck* does not explore those large issues, but pseudo-Gauguin does stand for more than a question about how far we can expect creative artists to be well-behaved.

The third question raised in the article is that of retrospective justification, and this is the widest, because it can arise beyond the ethical, in any application of practical rationality. It is the question of how far, and in what ways, the view that an agent retrospectively takes of himself or herself may be affected by results and not be directed simply to the ways in which he or she deliberated, or might have better deliberated, before the event. We may say that it is natural enough to be upset if things turn out badly, for oneself or others, as a result of one's action – in that sense, to regret the outcome – but that *self-criticism* rationally applies only to the extent that one might have avoided the outcome by taking greater thought or greater care in advance. Reflection will then naturally turn toward asking when it is true that one might have avoided the outcome; and this reflection may eventually lead to scepticism. But the question I wanted to press comes before that reflection. It questions, rather, a presupposition of dividing our concerns in this way. The presupposition can be put like this: as agents, we seek to be rational; to the extent that we are rational, we are concerned with our agency and its results to the extent that they can be shaped by our rational thought; to the extent that results of our agency could not be affected by greater rationality, we should regard them as like the results of someone else's agency or like a natural event.

This idea seems to me very importantly wrong, and examples I have given in *Moral Luck* and elsewhere have sought to press the point that, in more than one way, my involvement in my action and its results goes beyond the relation I have to it as an ex ante rational deliberator. My discussion of this matter has no doubt not been helped by the fact that I put together the three questions that I would now distinguish as being about morality, about the ethical more broadly, and about rational agency. But although the questions must be distinguished, there are also reasons for eventually addressing them together. Morality in the narrow sense is formed, in part, by the attempt to shape the demands of the ethical to these conceptions of agency. In particular morality's notion of guilt, of blame directed to oneself, is the notion of the rational self-criticism of a deliberator. This notion and others related to it support the powerful feeling that morality just is the ethical in a rational form. But, even leaving aside the standing invitation that it offers to scepticism, this conception of the ethical runs into impossible problems. In part this is because it is using what is in any case an inadequate idea of agency, which (as I just put it) effectively limits one's involvement in what one does to that of an ex ante rational decider. But further problems arise even if morality is granted this idea of agency. It cannot then meet all the demands of the ethical. Ethical beliefs express themselves, also, in rejection or hostility toward those (at least in the locality) who have the wrong ethical sentiments or none, and if morality is to limit genuinely moral comment to blame, and blame to what is available to the rational deliberator, it is faced with a vast epistemological demand, to show (as Kant appropriately thought) that the correct ethical demands are indeed available to any rational deliberator – as Kant was disposed to put it, 'as such'.

There are many ways in which the three questions are interrelated. This last argument traces one aspect of morality to its share in the more general idea of agency. Equally, it must be true that this idea of agency is itself formed by aspirations shared by morality, to escape as far as possible from contingency. Again, there are ways in which the demands of morality and rationality may resist being combined. Nagel, in his paper, made the good point that an agent may know in advance that if things turn out in one way he will have been guilty of an unforgivable wrong, and if in another, he will not. In Gauguin's case, this applies the theory of moral luck to yield an idea of moral hazard. This, in a sense, honours the demands of ex ante rationality, but in a way that it is not very acceptable to morality. Moral hazard is an idea that morality itself resists. If the downside risk involves a moral wrong, then (morality will say) one ought not to take that risk; if one ought, or may, take that risk, the downside cannot have those relations to morality. Rather similarly, morality resists the notion of a moral cost, in the sense of a moral wrong knowingly committed by an agent who is doing something that even from a moral point of view is better: in that case, it will say, the wrong cannot ultimately be a wrong, the cost cannot really be a moral cost.

To evaluate these replies, to assess the force of these invocations of the moral, we need to bring in another of the three questions: the placing of morality itself in relation to the ethical more broadly, and in relation to other human concerns. By pursuing such questions, we may be able to penetrate the misplaced reassurances that morality offers, and rid ourselves of some of the perplexities that it encourages. The oxymoron in 'moral luck' shows up a fault line to which, I still think, it is worth applying the chisel.

Notes

This paper was written as a postscript to a collection of papers on the topic, edited by Daniel Statman (*Moral Luck* (Albany, NY: State University of New York Press, 1993)). The name *Moral Luck* here refers to my article of that title, not to my book named after it. The article originally appeared in *Proceedings of the Aristotelian Society* S.V. 50 (1976), together with a reply by Thomas Nagel, referred to in this chapter; that reply is reprinted in Nagel's collection *Mortal Questions* (Cambridge: Cambridge University Press, 1979).

1 In *ELP*, chapters 1 and 10.

2 But not for the same reasons. Edward Craig offers an illuminating approach to this and related aspects of knowledge in *Knowledge and the State of Nature*.

3 Thomas Nagel, *The View from Nowhere* (Oxford: Oxford University Press, 1986.)

4 This idea of the voluntary is discussed in 'Voluntary acts and responsible agents.' I have argued that it is inherent in the concept of action and that it is essentially superficial, in *Shame and Necessity*, chapter 3.

5 Judith Andre, 'Nagel, Williams and moral luck', *Analysis* 43 (1983): reprinted in the Statman volume.

Index